THE
AMERICAN
CRAFTSMAN

by

SCOTT GRAHAM WILLIAMSON

*Hundreds of illustrations from photographs
and contemporary prints*

CROWN PUBLISHERS :: NEW YORK

PRINTED IN THE UNITED STATES OF AMERICA
BY J. J. LITTLE & IVES COMPANY, NEW YORK

TO MY FRIEND

LINCOLN ROTHSCHILD

ACKNOWLEDGMENTS

The author wishes to express his thanks to the following persons for their cooperation and valuable assistance in the problems of both the text and the illustrations of this book:

Mr. William B. Sprague, of the Early American Industries Association; Mr. H. Maxon Holloway, Curator, and Miss Bella C. Landauer of the New York Historical Society; Miss Winchester, of *Antiques;* Miss Grier and other members of the Staff of the Metropolitan Museum of Art; Miss Wright, of French and Company; Captain J. G. W. Dillin, for permission to use material from his volume, *The Kentucky Rifle;* Mr. Stephen Sleeper, of Boston, Mass. for the portrait of John Coney by Jeremiah Dummer; Mrs. Paul M. Hamlen, for the self-portrait by Dummer; Mr. E. H. R. Revere for the portrait of Paul Revere by Gilbert Stuart; and Mr. Wharton Sinkler for the Benjamin West portrait of Benjamin Franklin.

Further thanks are due to The Cleveland Museum of Art; The Frick Memorial Library; The Peabody Museum, Salem, Mass.; Colt's Patent Firearms Manufacturing Company, Hartford, Conn.; The Museum of Fine Arts, Boston, Mass.; The Boston Athenaeum; Fine Arts Gallery of Yale University; The Rookwood Pottery, Cincinnati, Ohio; The Atchison, Topeka & Santa Fe Railroad; The Newark Museum; The National Rifle Association of America, Washington, D. C.; The New York Public Library; and the Philadelphia Museum.

CONTENTS

CONTENTS

LIST OF ILLUSTRATIONS

POTTERY

THE AMERICAN CRAFTSMAN

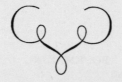

CHAPTER 1

AMERICAN BEGINNINGS

AMERICANS can make things. This attribute has been and is one of the primary factors in our national "genius". Our history has been, to a unique degree, a record of the ability to make just about anything; make it when it was needed; and make it fast! This has held true in many fields of endeavor, ranging from the production of arms and implements of war for the founding or maintaining of our Union, to the manufacture or handshaping of the humblest as well as the most complex items for our every-day use.

Even in Colonial days, when already manifested "Colonial" abilities were rapidly becoming a sore point and a matter of resentment to the stay-at-homes of England, a grudging recognition was accorded to American ingenuity. When the Colonies fought a one-sided war for Independence, which in terms of logic and reason they should certainly have lost, the resourcefulness and never-failing shrewdness of the rebels once elicited the exasperated comment from a British officer that ". . . . the ingenuity of these people is singular in their secret modes of mischief".

With the establishment of Independence, the new country forged ahead, with a renewed impetus toward craftsmanship and mechanical contrivance which continued to make it conspicuous in the world. Franklin and Fulton and many others carried

American inventions to Europe. The inventions of Europe were, in turn, adapted, improved, and often downright revolutionized by Americans. Out of this many-faceted ability rose a great modern industrial nation.

The latter day generations of Americans take many riches of their heritage for granted, and this is a pity. Many of the simpler and equally vital hand-processes which preceded our present high degree of industrialization had important aspects and values for our people which we can ill-afford to lose simply for the sake of production efficiency. We need not have lost what we may call, at the risk of seeming obscure, the philosophical and psychological concomitants of craftsmanship. America was once a nation of craftsmen. In a sense it still is, or still could be. The peculiar bent of the American toward craft accomplishments is not to be blindly or smugly attributed to the American air or to any singular quality in the bloodstream of the polyglot elements that make up the "American", even of many generations on the soil. There was good reason for the development or *renewal* of skills on the part of early Americans, which a little thought about the exigencies of colonization should make clear.

All around us, today, is our familiar America. We are surrounded by American "things": houses, furniture, objects of art, utensils, countless influences and variants of earlier origins which combine to constitute, or contribute to, our contemporary culture and civilization. Yet only a few hundred years ago, a relatively negligible span of history, there was nothing here but a wild continent, lushly endowed with raw materials.

When the Puritans, the Dutch, the Swedes, the Cavalier English of the South, and the French arrived at various times on the shores of America, they came to a wilderness. Widely divergent motives had prompted the adventure; a considerable range and contrast in equipment and wealth distinguished them. But the wilderness was common to them all. The best that the wealthiest of them brought was little in the face of it. The American wilderness was literally their "common wealth". Their welfare and hope of future prosperity rested largely in what they were to wrest, or make, from the plentiful materials at hand. There were trees and minerals, and clay and sand and water. There were such tools as had been brought from the homeland, such skills as the pioneer hands might possess through previous training or through the instinct of necessity. There were memories, sharpened by the migration, of the styles and fashions of their homelands, to be carried over, as far as possible, in the homes, furniture, and accessories that must be made in the New World. Above all these things were a relentless energy, an indomitable courage, and the spark of a common genius that was to make America. How well they wrought is eloquently told in their handiwork.

This was truly a pioneer society. Under the circumstances a prime requisite for survival and social usefulness was *the ability to make things*. Yet even this precious faculty, if too limited, was not enough. It required another quality, *versatility*. The settlers of America could not, at first, afford the luxury of specialization.

In 1711, which we must remember is by no means one of the earliest dates in our Colonial history, the Reverend John Urmstone, of North Carolina, wrote: "Men are generally of all trades, and women the like within their spheres. . . . Men are generally carpenters, joiners, wheelwrights, coopers, butchers, tanners, shoemakers, tallow-chandlers, watermen, and what not; women soap-makers, starch-makers, dyers, etc. He or she who cannot do all these things . . . . over and above all the common occupations of both sexes will have but a bad time of it; for help is not to be had at any rate, every one having business enough of his own."

Not all of those who ventured here were prepared to cope with these rigorous exactments. In the early days of the Virginia Company shiploads of "gentlemen" arrived in the search for easy money; a search, it should be said in justice to them, which had been fostered and for which they had been recruited by the fanciful representations of the Company. None of these gentry had taken into account or been warned against the realistic nature of the job of colonizing. Charles Beard tells us that it was the shrewd, practical and courageous Captain John Smith who wrote in exasperation to the Company in London: "When you send again, I entreat you rather send but thirty carpenters, gardeners, fishermen, blacksmiths, masons, and diggers up of trees' roots, well provided, than a thousand such as we have."

When every man was a jack-of-all-trades the bulk of his work was necessarily crude and primitively functional. This kind of production, at best, could only be a stop-gap. When the colonists had got their second wind, the skilled craftsman in a specific field began to stand out. This was the artisan, and it was natural that he should become a focal point in the developing community life of America. He formed the third in succession of the class strata of Colonial social order, ranking immediately after the dominant, landed and merchant families, and the second level of small, landed yeomen, or farmers. The qualities of character, temperament, and native talent which were often invested in the true craftsman tended to thrust him into leadership and prominence in public life. Craftsmanship amounted to more than merely a trade or "business." It was an art and an avocation. Statesmen and leaders of genius, such as Thomas Jefferson and Benjamin Franklin, found the time in their crowded lives to be craftsmen of the first rank.

The rank-and-file of these American craftsmen are the true representatives of the genius of a people. It is they who *are,* rather than who *make,* history. Political and economic studies give us little insight into the lives of peoples. It is by what they *did,* made with their hands for use and left for heritage, that we can truly know them. The folk-lore, the folk-craft and handi-work of a people are its history, written more enduringly than on the printed page. We can know our forebears by their fruits. We can appraise them through the work of their hands and brains. We can judge the products of their desires and necessities in the light of what we know about the handicaps that beset them. In this way we glimpse their idealism, courage, original-ity, and aspiration. In this way the qualities of a society can be interpreted through the products of its typical craftsmen.

Antiques and Americana

These factors raise the whole issue of "antiques," what they are and wherein their values lie. The antique cannot be dis-missed as a relic of past times appraised, as is often done, in terms of scarcity value.

The objects discussed and illustrated in the following pages are antiques of varying scarcity value. But our interest lies, so to speak, in first causes. We are concerned with why these things were made, who made them, and how it was done. We want the story of American objects before they acquired the external aura of antiquity. The collector often looks at the object with eyes that see nothing of its functions. It is hard to associate an object of display with a vital, simple utility which it may once have had. In a manner of speaking, the beauty of many antique objects must be regarded, historically, as a by-product of necessity.

In modern design a great point is made of "functionalism." The term is much abused and a certain angularity is sometimes called "functional" when it basically fails to fulfill the actual purpose of the object to which it is applied, whether this be a chair or a building. Our functionalism is frequently self-conscious and consequently false. Functionalism, as a luxury of swanky design, is a contradiction.

Most of the antiques from our very early Colonial period are truly functional. The term certainly never entered the minds of our Colonial craftsmen, but the factor of design for use was paramount. When we see a chair with a hinged back that will swing down and form a table this is Colonial functionalism, springing from a really urgent necessity to conserve space and materials and time. When we see a pottery bottle, in the form of a large ring, worn by the mower over his arm as he works in the fields, we are seeing a primary example of how to solve a problem in the simplest way. To view either of these objects, or countless others like them, in museums or private collections, without taking into account this measure of ingenuity-in-utility, is to have no real appraisal of them.

The conception of antiques as living documents of history, indisputably authentic, and eloquent in their tangible presence, is not new. It needs emphasis and stress. If we think too exclusively of antiques as they *are* we are led into cycles of antique reproduction, rather than genuine contemporary creativeness. At the same time, no very valid new creation springs out of the mere avoidance of what has been done before. These two failings; imitations of the past and forced strivings after the new, are only too evident in much of the furniture that is made today.

We must familiarize ourselves with antiques as they were,

viewing them as much as possible in the perspective of their own period, seeing them as a "gleam in their maker's eye." It is doing this that we imply, in the point made a few moments ago, that the products of our early craftsmen are genuine, incontrovertible documents of history: the epitome of Americana. It is not the beauty or rarity of these antique objects which primarily makes their historical-record value, for indeed some of them are not intrinsically beautiful and not all them are rare. It is their *use,* and so to speak, their personal histories, that constitute their chief investment-for-posterity value. To this their beauty is a generous dividend.

CHAPTER 2

WHAT IS CRAFT?

WHERE does craft production stop and industrial production begin? The answer is not so easy as it seems. In the spirit of this book we are not going to look upon craft in any narrow sense limiting it rigidly to hand production, or even to production of an entire object, or even production wholly controlled by the workman. Such terms characterized the worthwhile, yet relatively futile, "arts and crafts" movement launched by William Morris in England during the 19th century. We shall take the bull by the horns and run the full risks of controversy in our conception of craft as consisting of the *spirit in which,* rather than solely the *means by which,* a production process is carried out. This would appear to be the only conception of craft and craftsmanship which can hope to take root in this technologically advanced age. Certainly we cannot promulgate theories concerning the social and individual desirabilities of craftsmanship if such theories, fully realized, would imply the rejection, to a large degree, of the advantages and progressive aspects of industrialism. A return to the horse-and-buggy would be no more desirable in production than in politics.

Complex an adjustment as it may seem to be, people today are nonetheless eager for an understanding of the possible role of craft in modern life. We, in America, have suddenly waked

8

up to the richness of our background. We have become "craft conscious." Interest has revived in the whole conception of "craftsmanship." A score of advertising media are instinctively, yet blindly, trying to persuade us that craft flourishes now, in the midst of industrial life.

Large automobile companies, in elaborate advertisements, present their skilled mechanics as "craftsmen," making a title of the term. A certain absurdity, yet almost a pathetic intensity, of this tendency is revealed in the yearning for the myth of individual handicraft betrayed by such phrases as "Tomato Soup . . . . by Campbell." General Motors still clings to the lost carriage maker in the insignia and motto, "Body by Fisher." *Personal* names for *mass* products are at a premium. There is commercial value in "Fanny Farmer" candies, or "Mrs. Wagner's Pies." A sense of the public psychology is revealed in these oblique apologies by manufacturers for the industrial standardization of their products. This is not to imply that there are not many commodities which industry produces with better results than could the individual. But it's worth noting that when the sewing machine was first invented especially high prices were charged for clothing made on it. "Untouched by human hands" was once the miraculous advertising appeal for other milled or machined commodities. Yet today, the label "hand made" is worth an illogical amount in the retail value of many products.

It is pretty evident that the yearned-for craftsmanship in the modern world will have to be in terms of an enlightened and enriching attitude toward work. America has been profoundly shocked, today, by the spectacle of the devastating and brutal power of *malevolent* organization. In what is unquestionably a world crisis, America has become aware of the immediate need to tighten and bolster up its own organization and its entire field of productivity. Now, more than ever in our history, we must employ, to capacity, the American ability to make things, but we must do this through an extension of the American spirit, not through the fatal "organization" of totalitarianism. We must fight fire with *water*; quench it, not match its destructiveness.

The key to an understanding of the necessity for craft revival in modern terms is briefly found in the words of Allen H. Eaton of the Russell Sage Foundation. *"The time will come when every kind of work will be judged by two measurements: one by the product itself, as is now done, and the other by the effect of the work on the producer."* This enlightened concept is the vast gap between democratic and totalitarian production!

Labor and work are quite different matters. Labor is a commodity in terms of applied energy; work is an activity wherein the worker's personality effects or shapes his product. We need not fight the machine, but we must attempt to so use the machine that the material resources and powers which it places at the disposal of society shall be used to stimulate, rather than retard, the reviving impulse of creative workmanship present to some degree in every intelligent man or woman.

This is regarded as an age of science. Craft is a link which weds science to art, to the benefit of each. Science, for one thing, has greatly systematized the processes of invention. It might be said that invention has become more self-conscious since the advent of scientific perception of the attributes and uses of materials. But invention and craft have always had a great deal in common and still do.

Craft is the basis of most invention. The lack of craft, of the ability to apply manually the mechanical principles conceived by the inventor, would preclude a great deal of the inventive process. Craft instinct must still augment, and lend its creative qualities to, the scientific aspects of invention. What is craft but the perception of how to use something, even if that something is a formula?

The great contribution of science has been the clarification and organization of *facts*; the expediting of intelligent *discovery*; and the composition of new *materials*. In effect this is the shaping of new tools for the modern craftsman. To the craftsman a fact is as much a tool as a hammer; so is a discovery which he can apply, or a scientifically-compounded material he can use. If he obtains his facts through science instead of divining them by slow-moving instinct it merely expedites his work. His is still the creative intelligence. To argue the predominance in social importance of the fact-finder as against the fact-user is no more fruitful than the "egg or the hen" controversy.

There are pessimists who insist that the craftsman has disappeared forever from the American scene. But it is wiser to say that American craft has *changed,* rather than vanished. Perhaps by acquainting ourselves with the skilled workmen and artisans of our past history, attempting to understand their work and their personalities, we shall be stimulated to a better sense of the values and uses of the modern crafts.

We have a right to expect some significant link between the crafts that shaped our developing nation, and our contemporary life. Charles Beard has said: "In the history of social philosophy there is nothing more interesting than the tardy recognition accorded to the fact that modern business enterprise rests upon the whole heritage of western civilization—its religious disciplines, its laws and morals, *its crafts and skills, its sciences and arts,* (Italics mine), its tastes and aspirations . . . . In some mysterious way thought and the materials of life evolve together."

The artisans, in whose lives, functions, and influences we shall interest ourselves include carpenters, cabinetmakers, bookbinders, clockmakers, diemakers, glassmakers, gunmakers, ironworkers, lampmakers, leatherworkers, pewterers, potters, silversmiths, toolmakers, and weavers. We shall not try to be exhaustive, but merely representative, in considering the arts and crafts that have contributed to our American civilization.

CHAPTER 3

HOUSES AND HOUSE BUILDERS

THE Pilgrim settlers on the shores of New England disembarked from their ship to find themselves in a stark wilderness. They had no shelter but their ship; no abundance of supplies; perilously inadequate equipment, and only a few random trifles of furnishings for their new homes. The little band of religious rebels who made up the Plymouth party had been heading for Virginia bearing a document granting permission to settle. Upon finding themselves, instead, confronted by this relatively barren and forbidding land they abruptly decided to remain. Doubtless the prospect of continuing the voyage seemed no more encouraging than the prospect of remaining. It is also probable that the shrewd Fathers realized that the very handicaps of the place would subject them to a less imminent danger of further molestation than the more fruitful, predominantly Royalist, predominantly Church of England, South.

The immediate and urgent necessity was for shelter. They had not the time, the facilities, nor the materials for elaborate procedures. Accordingly the first specimens of American house-building were crude huts of branches stuck together with mud, wattle, leaves and other debris. These hovels were usually roughly conical in shape. The settlers fell into the habit of calling them "wigwams," although they in no way derived from the

13

Indian dwellings of that name. To the contrary, they were fashioned after the dwellings of the English yeomanry of the early 17th century when actual frame or brick houses were a luxury of the upper class.

Many variants or improvements were not long in forthcoming. Possibly the commonest of these was to excavate a hillside and build out from it, thus having one half of the house beneath the surface of the ground; an excellent safeguard against violent weather. One of the first New Englanders, Edward Johnson, commented on this in a curious book called *Wonder-Working Providence of Sions Savior in New England*. "They burrow themselves in the Earth for their first shelter under some Hill side, casting the Earth aloft upon Timber: they make a smoaky fire against the Earth at its highest side."

Another improvement in the clay and wattle house was the addition of a ridge-pole, supported by forked sticks. This did away with the cramping, conical shape, enabling the elongation of the entire structure.

After the immediate necessity for shelter had been met the colonists could begin to contemplate a more permanent type of dwelling. Their natural desire was to recreate the environment from which they had come rather than, as we might like to think, self-consciously build a new and appropriately original world. This understandable wish even blinded them, for a time, to the resources about them. They had come from a land where lumber was none too plentiful. Therefore it was some time before the fact of the new abundance of timber took effect on them. There was perhaps never any physical need for the twig-and-mud shelters except during the first weeks of the new colony, yet they persisted.

Once the fact of abundant timber did sink in, it resulted in widespread building. The first timber houses were made of logs, or planks, raised vertically and fastened together near the top. The roofs were of thatch; and the chimneys, of stick and mud. The colonists began to catch up with their resources by substituting shingle for thatch nearly two centuries before this trend occurred in Europe. On the other hand, the dangerous stick-and-mud chimney persisted long after the other primitive features had begun to disappear and was responsible for many fires until laws were passed against it.

Later, the use of the abundant stone of New England was to become an important factor in building.

Few of us realize that the traditional log-cabin, in the familiar style of horizontally placed logs, notched and fitted at the ends, is an important factor in the later expansion of the *frontier,* rather than of the colonies. The only settlers who arrived in America with a tradition of abundant timber were the Swedes. The first of these came to Delaware in 1638. It is to them that we owe the log-cabin form. Similar houses had long been used in the Scandinavian countries. Subsequently the advantage of the log-cabin for frontier construction, where it was necessary to cut down trees in any event to prepare the land for occupancy, was quite quickly grasped by everyone. It remained essentially a frontier form, however, because it had definite limitations and could not satisfy the early householders' desire for nicety. It persisted generally in colonial forts and prisons. It is often confused with the block-house, a structure built with squared logs smoothly joined. The block-house construction was not used for dwellings. For a long time, in Virginia, the term "log-house" meant "jail."

The crude houses of the first stage were made with simple implements by amateur labor. American need exerted some influence upon the tools used to meet it. Before we look to the still more elaborate period of house-building, where more specialized skills of workmanship are brought to bear, it will be interesting to examine the pioneer tools.

The means by which a primeval forest is partly cleared and made to bring forth a cluster of rude houses are worth knowing. Obviously the implements used by our American forefathers for this purpose were not of their own invention. Nearly all of them dated from Roman times, at least. In origin many of them had archaeological value in their interpretation of the implements of Babylonia, Egypt, and other ancient civilizations. These are the basic tools of mankind wherever he lifts himself above the most abysmally primitive levels. Such tools lose nothing in significance to us by not being American inventions. Rather, the few changes America did make in them take on added meaning in the face of their antiquity and seeming changlessness.

The prospective house builder, confronted by a forest, was faced with a series of at least nine different processes leading into the actual work of construction. These were: felling, splitting, sawing, moving, holding, surfacing, shaping, fitting, and fastening.

To begin at the beginning, the familiar cross-cut, two-man saw, stock-in-trade of the lumberman today, did not come into use until 1880. It was with the unaided axe that Americans cut their way through the great wilderness, with cities springing up in their traces.

If any one thing deserves to be the symbol of American conquest it is the axe. It is a simple implement, yet implicit in it is a large part of the difference between civilized and primitive races. The American Indian had no axe, for he had no iron. When he needed a log he was compelled to use one which had fallen of itself.

The axe that first came to America found an immediate ex-

1. PIONEER'S VILLAGE, SALEM, MASS. Reconstruction of English wigwams.

OLD STONE HOUSE, GUIL- FORD, CONN., 1639. Said to be the oldest house in the U.S.

3. JACKSON HOUSE, PORTSMOUTH, N.H., 1664. Note characteristic lean-to.

Antiques

4. A Typical New England Blockhouse.

5. Unusual Revolutionary Blockhouse. Said to have been built by a French engineer.

6. Parson Capen's House, Topsfield, Mass., 1683. Built for the Parson by his father-in-law. Gothic type. Note carved pendants on the overhang.

WASHINGTON'S BIRTHPLACE, WESTMORELAND CO., VIRGINIA. From a Currier and Ives Print.

DOORWAY DETAIL, PARSON
CAPEN'S HOUSE. Note
studded door and carved
ornament.

Antiques

9. Early Lumbering Tools. Note variety of axes.

10. Early Carpenter's and Wagoner's Tools.

12. Frows and Frow Clubs.

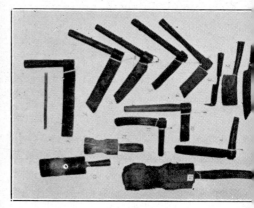

11. Carpenter's and Wagoner's Tools.

13. Cooper's Tools.

These pictures by courtesy of Mr. W. B. Sprague and the Early American Industries Association.

14. SPENCER-PIERCE HOUSE, NEWBURY, MASS., 1651. Left wing added later.

15. BUSSING HOMESTEAD, NEW YORK STATE, 1600-1699.

16. HOME OF JOHN WARD, AMERICAN CABINETMAKER, SALEM, MASS., 1684. Gothic type.

17. INTERIOR OF WARD HOUSE. Note architectural details, stools, and other furniture.

18. NELSON HOUSE, SHEEPSCOT, MAINE. Colonial period.

Antiques

19. INTERIOR OF NELSON HOUSE. Note Windsor chair and warming pan.

Antiques

20. ATTIC OF A NEW HAMPSHIRE FARMHOUSE. Note spinning wheel, bedstead, jugs, coal scuttle, etc..

Antiques

21. INTERIOR DISPLAY. Note Pennsylvania three-corner cupboard, "baby grandfather clock," left, also miniature Chippendale chair for child.

22. Home of David Rittenhouse, American Clockmaker and Friend of Benjamin Franklin, Philadelphia.

23. Sayre House, Summit, N. J., c. 1700.

24. Eleazer Arnold House, Lincoln, R.I., c. 1687. Known as "stone-end" type of structure.

5. Long Island Farmhouse. Early 19th century. Painted by William Sidney Mount.

26. Timothy Ball House, Maplewood, N. J. 18th Century.

28. Typical Pennsylvania-German Stone and Wood Barn. Note decorative symbols.

Antiques

27. Pennsylvania-German Stone House, 1714.

Antiques

29. COMMUNITY DINING ROOM, OF SHAKER TYPE. Museum display with authentic pieces.

30. COLONIAL INTERIOR, NEW BEDFORD, MASS. Museum display. Note wall paneling, chandelier, and Windsor rocker.

Colonial Capitol, Restored, Williamsburg, Virginia.

32. Independence Hall, Philadelphia. An old engraving.

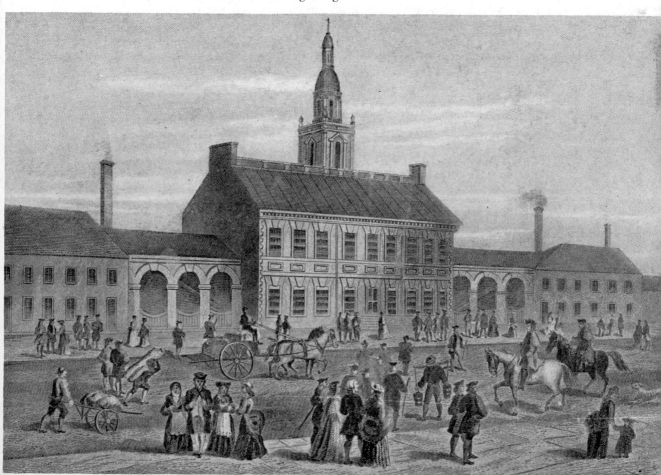

33. Old Botsford Tavern, New England.

Wickwire House, Cortland, N. Y. 18th Century.

35. WICKWIRE HOUSE, DOORWAY DETAIL.

36. FAÇADE DETAIL. ST. JOHN'S COLLEGE, ANNAPOLIS, MD., 1770.

37. WASHINGTON'S HEADQUARTERS, MORRISTOWN, N.J.

38. FANEUIL HALL AND THE OLD FEATHER STORE, BOSTON, MASS. An old print.

change value with the Indians and hence quickly became known as the "trade axe." The top edge of its blade forms a right angle with the handle in a manner which most of us associate with the Indian "tomahawk." As a matter of fact, this deadly head-splitter was a conception of early American blacksmiths, a miniature model of the standard "trade axe." It found ready acceptance as an article of barter among the Indians, and was thereafter buried in more than one American blacksmith's skull.

The "trade axe" had no poll. The "poll" is the hammer part of an axe, opposite the blade. Another type of axe, now known as the "Anglo-American felling axe," had a small poll and each edge flared at an acute angle to the haft.

An American axe did develop. It was made only in America and when found in other countries may be known to have been imported from America. The head of this axe was rectangular, the cutting edge was a straight line instead of an arc (as in all previous types), and its most particular characteristic was that *the poll weighed more than the blade.*

Some explain this by the theory that America originally had many inexperienced tree-fellers. These inept men presumably found it difficult to keep the axe blade from wobbling during the forward stroke, and to obviate this kept thinning the blade by grinding, until they eventually arrived at the idea of making the poll heavier than the blade in order to facilitate a straight stroke. This is a plausible theory, yet the fact is that this type of axe is more efficient for both inexperienced and experienced woodsmen. It must be set down as one of the first great communal inventions of America due, not so much to our inexperience, as to the fact that we were confronted with more unfelled trees than any other people in civilized times.

The American axe reached its full development before 1750 and in common with all other early axes (before 1850), had a straight handle. The well known type of the double-edged axe did not come into general use until well into the 19th century. It was feared by lusty woodsmen as a "back-wounder."

Once down, the log had then to be moved by power of oxen, horses, or men. This involved the use of a "drag-shackle," which worked on the principle of the familiar ice tongs. The log was then split into segments with an ancient type of iron wedge and wooden mallet, sometimes called a "beetle." These implements are still in use, although for different purposes.

An essential early tool, now almost extinct, was the "frow." This was a steel blade with a wooden handle at a right angle to it. In variously modified forms it found a use in every early form or process of woodworking. It was used by the settlers for splitting segments of log into lathes or shingle material. It was steered with the handle and pounded on the opposite end of its blade with a wooden implement called a "frow club." Used in conjunction with this was the "frow horse," a sort of forked bench for bracing a block of wood while it was being split into shingles by the frow.

The rough shingles were then held in a "shaving horse" and worked over with the draw-knife, an implement the same as that in use today. In most parts of the country the shingle was thinned only at the top, but in Pennsylvania it was the custom to overlap them at the sides as well and this involved thinning them at top and side. Then they were sheared off in a device called a "shingle cutter," similar to the familiar stationer's paper cutter.

The conversion of logs into planks was the most important of the early processes. This was accomplished not by splitting but with a very ancient implement known as the "framed pit saw." This was a long saw blade, vertically bisecting a rectangular frame of wood. It was worked by two men. The so-called "open pit saw" dispensed with the frame, depending for strength upon an additional rigidity of the blade. The former was more widely used. The importance of the pit saw cannot be over-stressed, for it was the sole means of obtaining planks before the development of the power saw turned by water or horsepower.

The "spirit level" was invented in 1660 but did not come into general use among American carpenters until after 1830 due to the difficulty of getting accurately blown glass tubes. The level in common use employed a miniature plumb-line suspended from an arc into a gauged crevice.

There was an early brace, of wood, but it did not replace the augur because the leverage it could apply was limited and there was greater need for holes of large diameter due to the custom of joining with wooden pegs rather than metal bolts, screws, or nails.

The adze, a hoe-like cutting implement, was used more in boat-building than elsewhere. Planes were much the same as today except that their bodies were more often made of hard wood than of metal. Hammers, screws, bolts, and wrenches all bear antique pedigrees. Calipers, measuring sticks, plumb lines, squares, compasses, vises, and chisels were practically the same as those in use today. This is also true of the handsaw, key-hole saw, and scroll saw.

The beams, rafters, and trusses of early houses often were not sawn but hewn with the broad axe. Joints were usually mortised and fastened with pegs, bolts, or nails for additional strength. The previously mentioned draw-knife was used for the "chamfering," or bevelling, of beams which constituted one of the main decorations of early American houses.

There was a limit to the skill and resourcefulness of the amateur carpenters who so admirably rose to the occasion in building the first homes on American shores. Their creations were crude and far from adequate to a graceful or comfortable way of life. Accordingly, when the first push was over, they welcomed eagerly the gradual influx of skilled carpenters and related craftsmen who steadily and unobstrusively set about the task of building up American homes on the basis of permanence, genuine comfort, and a certain amount of beauty. Such men were not long in coming, men skilled in the mysteries of building a frame house that would really stay together. But there are no great names among them for our story. Their relative talents must remain unknown to us. That they were generally inventive and skilful there is no doubt. But the rest is cloaked in a veil of anonymity.

A little bit of information can be found about certain of the Dutch carpenters of New Amsterdam. The handful named, about whose lives any details at all can be discovered, certainly cannot give any comprehensive picture of the times. But the hint thus afforded gives us some ground for surmise concerning the lives and habits of early American builders. The Dutch carpenters are of special significance, for they are responsible for the only really indigenous type of American architecture prior to the skyscraper.

In those days a man who called himself a carpenter might also be a glazier, upholsterer, mason, shipbuilder, joiner, and some form of metal worker. In addition to their versatility the carpenters of New Amsterdam appear to have been possessed of active and obstreperous dispositions. Apparently they never paid a debt without an argument or expected to collect one without litigation.

Men whose negotiable wealth is carried within them in their brains and hands are sometimes more independent of spirit than men whose wealth is external. That is partly why, in the field of the arts and crafts, there has existed the tradition of Bohemianism. In the early days of America the craftsman was the social equivalent of the artist. Because his knowledge and skill were so vitally necessary to the material and aesthetic welfare of the community he was more inclined to eschew respectability than were the members of any other group.

Early manuscripts reveal the following list of carpenters of old New Amsterdam. All called themselves carpenters except for the three otherwise designated. Asterisks indicate those who acquired for themselves, in one way or another, reputations as troublemakers.

1. Frederick Arentsen * (turner)
2. Cristyn Barentsen
3. Jan Clyn *
4. Frederick Flipsen *
5. Adrian Jansen Hagenaer * (probably a joiner's apprentice)
6. Jan Jansen Hagenaer
7. Jan Hendricksen *
8. Abrams Jacobson *
9. Albert Jansen
10. Frans Jansen *
11. Thomas Lambertzen *
12. Arent Lourizen
13. Adolf Pietersen
14. Pieter Pietersen *
15. Gerrit Jansen Roos
16. David Wessels * (chairmaker)
17. Cornelis Willemsen *

A few items of interest, concerning some of these, turn up in the public records. Frederick Flipsen was accused of drinking brandy at Andres Johginsen's taphouse on the Sabbath "while the first preaching was going on." He was further charged with disturbing the peace by inducing "Steenwyck's Negro," also influenced by brandy, to play the jew's-harp at one Govert Loockerman's. In 1662 Flipsen tried to collect some brewing equipment in payment for a debt. On another occasion he ungallantly took possession of a widow's petticoat as security for a less important account.

A notation in the records, in 1658, tells us that "Albert Jansen requests, as he is about to build a house, and his lot is too little, that an adjoining lot be granted him." There is no indication as to whether or not he obtained it. But at another time Jansen claims "that he made for Mr. Stickly two pillows, two cushions and a bench, on which they sleep, and one bedstead for which he should have 500 pounds of tabacco." One could wish to know why the Stickly family slept on the bench and what they did with the bedstead.

Frans Jansen was apparently in hard case. It was stated in court that he, "in company with Abel Hardenbroech and others, broke windows and made a noise in the street." He denies this, "but admits he was in company." Another accusation affirms that he had "at night and at unseasonable hours in company with some soldiers created an uproar and great insolence in the street." Charged with the offense the defendent "denies having committed it, acknowledging that he was with company, but had no hand in breaking the windows, saying further he did not even know where those live whose windows were broken." Jansen ended his career as a professional beer-carrier.

The most involved case is that of Cornelis Willemsen. To begin with, he could not pay Symon Jansen for his woodworking tools, and, furthermore, would not surrender them. He held out for quite a while and then, one day, the bailiff went to fetch him, only to find him gone. He had sailed away, taking with him Stoffel Eduaart's boat and Joseph Waldron's son.

Behind him he left "At Joseph Waldron's one bed and appurtenances as a bolster with two pillows, one quilt, two sheets, one pillow case, one gun, a grindstone, one chest with old rag of no value. At Geerje Hoppi's widow of Andres Hoppe, was found an octagon little table and an old workbench. With Dom. Drisus is remaining . . . . the sum of Fl. 60 in Zeaway (wampum, or Indian shell work) which he earned there in wages."

It later appears that Joseph Waldron went to other colonies in search of his young son, whom Willemsen had lured away from New Amsterdam, but returned without success.

In the last entry of the case there is a certain pathos: ". . . . request of Joseph Waldron wherein he asks to be allowed to sell the goods in his house belonging to the fugitive Cornelis Willemsen, Carpenter."

At a much later date, when genuinely distinguished names appear in the field of American house-building they are the names of amateur and professional architects, rather than craftsmen. The exception to this is Samuel McIntire, in the town of Salem, 1782–1811, who was an architect, contractor, carpenter and woodcarver, celebrated for ship's figureheads.

As we pick up again the thread of development of American houses, emerging from the primitive-pioneer status, we can begin to speak in terms of "architecture." In the narrowest sense architecture cannot be classified as a "craft." But for practical purposes within the spirit of this book it must be considered. For architecture is a highly communal proposition. On its broadest representative level, in any given era, it is truly typical of a people: exalted, debased, or mediocre. It remains highly communal even when much of its work passes into the hands of the individually creative or interpretive specialist. It is thus, in a sense, a magnificent culmination of crafts.

Early frame houses of New England followed the Gothic tradition. Their characteristic features were the steep roof, leaded casements, clustered chimney stacks, second story overhang, and exposed beams. The ground floor was usually only one room deep and one, two, or three rooms long. Its central feature was the fireplace; usually in the middle facing front; occasionally one at each end of the room. The more pretentious houses in the English Colonies were often two-and-a-half stories high, the second floor being devoted to bed chambers and the attic to storage.

The spacious baronial interiors owed what beauty they possessed to the functional lines of the exposed beams. These beams were usually "chamfered," that is, had bevelled edges, to detract from their stark angularity. The characteristic overhang of the second story was sometimes made more decorative by the addition of outdoor molding or pendants. Space, strength, and simplicity were the chief aims.

The Dutch, in the New Netherlands, developed a special style of house which we have previously mentioned as being possibly the only American creation in architecture previous to the skyscraper. It is certainly not a reproduction of any house common to the Netherlands, in the manner of the English reproductions. In typical form this Dutch house was one-and-a-half stories high. The lower part was made of roughly hewn native stone of varying sizes; the upper part of planes or shingles. The roof was quite steep, with an exaggerated overhang of the eaves, usually curved slightly upward to prevent an appearance of top-heaviness. The stones were fastened together with clay mixed with straw or hog's hair. The stone walls were whitewashed.

As time passed the pitch of the roofs became less steep and near the end of the 17th century the "gambrel roof," an English idea, was added to it. This is a roof with an additional obtuse angle on each side of the ridge-pole, causing the profile to approach closer to an arc than a wedge.

The Renaissance architectural influences did not come to America until 1700, and then strictly in an English version. In general, the ideal of our Colonial Architecture was the very natural imitation of the English.

A new form of life, for those who could afford it, was implicit in the new architecture. In the old Gothic-survival type of house there was a minimum of privacy. The great room of the ground floor was generally kitchen, dining-room, parlor and, in some cases, town meeting-place as well. On the second floor there was often no hall, so that to get to the last bedroom one had to walk through all of them in the manner of the dismal "railroad-flat" of the modern city. This predicated a mediaeval family life in which all members were practically vassals to the head of the house.

The new houses were designed for privacy. Floors were divided, as a rule, into four rooms. The novel idea of privacy for each member of a family was in itself a preliminary assertion of the Rights of Man.

In addition to this came an emphasis on the ideal of symmetry. The abstractions of space, mass, line, and surface became important. Interiors were panelled and a molded chimney-piece was built around the heretofore purely functional fireplace.

This was the dwelling of a comparatively wealthy man. The Colonial, or Georgian, style reached its full splendor in America in the fifty years preceding the Revolution. It took unto itself rich doorways, pilasters, porticoes, carved staircases, ornamental ceilings, and Palladian windows. America had, now, a truly

wealthy class. The Tidewater planters of the South, the Pat-
roons of the Hudson River Valley, the merchants of New York,
Philadelphia, Salem, and Boston, had money in their pockets.
(The great English potter, Wedgwood, wrote in 1765: "We can-
not make anything too costly for the American market. . . .")
Luxuries that could have found no buyers in England or on the
Continent had a ready sale in America.

During these times a knowledge of architecture became a
part of the equipment of every true gentleman. There were very
few professionals. A knowledge of the art was disseminated
through books, such as those by the Englishmen, Wren and
Jones, or by the classic Palladio. American carpenters were con-
versant with these books and a gentleman with housebuilding intentions could discuss with his carpenter, on equal terms, the
artistic and technical intricacies of the home he desired to own.
Certain gentlemen, such as Peter Harrison of Newport, were
so gifted as amateur architects that they were greatly in demand.
Some frequently accepted payments for their consultations.

Many lovely houses were built, and are much admired by
amateurs in Americana. Yet there was nothing "American"
about them; nothing whatever was added to the English styles
of the same period.

Histories of architecture, as a rule, deal only with the domestic architecture of the rich or with public or ecclesiastical buildings. This is unfortunate, for the histories of such structures,
since the Renaissance, have been largely a series of reversions to
past eras.

The architecture of the common people has usually been of
more interest and originality but little has been written about
it. Documentation of the subject is virtually non-existent. There
are marked regional differences in common dwelling places and

they do not shift from style to style as public or wealthy architecture does.

The farm houses of New England developed the lean-to, a long, low structure at the back of the house, and the massive central fireplace, anchoring the center of the building. These can be found, and are still built, in our time. In the South there was no middle-class to speak of, hence no architecture between mansion and hovel. But many Southern dwellings developed the style of the kitchen in a separate building, connected by a covered walk. Such items as these, along with our adoption and improvement of the Swedish log-cabin, and the Dutch-Colonial stone and wood house are almost the whole of American architecture, prior to the modern period. It is unfortunate that we know so little of these aspects and so much about our Georgian, Roman, Greek, Gothic, and sundry other imitations.

We can conclude our talk of architecture with a word about "period." So far as any one section of America is concerned, such as the area of the original colonies, it is possible to trace fairly definite successions of "periods" in architecture (and, of course, in furniture). But there is always one complicating factor which is too often overlooked.

To a considerable degree "period" is a matter of class, and economic position. For example, in Tudor England it was only the upper class that was Tudor, the rest of the people were early Gothic. Pursuing the parallel to our own times, the greater number of average homes fall into the category of the late Victorian style. With rare exceptions it is only a handful of the wealthy who are "modern." Thus, at any given time, we find a great diversity of periods within the same community with the poorer classes, who are always in the majority, lagging as much as a century behind.

Early America added an extra complication. The historian, A. G. Simons, says: "While the frontier existed, this was the only country in the world that for many generations permitted its inhabitants to choose in which of the historic stages of evolution they would live." This also means, of course, in what "periods" they would live. Thus, in this country, as long as the frontier existed, we find a consistent recurrence of periods as we move away from any center of settlement.

So far as "period" in the architecture of the people at large is concerned, it is a slow-moving process. When the buildings change a people has changed. Next in turgidity, resistance to change, is furniture, the leading character on the stage of architecture. It is logical, therefore, that our next step in surveying the scene of American crafts, should be a look at the furniture which the early American craftsmen constructed to equip the homes they had established.

CHAPTER 4

FURNITURE MAKERS

WHEN the Colonial settlers of America had built their first rude houses they had to furnish them. Little or no furniture, mainly chests, had been brought from the home country. Importation was not immediately practical and would have been highly inappropriate in any case. The people who had built their houses of logs, crude planks, or wattles were not inclined to deck them out with the best style of English furnishings.

It fell to those most skilled in general handicraft, to knock together makeshift furniture. So far as possible this was made in imitation of the remembered furniture left behind them. Accordingly the first pieces made and used by the English colonists were strongly reminiscent of English cottage furniture. In general style it was mediaeval, Gothic. Only slowly did it begin to manifest the influence of the prevailing modes of Court, or upper class furniture, from England. Even the Gothic, or Tudor, forms were subject to certain modifications arising from functional requirements, the necessary simplicity, and the use of the types of wood immediately available. It is easily understood that the rigors and feverish activities of the task of colonization left little time for the embellishment of house furnishings.

The men who were our first professional makers of furniture were usually carpenters, or general workers in wood, who called themselves "joyners." Their craft, in this stage, was relatively simple.

The first trained woodworker in America was that same John Alden, traditionally supposed to have triumphed in love over the rivalry of his friend, Miles Standish. In any event, it was certainly his trade which procured Priscilla's lover his passage to America. The English law required that no ship should set sail on a long voyage without a cooper to take care of the barrels in which provisions and water were stored. John Alden was that cooper, on the Mayflower, and sailed with the option that he might return with the ship or not, as he chose. Whether Priscilla influenced his decision or not, he elected to remain, and to practice his craft of coopering, and later of "joyning." In other words, he turned to furniture making and probably could be credited with some of the early New England pieces now in museums or private collections, all of which, of course, are unidentified by markings.

Another of New England's early joiners was Governor Winslow's brother, Kenelm. Kenelm Winslow arrived in 1629, and apparently found plenty of work to do. In 1640 he was appointed Town Surveyor and in 1641 was fined ten shillings for neglecting the highways, an offense which sounds a little strange, considering the period. He finally abandoned the joiner's trade and spent his later years as a farmer and shipper.

The wave of migration which swept into Massachusetts Bay after the third decade of the 17th century brought with it a great many joiners. Nearly all of them are listed in local records for it was customary to refer to a man's trade, along with his name, as a means of additional identification in all legal procedures. There are no names for special discussion, for the work of individuals, however meritorious, cannot be identified. A rare exception to this prevailing situation is a chest made by Nicholas

Disbrowe, who came from England and was living in Hartford, Connecticut, in 1639. The chest, which was discovered by Mr. L. V. Lockwood, has written inside of it: "Mary Allyns Chistt Cutte and Joyned by Nich. Disbrowe."

Nicholas Disbrowe was later charged with witchcraft by a customer who did not like the bill rendered and purported to find something occult in the matter. After some trouble the joiner was acquitted.

The most characteristic feature of the joiner's furniture of our early period is its construction. It is composed of straight members, joined at right angles. The curve is entirely absent in the structural sense and barely begins to assert itself in the decorative aspects.

The most basic item of furniture in the early American home was the chest. It was simple to build, could be used as a storage place in the home, as a trunk in travel. It served as a seat and, if necessary, as a low table. Its usual decorative features were plain panels and simple moldings. Appliqué ornamentation appeared later. Molding and appliqué were usually painted black to resemble ebony. Carving was also practiced, usually of the simplest, flat kind, with only two parallel surfaces. Such carving was often accented by painting the two surfaces in different colors, generally red or black.

An evolution began, in the chest, with the addition of drawers to its lower section. As it was found convenient to add more drawers the chest naturally became higher. This drawer-adding was more rapidly adopted in America than in England, for natural reasons of usefulness. The top continued to be hinged. As the chest took on height and could no longer be used as a seat with any degree of dignity, it was natural that its top should be used as a repository for objects of pewter, silver, pottery, or glass. This development made the hinged top impractical. Accordingly the drawers were continued all the way to the top. Thus the well known chest-of-drawers evolved.

At the end of the 17th century, for greater convenience in using the bottom drawer, the chest was raised on short legs, producing the highboy, an object especially suited to American tastes by its immense practicality.

In sheer terms of furniture height, the 17th century American home was dominated by the cupboard. There were two primary types. The "Court Cupboard" had doors above and below. The "Press Cupboard" had doors above and shelves below. These followed the rectangular joining and simple ornamentation of the chest and were used for the storage of things that had to be readily accessible, such as food and tableware. The cupboard failed to evolve beyond the 17th century, though it is probably the grandfather of the built-in cupboard and the "sideboard."

The early desk-box was a small chest intended for writing implements and other odds-and-ends. Its sides and front were often of oak; top and bottom, of pine, securely dove-tailed and often ornamented with much greater lavishness than any of the larger pieces. Sometimes the lid was slanted forward, the better to display its decoration. From this it was but a step to the desk-box on legs, connected by stretchers. This produced the slant-top desk of the 18th century, which is still made much in the same manner.

Commonly in use for sitting were stools and forms. The stools were rectangular and added much to the effect of a room, for they were often topped with pads of brightly colored upholstery.

Three types of chair were in use and a certain amount of ceremony was associated with them. This was especially true of

ohn Alden, America's First "Joyner." Imaginatively conceived in
he of the Rogers groups of American figures.

40, 42. Chair Table, c. 1675. Said to
        have been owned by Peregrine
        White, born on the *Mayflower* in
        1620. Rectangular top rests on
        slightly shaped arms and strips on
        underside of top. White oak with
        pine top. Shown as both chair
        and table.

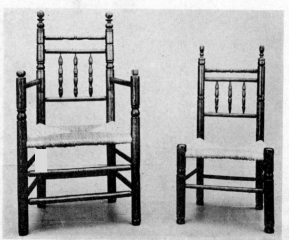

41. Governor Carver Chairs, 1650-1700. Note
spindle construction.

43. CHEST DECORATED WITH SCRATCH CARVING.
Pine. Constructed without stiles and rails.
c. 1650.

Metropolitan Museum

44. OAK CHEST, ATTRIBUTED TO THOMAS DENNIS, IPSW
MASS., c. 1675. Raised on feet.

Metropolitan Mus

45. CHEST WITH ONE DRAWER. Retains hinged
top. 1650-1675. Oak.

Metropolitan Museum

46. CHEST WITH TWO DRAWERS, ATTRIBUTED TO NICHOLAS
DISBROWE, c. 1675. Oak.. Top will not lift.

Metropolitan Museum

47. CHEST WITH TWO DRAWERS. Retaining hi
top.

Metropolitan Mu

Chest of Drawers, 1675-1700.

Metropolitan Museum

49. Chest with Drawers. Raised on Frame.

Metropolitan Museum

Early Highboy, 1690-1700. Pine.

Metropolitan Museum

OM CHEST TO HIGHBOY

51. The Ultimate New England Highboy, 1725-1750. Walnut burl veneer, decorated with inlay and gilded shell.

Metropolitan Museum

52. CHAIR TABLE with Square Top.

Metropolitan Museum

53. PINE SETTLE, 17th century.

Metropolitan Museum

54. TRESTLE TABLE, c. 1650. Much reduced in scale.

Metropolitan Museum

55. CRADLE OF OAK, 1625-1675.

Metropolitan Museum

58. CHEST ON CHEST. Mahogany. Another New England refinement in the chest evolution.

Metropolitan Museum

6, 57. PENNSYLVANIA-GERMAN DOWER CHESTS. Painted pine. With and without drawers.

Metropolitan Museum

59. PINE AND OAK CUPBOARD. Painted in Grisaille. 18th Century.

Metropolitan Museum

60. PENNSYLVANIA HANGING CUPBOARD, 1725-1750. Walnut.

Metropolitan Museum

61. PRESS CUPBOARD, 1660-1680. Carved oak.

62. BUTTERFLY TABLE. 17th century.

63. DROP-LEAF TABLE, MASS., c. 1675.

64. Press Cupboard, 1650-1675. Oak.

Metropolitan Museum

65. Walnut Dresser, Pennsylvania, c. 1750.

Metropolitan Museum

66. Corner Cupboard. Pine. 18th Century.

Metropolitan Museum

67. Sawbuck Table of Walnut and Oak, Pennsylvania, 1700-1750.

Metropolitan Museum

70. Wainscot Armchair, Sometimes Called "Master's Chair." Carved oak. 17th Century.

Metropolitan Museum

68, 69. Chest of Drawers, with Label. Jonathan Gostelowe of Philadelphia, c. 1790.

Philadelphia Museum

Jonathan Gostelowe,
CABINET AND CHAIR MAKER,

At his shop in Church Alley, about between Second and Third-streets,

BEGS leave to inform his former Custom and Public in general, That he hath again fumed occupation at the above mentioned place: A renewal of favours will be thankfully received; and his best endeavour shall be used to give satisfaction to those who please to employ him.

71, 72.   SECRETARY DESK BY JOHN GODDARD, OF NEWPORT, R.I. Note characteristic shell design and flame finials. Open and closed view.

Metropolitan Museum

Metropolitan Museum

73.   BLOCK FRONT DESK, MAHOGANY. Has Goddard's characteristic design. Compare with secretary above.

Metropolitan Museum

74.   NEW ENGLAND BLOCK-FRONT DESK, CABINET TOP. Mahogany. Carved figures attributed to John and Simeon Skillin.

75. HIGH STREET, WITH THE FIRST PRESBYTERIAN CHURCH, PHILADELPHIA. Jonathan Gostelowe's Shop was the little two story building.

76. CARD TABLE, WITH LABEL OF STEPHEN AND THOMAS GODDARD. Mahogany, Pine, and Satin wood.

77. CARD TABLE, BY JOHN TOWNSEND, OF NEWPORT, R. I., 1766.

79, 80, 81. Library Table, Arm Chair, and Side Chair, in the Style of Duncan Phyfe.

78. Colonel Marinus Willet, Cabinetmaker, of New York.

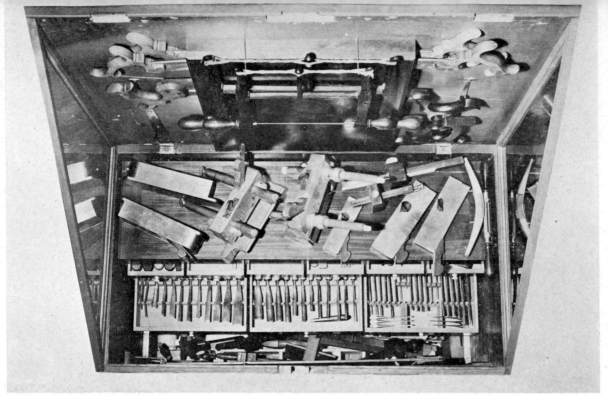

82. Tool Chest of Duncan Phyfe.

83. Duncan Phyfe's Shop and Warehouse on Fulton St., N. Y., c. 1820.

French and (

84. This is the only extant likeness of Duncan Phyfe. It is painted on ordinary blue and white upholsterer's ticking, in furniture paint. It is presumably the creation of one of his shop workers. Phyfe wears an upholsterer's smock, his celebrated Scotch cap, and holds a cabinetmaker's saw.

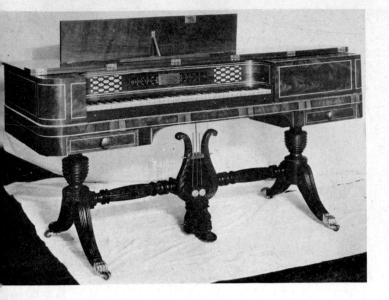

85. PIANO, BY DUNCAN PHYFE.

Antiques

Metropolitan Museum

6. DROP-LEAF TABLE IN THE STYLE OF PHYFE.

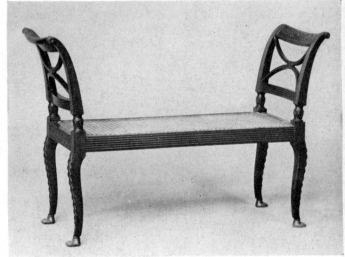

Metropolitan Museum

87. WINDOW SEAT. Probably Phyfe.

Metropolitan Museum

88. MAHOGANY DINING TABLE BY DUNCAN PHYFE.

89-93.   TYPES OF AMERICAN WINDSOR CHAIR.

Metropolitan Museum

94.   TRADE CARD OF A FANCY AND WINDSOR CHAIR MANUFACTURER, 1825.

N. Y. Historical Society
Bella C. Landauer Collect

95, 96. Two Views of the Factory of Lambert Hitchcock.

Antiques

97-101. Chairs by Lambert Hitchcock. Note Rocker, and detail of decoration.

Antiques
Brooklyn Museum

the "wainscot chair." The back of this chair was a solid panel. It had turned arm-posts and followed the usual rectangular joining. It was thought of as the "Master's chair," an aura which may have prevented it from becoming more common in use, for it was easy to build.

A more popular type of chair was the "slat-back." This had turned back-posts, connected by three or four horizontal slats. Its primary decorative feature was the high finial of the back post.

Most common were the chairs made with turned posts connected by turned spindles. Although they did not originate here, two variants of this chair are known in America by the names of Colonial Governors Carver and Brewster. The Carver chair is mainly distinguished by a back composed of three horizontal spindles, set between the back-posts, and three vertical spindles set between the lower two horizontal spindles. The Brewster chair is more elaborate, having two sets of vertical spindles, one rank above the other, in the back; and a greater number of other spindles between the arm-rail and the seat-rail. The addition of all these simply turned spindles did not add greatly to the strength of the chair but merely presaged the general yearning for greater elaboration of design.

The earliest American tables were of the trestle type. These could be taken to pieces easily when occasion required. As the term implies they were merely long boards set atop H-shaped trestles, the trestles themselves being joined by a stretcher. At first the top was not fastened, but later was fixed to the trestles by wooden pegs (dowels).

In the 17th century the rectangular table became more popular. This was a simple, four-legged table with a rectangular top. If the legs were turned they were left square at the top and bottom so that the narrow skirting of the top and the stretchers at the bottom could be mortised into it in customary right-angle form.

The "gate-leg" is a rectangular table with drop-leaves and hinged gates which swing out to support them. Sometimes generously shaped flaps replaced the gates, and these are called "butterfly" tables. Another common table of the earlier period was called the "tavern table." It was rectangular, with an unusually wide skirt in which, sometimes, a drawer was placed.

Beds were extremely simple, being merely rectangular frames strung with leather thongs to support the mattress.

CABINETMAKING

The second period of American furniture involves the evolution of craftsmanship from simple joining to the full status of the art and craft of cabinetmaking. This marked the end of the exclusive use of the rather elementary rectangular joining. The structural use of curved members began. The "cabriole leg" appeared and flourished. Ornamentations aimed at refinement: inlay veneering, japanning, and more intricate carving were used. Yet the important tendency was to achieve beauty by construction, rather than by decoration. Heretofore furniture had not been made with any general decorative scheme in mind. Now it was made in sets, with an eye to grouping and elegant effects.

The craft of cabinetmaking required not only technical skill but a considerable education, at least a knowledge of plane geometry, and familiarity with the standard "pattern books" of the day. The amount of furniture in use increased greatly. The affluence of the Colonists, reaching its high point about 1750, made the employment of cabinetmaker highly remunerative.

The same tendencies toward more gracious patterns of life which affected housebuilding and the development of architec-

ture in America, also made themselves felt in furniture. An unusual fluency in the use of classic forms began. Furniture became
almost entirely architectural in structural elements and ornament. The fluted column, the architrave, the pilaster, the abacus
were essential features of its construction. The general effect was
a greater formal elegance, lightness, and aloofness.

This is a period in which more distinct personalities emerge.
The work of a good many cabinetmakers is identifiable because
of the new custom of attaching labels, which even then was none
too widely practiced.

Outstanding in this era were William Savery (1721–1787),
Jonathan Gostelowe (c. 1745–1795), and Benjamin Randolph (c.
1762), of Philadelphia; Andrew Gautier (1720–1784), and
Colonel Marinus Willet (1740–1830), of New York City; John
Goddard (c. 1750) and his relatives by marriage, Job, Christopher, and John Townsend, of Newport; Aaron Chapin (c.
1783) of Hartford, Connecticut; and Major Benjamin Frothingham (c. 1734–1790), of Charlestown, Massachusetts.

These men all worked in the manner of Thomas Chippendale. To work in the style of another artist or craftsman, without falling into mere imitation, is a difficult feat. Yet a good
number of American cabinetmakers accomplished it, making
definite contributions and clearly imprinting their own personalities upon their products.

The Quaker, William Savery, accomplished this adaptation
to perfection, particularly in his chairs and highboys. He served
a clientele of wealthy Quakers in a style which might be called
a restrained Chippendale. He used the cabriole leg, claw-and-
ball foot, fiddle-back, and other Chippendale elements with his
own modifications. He was appointed Ward Assessor in 1754,

and seven years before he died was in possession of property valued for taxation at $46,000.

Jonathan Gostelowe, Savery's younger competitor, was a good cabinetmaker, a vestryman in his church, a Major of Artillery during the Revolution, and a leading light in his guild: "The Gentlemen Cabinet and Chair Makers of Philadelphia."

A contributing reason for the pompous title of this craft guild was the fact that many real Gentlemen (in the economic definition which largely prevailed) were wont to familiarize themselves with various crafts. We have seen this in architecture and the same is true, to a somewhat lesser degree, in the field of cabinetmaking. As a matter of fact, many early books describing the techniques of even such crafts as glass-blowing, iron forging, weaving, and so on, are addressed to Gentlemen (and Ladies!) "who may be interested in practicing these Mysteries." "Mystery," it might be explained, derived from the early English *misterie,* meaning trade.

The guilds entirely accepted this affectation of the gentry and perpetuated it in their official name, partly we may suppose, as a means of strengthening their effort toward exclusiveness. The natural function of such an organization was the betterment of general trade conditions and economic returns. At this stage of the game it was, however, more akin to an employer's protective association than a union as we know it today. Its primary efforts were directed toward the restricting of competition by making it difficult for newcomers to enter the field.

Another member of the Gentlemen Cabinet and Chair Makers, Benjamin Randolph, was particularly noted for fine chairs.

John Goddard, of Newport, Rhode Island, was celebrated for his Secretary Desks. These pieces were referred to, by collectors, as Rhode Island Desks for many years, until they were finally identified as all being the work of Goddard of Newport. They are of mahogany, with block fronts. They are characterized by the shell carving on the front of the writing-leaf, on the doors of the bookcase compartments above, and on the pigeon-hole drawers of the interior; also by Goddard's fondness for the broken-pediment top with flame finials.

John Goddard married into the Townsend family and probably served his apprenticeship under Job Townsend. This latter craftsman was in business with his brother, Christopher. But Christopher's son, John Townsend, excelled both of them, especially in his block-front chests of drawers and secretaries, in which field he nearly excelled the master, Chippendale. He, with John Goddard's son, Thomas, carried on the Goddard-Townsend association almost until his death in 1858.

Benjamin Frothingham, cabinetmaker, was the son of Benjamin Frothingham, joiner and cabinetmaker, and was born in Boston, in 1734.

Marinus Willet rates with Paul Revere as a craftsman-patriot. He was born in the town of Jamaica, Long Island, in 1740. A most aggressive fighter for freedom on all fronts, he was one of Revere's fellow message-carriers. One of the most daring men in the Revolution, he led the Sons of Liberty when they attacked and seized the wagon trains that were starting from New York City to relieve the British Garrison at Boston on July 6, 1775. He was later a leader in other military victories, most important of which was the defense of Fort Orange, an event which prevented the reinforcement of "Gentleman Johnny" Burgoyne's force and made possible the great American success at Saratoga.

The third period of our early furniture, the classic revival, was dominated by the dour character and skilful hands of Duncan Phyfe.

Nearly all that is known of Phyfe is derived from the researches of another cabinetmaker, Earnest Hagen, who became interested in the Scotchman and began, about 1880, to collect his work as well as the meagre documentary information concerning his personality. Museums and collectors today base their judgment of what is and what is not Duncan Phyfe's furniture largely on the opinions of Mr. Hagen.

Due to his own idiosyncrasies, not much is ever likely to be known of the character of Duncan Phyfe. His father, Gabel Fife, with his wife and approximately eight children, made the voyage from Scotland to Albany in 1783. Some commentators feel that Duncan may have been apprenticed to a coachmaker in Albany, as the Scots were masters of that craft at the time. In any event, he appeared in the New York City Directory of 1792 as "Fife, Duncan, joiner, 2 Broad St."

In the next Directory appears, "Phyfe, Duncan, cabinetmaker, 3 Broad St." He is supposed to have been taken up as a protégé by a daughter of John Jacob Astor, which may have contributed to his phenomenal rise. That the other members of the family disliked the affectation of Duncan's P-h-y is indicated by the fact that they did not adopt it until to be linked with him was an assured honor. Even then, a widow of the clan reverted as far as "Fyfe" some forty years later.

Phyfe's career was launched apparently without struggle. He rose to the top like a cork and stayed there. In 1806 he moved to Partition Street, (later Fulton Street), where, by 1811, he had three buildings for his home, shop, and showroom. A few years later he moved to a home across the street and used the former mansion as a warehouse. By this time he was employing nearly one hundred workmen. Long before this he had become *the* cabinetmaker of New York City, and his name was well known in Philadelphia and Boston. He received much higher prices for his work than any of his contemporaries.

He never advertised, which is strange when we reflect that there were no limits to the production he could have attained inasmuch as he was able to employ many men and produce his own type of work by means of supervision. He never belonged to any of the customary societies, guilds, fraternal orders, churches, political clubs, or organizations of any kind, by means of which most craftsmen sought business. Apparently he was willing to depend solely upon the perfection of his product to advertise his presence and ability. He is mentioned in none of the contemporary gossip columns, travel books, or diaries. It would seem, almost, that he never left his workshop.

It is said that he wore, at all hours of the day, a beaverskin cap, and that he kept a short-stemmed pipe in his mouth. He is said to have paid equal attention to those who had the money to buy his product and those who merely expressed a technical interest in his work. Famous travellers and personages were given no more attention than the ordinary customer or visitor. He was terse, polite, and precise.

In 1825 New York City celebrated the completion of the Erie Canal with a vast parade and elaborate ceremonies. The whole town turned out, marched, waved, yelled, shot things off, applauded, got drunk, burned colored lights, listened to orations, and otherwise showed its heartfelt anticipation of the wealth that was to flow through the new channel. In the great parade hundreds of cabinetmakers and chairmakers marched behind a flag which read, "By Industry We Thrive." The name of Duncan Phyfe does not appear in the official list of the marchers. He must have been in his workshop. But the records do show that the cedar boxes for the various medals, and the casket for the bottles of Lake Erie water which were sent to Lafayette in France, were made by Duncan Phyfe.

In 1846 Phyfe closed his flourishing business. His sons, whom he had briefly taken into partnership, were apparently either unable or unwilling to continue. Having made a sizable fortune he retired to his home across the street. In the backyard he had built a workshop. Here, as he moved toward death, he puttered among his familiar tools. Here he made doll-furniture for his little relatives. Here as an old man, he played as he had once worked, at his craft-art of cabinetmaking, until he died in 1854.

From about 1820 the exquisite quality of Phyfe's work had deteriorated under the pressure of popular taste demanding heavy imitations of Empire styles. Apparently this was a trend with which Phyfe could not cope. Unquestionably it stunted his real contributions at an untimely period, for he yielded and engaged in the production of what he himself, in 1830, called "Butcher furniture."

During the period of Duncan Phyfe, cabinetmakers became so numerous in America that any attempt to enumerate even the outstanding ones would be impractical. The census of 1810 states that the annual value of the American cabinetmakers' output was $1,426,047, not counting chairs which were valued at $105,185. It lists 596 cabinetmakers, in the 17 states, plus the District of Maine and the District of Columbia. Since a study of early directories and newspapers would make this figure appear to be not more than one third, at the most, of the actual number of cabinetmakers, the production figures should be similarly multiplied.

Lochlin Phyfe deserves mention. He worked with his celebrated brother throughout his career and made at least one trip

to England in search of brasses to be used on Phyfe furniture.
Many commentators conclude, from this, that Phyfe imported
his brassware from Britain. On the other hand, it is highly
possible that these were used, for the most part, only as models
and that the greater quantity of Duncan Phyfe's brasses were cast
by his relative by marriage, the brassfounder, Wintringham.

One of Phyfe's chief competitors was the Frenchman,
Charles Honoré Lannuier. In his technique, he added English
touches to essentially French furniture. (Phyfe's had been to
some degree the reverse of this procedure.) Lannuier was born
in France in 1779. He came to America in 1790 with his two
brothers, Augustine, pastry-cook, and Stanislow, mantua-maker,
and despite his meagre eleven years he himself is listed as an
"ebeniste."

He first appears in New York City as "Lannuier, Henry,
cabinetmaker, 60 Broad St." He died a young man, in 1819,
yet was responsible for a great deal of early New York furniture,
including probably a considerable amount, if not all, of that
used by the first Congress of the United States when it sat in
Federal Hall, New York City, in 1789.

Another note concerning Lannuier crops up in the records of
the Common Council of the City of New York. In 1711 the
Common Council ordered "Eighteen Rush Bottom Chairs." In
1721, the Council ordered "Eighteen Leather Chairs," from one
Arnont Schemerboorn, for £16:6. In 1765, "24 Mahogany
chairs" from Andrew Breestead, £39. And finally, in 1812,
"$409 worth of chairs from Henry Lannuier."

Henry Connelly (c. 1770-1826) was the Phyfe of Philadelphia. Other cities also boasted their masters. In the following
pages we shall take occasion to mention a few more, with
emphasis upon their identification with essentially American
types of production.

AMERICAN CHARACTERISTICS

Identifying early American furniture is an ability which grows out of the study of a great many ornamental details and is always questionable. One must learn the origin and biography of each of hundreds of motifs, and the peculiar translations given to them by individual craftsmen at different times and in different places. There is no shortcut to this knowledge. Perhaps the best way to acquire it is to study carefully such a work as L. V. Lockwood's two huge volumes, *Colonial Furniture in America;* frequent museums to observe actual specimens; then return to the multitudinously illustrated volume.

As in all fields of the antique, there is much fakery connected with the glib identification of early American furniture. However, in deciding whether or not a piece of furniture is pre-machine-age there are certain simple clues. Early cabinet-makers did not bother to finish wood where it was not necessary, hence the insides of cabinets, bottoms of chair seats, and so forth, will reveal the ridges left by the jack-plane. A close examination of sawed ends will reveal straight serrations if the piece is early. Modern work will show the slightly arched ridges left by our circular saw. The dove-tailing of early drawers will not be done with the mathematical precision of modern work. Early dove-tailing employs large, uneven wedges. Modern nails and screws, if it is possible to examine them, are easily distinguishable by their precise design. Appropriate signs of wear, especially the flattening of the chair rungs, are easily distinguished from the too regular indentations sometimes created by the manufacturers of bogus antiques.

So far as the influence of American craftsmen upon European furniture forms is concerned, this must necessarily have been limited. The first furniture was made under the influence of recollections of the furniture of England. Later furniture was influenced by the varying trends in European importations. This was natural to our non-indigenous culture.

As in all the crafts, our influence was one of simplification, restraint, stronger construction; with a general tendency to promote the gadget, the space-saver, labor-saver, or other trickily arranged device. Various forms of drop-leaf tables, chair-tables, and other folding models found ready acceptance and development here.

The rocking-chair is probably as American as anything could be. In some quarters the rocking-chair is claimed as an American invention. Some authorities go so far as to attribute it to Benjamin Franklin. Research, however, seems to indicate rocking-chairs in the early 18th century. Moreover, since the cradle principle was well known in Europe it is probable that some experiment with rockers for chairs must have been tried.

Unquestionably, though, it was in America that the rocker achieved vast popularity. Before the vogue had passed, nearly every type of American chair was fitted out with rockers, including the hideous and massive over-stuffed armchair mounted on rocker-rails. It is interesting to note that in modern Russia and various Balkan nations the rocker is still referred to as "an American chair."

Skipping matters of decoration, and with a backward reminder of certain distinctive features of design already discussed in the consideration of specific craftsmen, we can next regard the highboy as something of a special matter. Europe had likewise developed this piece but had largely discarded it by the end of the first quarter of the 18th century. We continued to produce highboys, in a successive variety of styles well into the 19th century. Thus the highboy can be claimed as a distinctively American piece by sheer virtue of its persistence.

Perhaps our most complete adoption was the Windsor chair. Legend has it that King George the Third wandered, during a storm, into a peasant's cottage near Windsor Castle and sat in a chair, the back of which was made of many upright spindles. He is supposed to have been so struck by the rare comfort of this chair that he had it copied, and thence sprang the Windsor chair. This is probably apocryphal, for there were mediaeval chairs of a more or less similar type. But origins aside, the chair found an enormous acceptance in America. The many modifications of it are among our triumphs of early craftsmanship and design.

It seems first to have been introduced into Philadelphia, about 1760 and was called, for a short time, a "Philadelphia chair." It spread quickly throughout the country and was so popular that specialists sprang up, calling themselves "Windsor chair makers."

The original form has a U-shaped back, with from ten to twelve plain, slightly tapering spindles. From that developed the "hoop-back," the "fan-back," the "bow-back," the "comb-back" and the combinations of all these forms.

Sometimes a country gentleman bought the turned parts in town and made his own Windsor chairs during the dull winter months. The vogue lasted well into the third quarter of the 19th century.

A highly original chair designer was the enterprising Lambert Hitchcock. His father, John L. Hitchcock had been a worthy fighter in the Revolution and was lost at sea in 1801. About seventeen years later Lambert began a factory at Barkansted, Connecticut. The term "factory" is justly applied to this early enterprise, for Lambert's intention was to manufacture *parts* for chairs and ship them South, mainly to Charleston, South Carolina.

The South, with virtually no middle class and no artisan class, preferred to import its luxuries from Europe and generally found the work of local craftsmen suspect. Charleston, however, became such a mercantile center that it took on more of the character of a Northern metropolis and became a ready market for the craftsmen-manufacturers of the North. Thus Hitchcock's plan was not illogical. It became so immediately successful that it demanded expansion.

Hitchcock popularized the distinctly American "fancy chair." This was a plain chair of which only the front legs and front rungs were turned. The other parts were made flat, in the manner of a slat-black chair, but in various forms, the main point being that the back was decorated with a very fancy, stencilled design in gilt and other paints. Horns of plenty, fruit and leaf patterns, fountains with drinking birds, in blue, red, white, bronze, gold, and grey, were common designs.

To say that the company prospered is understatement. "Fancy chairs" became the most popular furniture form in America. Hitchcock shipped his chairs not only to the South, but in all directions. They were generally priced at about a dollar-and-a-half.

The children and women who worked in his factory applied the designs by dipping their naked fingers first in linseed oil and then in the dry powder of gold or bronze. A local observer comments that "their fingers became as stiff as boards."

Hitchcock usually imprinted his name on the underside of chair seats, making them easily identifiable. In 1826 he built a large factory of brick. His enterprise included the first commercial manufacture of rocking-chairs.

In 1829 Hitchcock went bankrupt, due to the common failure of over-reaching himself. But in a few years he had recovered. He married Eunice, the sister of his former book-keeper, Arbro Alford, and took Alford into partnership. Again they prospered.

Before his death, Lambert achieved the dignity of a State Senatorship. As an ignominious anti-climax, however, in 1866, some time after his death, the town of Hitchcocksville changed its name to Riverton to avoid being confused with the town of Hotchkissville.

Though otherwise undistinguished, between 1790 and 1820, Baltimore artisans achieved fame for the exceptional quality of their veneer and inlay work. A characteristic identification of the Baltimore furniture of this period is the use of a decorative oval on the doors of secretaries, and other appropriate places.

Louisiana also developed certain characteristics, partly due to natural French and Spanish influences, partly due to modifications necessitated by climate. The dampness, for example, made all forms of veneer impractical. Since mahogany is at its best in veneer, mahogany did not achieve the universal acclaim in Louisiana which had been accorded it elsewhere. Rosewood largely replaced it. Brass, ball-shaped feet, and marble tops on tables and chests-of-drawers were other characteristics necessitated by the climate. The four poster bed persisted in this region long after its disuse elsewhere, as a support for the essential draperies of mosquito-netting.

François Seignouret was the greatest cabinetmaker of early Louisiana. He was born in France in 1768 and was working in Louisiana between 1810-1815. He was especially fond of flowing carving, always raised on the actual wood of the piece, never applied. He was accomplished at a rippling sort of free-for-all beading and managed to lend a genuine elegance even to the most awkward pieces he was required to execute. He was the inventor of a special type of chair. The "Seignouret Chair" has a back which curves forward, forming rudimentary arms carved of one piece of wood with the seat band. This actually lends a maximum strength to the chair's construction and is hence a definite invention.

By the middle of the 19th century, machine influences and the prevailing mediocrity of taste had greatly debased furniture production generally. The great period of American cabinet-making had passed. The "Grand Rapids" era of American middle-class furniture had begun.

CHAPTER 5

CRAFTSMEN IN CLAY

WITH carpentry and cabinetmaking, pottery-making was among the first crafts practiced on a wide scale in America. There is a natural logic to this, the logic of people who occupy their time and skill with necessities in a more or less natural succession of importance. American settlers arrived and built their houses. The importation of furniture on a large scale being impractical, they set about building it. Simultaneously with the need for houses and furniture arose the need for the utensils of everyday life, of which the products of the potter are among the most predominant. Again large scale importation was not immediately practical or desirable. By a curious irony, it was only after a fairly well established American potters' industry existed that importation loomed as a large factor, throwing the American potter into competition with European manufacturers.

In Colonial America every community of importance must have had its pottery. Yet the records of these enterprises are surprisingly meagre. The town-clerks, diarists, and travellers of that day apparently felt that there was nothing worth noting about the mere existence of a pottery. To all intents and purposes we have little evidence, prior to 1684, except that they were there.

In 1684 a large pottery was founded by one Daniel Coxe,

102. Map of the City of New York, 1742-1744, greatly reduced from the original manuscript drawing by David Grim in 1813. The Remmey, Crolius Pottery Buildings are indicated by a circle, the Corselius Pottery by a dotted circle.

N. Y. Historical Society

103. CLARKSON CROLIUS, SR., AMERICAN POTTER, 1773-1843. Portrait by Ezra Ames, in 1825.

near Burlington, New Jersey. Coxe himself is not one of our early potters, however. So far as we know he may never have visited America. He was one of the "proprietors" of West New Jersey and organized his enterprise, strictly as a business proposition, from his London home.

An inventory of his properties tells us, in part, "I have erected a pottery att Burlington for white and chiney ware, a greate quantity to ye value of £1200 have been already made and vended in ye Country, neighbour Colonies and ye Islands of Barbados and Jamaica where they are in great request. I have two houses and kills with all necessary implements, diverse workemen and other servants."

The "chiney ware" may have been a good grade of salt-glazed white earthenware but, as we shall understand later, was certainly not real chinaware, or porcelain. Coxe had trouble with his white ware. There is a record of a plant superintendent, Edward Randall, imported from England at some expense to handle this product. Randall was subsequently sued by Coxe for failure to produce the goods. He was defended by a potter named William Winn who testified that there was "noe Clay in the County that will make white ware." Of the actual prosperity of the Burlington pottery we have no record.

The early American pottery industry is characterized by the existence of large numbers of small enterprises scattered all over the colonies, with a heavy mortality rate among them. Success in any of our early manufacturing efforts, even such fundamental ones as pottery, was the exception. In our scanty records there was apparently no room for accounts of those who fell by the wayside.

By 1750 there was such recognition of the necessity for domestic manufactures for the general welfare of the colonies that public subsidy was not uncommon. Yet, as always, it was more often sought than granted. Two partners, Goussin Bonnin and George Anthony Morris, started a pottery in Philadelphia in 1769. In 1771 they hopefully sent specimens of their work to the Legislature observing that they "would not wish to aspire to the Presumption of dictating the Measure" of the Legislature's encouragement, "but with all Humility hint at the Manner." Unfortunately the hint was futile and the Philadelphia pottery failed in 1774.

New York was naturally a center of manufacture. Two of the earliest names in the records are those of John Remmey and William Crolius. These men are believed, by some, to have been partners. In any case a map was drawn by David Grim in 1813, purporting to show New York City as it was between 1742 and 1744. On this map, a group of buildings on Potter's Hill is labeled "Remmey and Crolius Pottery." Whether or not these buildings represented separate manufactories and Grim's notation was meant to imply that *both* the Remmey and Crolius potteries were here located is of little concern to us. Evidence clearly reveals a link, formal or otherwise.

The Grim map shows very distinctly, a short distance to the southeast of the other buildings, a "Corselius Pottery." As it happens, John Remmey and William Crolius married sisters by the name of Corselius and consequently were brothers-in-law. I. N. Phelps Stokes, in his *Iconography of Manhattan Island,* says: "The first stoneware kiln or furnace in the United States was built in this year 1730 in this city." He then quotes the noted potter, Clarkson Crolius, as saying, "It was first called Corselius Pottery, afterward Crolius Pottery . . ." In effect, William Crolius and John Remmey married the Corselius Pottery and afterward divided it.

John Remmey carried on his pottery until his death in 1762. His place was taken by John 2nd. He, in turn, took his own sons,

Henry and John 3rd, into partnership in 1790, dying two years later. The two brothers remained in partnership for two more years after their father's death. In 1794 Henry left John and went into business independently. He subsequently left the potters' trade altogether. The last accounts of his activities indicate that, after a variety of enterprises, he fell upon evil days, ultimately fleeing the city to escape the consequences of the embezzlement of public funds.

The third John Remmey, however, maintained the old Pottery on Potter's Hill. He took a dignified part in the city government as became a noted scholar. He was Assistant Alderman of the Sixth Ward from 1817–1818. (The same post, incidentally, was held by John Crolius, Jr., 1799–1800, and Clarkson Crolius, 1802–1805, apparently being something of a potter's prerogative.) He was one of the five members of the Committee on Arts and Sciences, 1817, and thus assisted at the rendering of many wise decisions. For example, ". . . . resolved that so large and growing a City as New York should not long remain without its latitude being accurately ascertained."

He never travelled, yet was the author of a scholarly book, *Egypt As It Is*. He owned one of the largest libraries in New York City, in his time, maintaining it as a lending library, at so much per annum for "Gentlemen and Ladies of Quality." He continued the active operation of the Remmey Pottery until 1831, some eight years before his death.

The Crolius family was prolific. The original William, who married Veronica Corselius, was in partnership for a time with his brother Peter. Peter was issueless. William, on the other hand, was followed in the stoneware craft by five more Williams, five Johns, one George, and two Clarksons, making fifteen Crolius potters in all.

The first Clarkson Crolius, grandson of William, became active in city politics. He served on a diversity of committees protesting elections, inspecting elections, etc. When he held office as Assistant Alderman of the Sixth Ward, however, he was scant in attendance at meetings.

His career in office hardly appears to have been notable. He sponsored "A law to prevent dogs from running at large." The measure was passed and soon revoked. In 1803 he was one of only two Assistant Aldermen favoring a revision of the City Charter. The conservatives of the Council were stern in their defense of the document. "It is perhaps inexpedient for the Common Council at this time to express any opinion of the motives of those who appear solicitous to obtain alterations in the charter or to animadvert upon the means which have been used and are now pursuing to accomplish their views."

Of course to advocate change in a charter is far from being necessarily suspect. On the other hand, whatever the merits of the particular case, the subsequent activities of Crolius hardly show him in an enviable light. In spite of his habitual absence from meetings he had a great desire to be re-elected to his office in 1808. He had lost the confidence of his constituents and exercised considerable ingenuity trying to regain it. An affidavit of the election states that ". . . . while the Inspectors were engaged in the manner above stated (counting the votes) they were interrupted by a person of the name of John A. Crolius who proposed to them a different mode of counting." And in addition to John's proposal, whatever it may have been, ". . . . Mr. Leonard Seaman one of the Inspectors (related to Crolius by marriage) did make the proposition that said Inspectors should take each for himself a separate parcel of ballots and examine it." By means of these special systems of ballot-counting variously endorsed by Cousin John and his wife's relative Leonard Seaman, Clarkson Crolius was elected. But the election was held over again, and when tallied by more conventional methods was won by Crolius' opponent.

The second Clarkson succeeded his father, and Crolius Pottery continued to be made far into the 19th century. Both the Remmeys and the Crolius made stoneware, usually of a light grey or tan color, salt glazed, and decorated with flowers and formal patterns in cobalt blue. It was extremely hard and sturdy and may be taken as representative of the best in early American stoneware.

Other New York potters were Dirick Benson, John Eutatse, Henry Bensing, Jonathan Durrell, and Thomas Campbell. Probably no other colony supported so many, but there are records of potters at Salem, Peabody, Braintree, Weston, and Boston, in Massachusetts; one in Litchfield, Connecticut; one somewhere in South Carolina; one each in Huntington, Long Island, and East Greenwich, Rhode Island. There were others in Montgomery and Bucks Counties, Pennsylvania. These, in addition to those already mentioned in more detail.

THE POTTER'S CRAFT

Before passing from the early American potters to those who flourished largely after the War for Independence, we can pause to review the actual *craft* or method of the potter. We might begin this with a reminder that pottery-making is hardly a craft in which we should look for developments or techniques, other than those related to design, which are characteristically American. The origins of the potter's craft are lost in the remotest antiquity. There are ceramic records of races who left their history in no other form. As a craft its antiquity probably rates second only to that of rock-chipping.

Pottery-making is based upon the two essential facts that

clay, when mixed with the proper amount of water, can be easily shaped into almost any form, and that when baked it solidifies into a substance that is hard and resists heat and fracture. Clay is a form of earth that occurs quite commonly in most parts of the world. Its chemical composition varies according to the nature of the finely divided mineral substances that it contains; these are usually hydrous silicates of aluminum, iron, and alkaline salts. The distinguishing quality of clay is the smallness of the particles of which it is composed. In good clay these are not more than five thousandths of a millimeter in diameter. A good clay should also be free from pebbles and humus.

There has always been a mystical and poetical aura around the subject of pottery because of the idea that it is composed of the same substance as Man himself. This theme has appeared widely in "literary" and especially in folk poetry. That it has greatly impressed the potters themselves is evidenced by many such signs as the following characteristic verse on a piece of early Pennsylvania-German slip ware:

"This dish is of earth and clay
And men are also thereof."

Or this inscription from an English piece:

"What handycraft can with our art compare
For pots are made of what we potters are."

In spite of the prosaic fact that man is not made of clay at all, the mystical halo surrounding the potter's craft goes deeper than substance and is not to be dispelled by chemical analysis. It derives, in fact, from a reverence for the process of creation, which in the case of the potter is unusually intimate, in that he commonly shapes his creations with his bare hands.

The making of pottery entails three or four processes. First is the preparation of the clay; cleaning it, picking out pebbles, grinding, to break it up into its integral particles, and mixing it to the desired consistency with water. Second is the shaping. This may be done by any of three means: by building it up with the unaided hands, by "throwing" it on the potters' wheel, or by forcing it into a mold.

The first method is the most ancient. Primitive men employed several methods. Sometimes they built up their pot in layers, or snake-like spirals, and sometimes they just kneaded it from a simple lump. But while it is not as old as pottery-making itself, the potters' wheel does go back to very early times. The first ones were simply horizontal wheels which the potter turned with one hand while he shaped his clay (on the center of the wheel) with the other. Later a second wheel was attached to the same axle so that it could be turned with the foot, allowing the craftsman the use of both hands on his clay. A great deal later a cord was attached to the lower grooved wheel so that it could be turned by an assistant. This was the method usually employed in early America.

When molds were used they were usually made of plaster-of-paris in two or more parts. The clay was forced into the mold, excess clay cut off with a wire, allowed to set (the plaster-of-paris rapidly absorbing the water), and removed for baking.

The potters' wheel was generally used, the mold serving to shape handles or other attached parts. The motions of the potter's hands on the complacent clay are rhythmic and fascinating to watch, like those of a magician.

After being shaped the piece must be allowed to dry until nearly all of its moisture is gone. Otherwise it will crack in the oven. Then comes the actual baking: the time varying from about fifteen to twenty-four hours for crude earthenware up to three days for very hard stoneware. The ovens used in this country were usually round, with either a round or conical top; the former for common pottery, the latter for hard pottery. The furnace was usually divided like a bee-hive by plates of baked clay, enabling the articles to be placed in separate cells. But in the case of porcelain, and sometimes hard pottery, the ovens were not thus divided. Saggers (or *seggars,* old spelling) were used. These were circular trays of baked clay, with vertical, perforated rims. The pieces were placed in the saggers, which were then stacked in the oven like pie-plates, one on top of the other, each acting as a cover for the one beneath. The ovens themselves were built of clay with the insides sometimes glazed to prevent particles from falling onto the objects being baked.

After the pottery has been cooled and removed from the oven we have what is known as "biscuit," that is, unglazed pottery. Often this is the finished product. Biscuit is naturally slightly porous, a quality which does not always lessen the value of the ware, according to the purpose for which it has been designed. The *ojas* of the American Southwest are an instance in which the porosity of biscuit-ware is a definite advantage. These are water jugs, usually of red clay. The clay absorbs a very small quantity of the water which continually evaporates from the surface, thus refrigerating the water.

The purpose of glazing is threefold: to prevent porosity, to resist chemical action, and to decorate. Glaze, as the word implies, is a thin coating of glass applied to the surface of pottery. Sometimes the substance is actually glass to begin with, in a finely powdered state; or the fused components of glass. Sometimes it is merely the alkaline or metallic-salt part of glass, which finds its silica in the clay of the pottery itself.

One way of glazing is to mix the necessary substances with water to a thin consistency and to paint it onto the ware, after

104. CROLIUS JAR.

105. DRINKING JUG BY JOHN CROLIUS, 1775.

6. BUTTER CHURN BY CLARKSON CROLIUS, SR. An unusual piece.

107. TEAPOT BY CLARKSON CROLIUS, JR., 1805-1887. Flower and acorn design with squirrel lid.

109. JUG BEARING U. S. COAT OF ARMS. This establishes it as the work of either the 2nd or 3rd John Remmey, probably the latter. Salt glazed stoneware.

108. STONEWARE BATTER JUG. One of the finest pieces by Clarkson Crolius, Sr. Dated, February 17, 1798. Note salt glaze and incised, cobalt blue decoration.

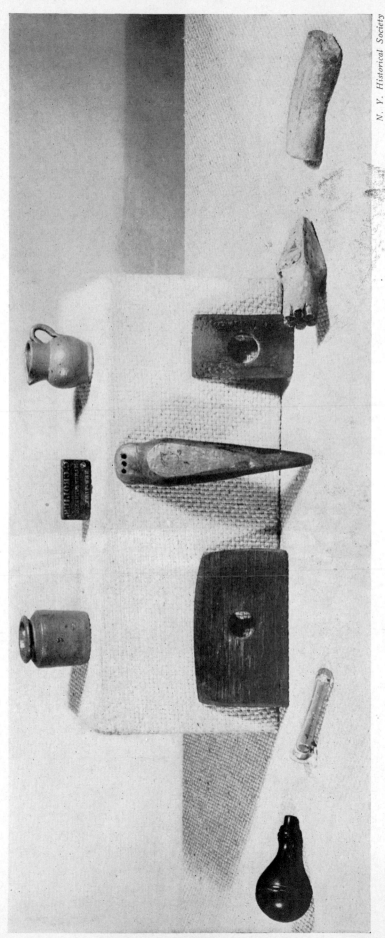

110. RELICS OF THE CLARKSON CROLIUS POTTERY. Note the Rosette die, the "C. Crolius" die and the miniature "samples." The little glass tube contains the Cobalt Blue dye used in most Crolius decoration.

111. Pennsylvania—German Slip-Ware, Sgraffito Decoration. This is sometimes known as Tulip ware because of the prevalence of the tulip design.

which it is placed in the glazing oven until it achieves a complete fusion with the surface of the pottery. In another method, known as "salt glazing" and frequently used on early American stoneware, the process is made part of the original baking. While the ware is at high temperature in the oven, salt is thrown upon it by hand. Most of the salt is converted into a vapor before it strikes the pottery. This produces a fine transparent glaze, characterized by the fact that it is slightly pitted where particles of unconverted salt have struck it.

A glaze may be either transparent or opaque, colored or colorless. In using transparent glazes the decoration, if desired, is applied to the biscuit and is then covered with the clear glaze. In using colored or opaque glaze, the design may be applied in a glaze of two or more colors, or the glaze of one opaque color may be scraped off to reveal the background material in the desired pattern. Glazes are colored by the same means as glass, that is by the addition of metallic oxides, a process the chemistry of which is still as obscure as it was in the 17th century.

The word "slip" in connection with ceramics refers to a very fine grade of clay which is applied to pottery either for decoration or as a corrosion-resistant lining. This "slip" is made by mixing the clay with water to the consistency of cream and usually some coloring substance is added, such as cobalt, to produce blue.

The terms *pottery* and *earthenware* are synonymous. They are distinguished from *porcelain* or *china,* also synonymous terms, by the fact that *they are not transparent or translucent.*

Earthenware is divided into "soft-paste" and "hard-paste." Soft-paste is, as one would naturally suppose, softer and more porous. Examination of a fractured edge of this type of ware will reveal separate particles incompletely fused. When touching such a fracture with the tongue the sensation of absorption is perceptible. Examination of a fracture on hard-paste pottery does not reveal separate, unfused particles, nor will it exhibit the phenomenon of absorption to any appreciable degree. Stoneware is a type of hard-paste, glazed earthenware that was extremely popular for practical purposes in early America.

"Slip-ware" is pottery that has been decorated with a slip of one or more contrasting colors by means of the same technique used by bakers in decorating the top of a cake. The cream-thick slip is placed in a funnel with a small hole for its emission and then the craftsman simply "writes" his designs or mottoes onto the body of the ware. This craft was so popular with the Pennsylvania-Germans that many people make the mistake of associating it exclusively with them.

In what is known as "sgraffito ware" an opposite technique is employed. The object of unbaked clay is completely covered with the slip, usually of a much lighter color, and before it has completely dried parts of it are scraped off to reveal the clay beneath in the form of the desired ornamentation or inscription.

POTTERY-MAKING AFTER THE REVOLUTION

Having acquainted ourselves generally with the processes of the potter's craft, we can proceed to follow the development of the manufacture after the rift between the Colonies and the Mother Country had actively developed.

The effects of the Revolution upon American pottery-making may be considered typical of its effect upon all non-luxury manufactures. Great Britain had been the major source of commodities for America. When this source was cut off by the war only three courses were open in regard to any given commodity: one was to do without it, another was to find a substitute, and the third was to stimulate home manufacture. Silks and satins can be given up. Even the most fashionable belles can array themselves in domestic homespuns at a time when it is fashionable to be patriotic. The drinking of tea can be substituted for by the brewing of insipid sassafras and other home-grown weeds; *was,* in fact, to such a degree that America never again became a tea-drinking nation. But pottery was something that we could make, and did.

The complete cessation of English imports threw the great American market into the laps of American manufacturers and they were not prepared for it. It stimulated the organization by inexperienced men of hundreds of very small and ill-equipped enterprises. In the usual case of the period, there was an abundance of material resources, fuel and clay for the asking, but a shortage of skilled labor. The war aggravated this condition, for many of the English craftsmen had returned to Britain at the sound of the first bugle-calls. Others, deeming themselves American (in those days more or less a question of temperament), had joined the gathering ranks of the Continentals. The result was a great increase in the quantity and a sudden decline in the quality of American pottery, from 1776 to 1783.

When the shooting was over America found itself a vast new entity among the powers of the Earth. Another sudden and typical metamorphosis occurred in American pottery-making. First of all there was a tremendous burst of energy on all sides. Talents and life-forces that had been caught up in military action were released all over the continent in enterprises of exploration, commerce, invention, education, manufacturing and craftsmanship. American craftsmen now had a national as well as a personal integrity to uphold in their work. The result was immediately apparent in greater beauty of form and refinement of ornament.

In addition to this there was a tremendous influx of craftsmen from foreign countries. In 1776 Silas Deans had made a prophecy to the secret committee of Congress in Paris. "The present Contest," he said, "has engaged the attention of all Europe. The good and the wise part, the lovers of liberty and human happiness, look forward to the establishment of American freedom and independence as an event which will secure to them and their descendants an asylum from the effects and violence of despotick power, daily gaining ground in every part of Europe. From these and other considerations on which I need not be minute, emigration from Europe will be prodigious immediately upon the establishment of American Independence." This proved to be correct, and the effect on American pottery-making, and craftsmanship in general, was to add skill, new techniques, and more foreign influences to leave their marks upon the growing variety of American design.

Simultaneously occurred a great surge of national consciousness. We were proud of ourselves. We liked to think that we were not only better fighters but also better manufacturers. There was no need, at this time, for a "Buy American" campaign. Patriotic slogans, portraits of American statesmen, Eagles and other national symbols were the popular decorative motifs of the day.

English manufacturers were desperate to recapture the rich American market. Their spies came, saw, and reported the new American tastes. No more birds and flowers, but profiles of Washington and Adams, eagles with talons full of arrows, violent and victorious revolutionary slogans. Such are the uses of competitive merchandising! The English began to manufacture and ship vast quantities of these things. They vied with our most ebullient craftsmen in expressing in pottery, glass, silver, brass, and textiles rabidly patriotic American and outright anti-British sentiments.

Immediately after the Revolution there were numerous new potteries in all the States previously mentioned. Among these, was that of Thomas Commeraw, of Coerlear's Hook, New York City, which became a strong competitor of Remmey and Crolius. Commeraw made stoneware similar to the latters', but his favorite ornament was a pair of crescents, with the four tips touching, leaving the center space thus formed, open in the shape of an oval. He continued in business until about 1820.

There were new establishments in West Virgina, Vermont, Kentucky and Ohio. The products of these were at first similar to those of the older colonies, the greatest volume being of tan and grey salt-glazed stoneware, red earthenware, and lead-glazed ware in simple, useful shapes.

With the first decades of the 19th century we find more and more local differences in the types of pottery. Many of these variations were the reflection of economic differences; occasionally, as in the case of the Pennsylvania-Dutch, of cultural differences. The simple, utilitarian forms prevailed along the westward frontiers. But in Philadelphia, New York and Boston, a finer ware was being produced; pottery that imitated silverware in its forms, with infinite varieties of color, lustre, and ornamental pattern.

For fifteen years after the signing of the Declaration of Independence, the arrogantly individual little territory of Vermont maintained its own sovereign independence. Finally, in 1791, it joined the Federation of States. Two years later, in a very unobtrusive fashion, began the enterprise which was to lead to quite the greatest pottery of the new country. Captain John Norton, who had distinguished himself in the Revolution and had been one of the guards at the execution of the unfortunate Captain André, founded on his farm at Bennington, Vermont, a single kiln for the making of pottery.

This was partly for the convenience of his own large farm and partly for that of neighbors, but popular demand soon made it a more ambitious enterprise. Within a year he had two kilns. He himself, albeit a gentleman, was a skilled potter. His knowledge of variegated techniques is indicated by the versatility of his original productions: red earthenware, brown slip-ware, lead-glazed and salt-glazed stoneware. Though these are all crude wares they are notable for what was little more than a household manufactory. It's interesting, by the way, to note the prices of the period: 144 milk pans, $18; 12 large platters, $1.00.

In 1813 the Captain retired leaving his two sons in the business, Luman and John. John Norton (2nd) left the partnership in 1827 and Luman took in his own son, Julius. All these men were craftsmen-employers, thoroughly skilled and active far beyond the function of ownership. Julius turned out to be an innovator, and a business man of great abilities. This was a relief to his father who had always had leanings toward the scholar's life. (Shades of John Remmey, 3rd). They moved to a new location in Bennington where they could use waterpower instead of horsepower, and the expansion of their business was phenomenal. In 1840 Luman retreated into his library and left the entire pottery to his highly efficient son.

Julius commenced the manufacture of much more varied articles than had ever been made by his father or grandfather. He had artistic aims. Inkstands, flowerpots, and other intricately decorated articles began to come from the Norton kilns.

In 1845 Julius Norton took his brother-in-law, Christopher Webber Fenton, into partnership. This was not a particularly momentous event for Julius, but in the history of American ceramics it looms large.

In 1847 Fenton left Julius Norton and started his own business, called the United States Pottery. It is reported that C. W.

Fenton was not, himself, a remarkable potter. Nevertheless, he possessed extraordinary talents in other directions. He had the average district school education, by no means equal to that of the other potter-employers yet above that of the ordinary potter. He was a man of some temper, fond of political argument. A constant "dram-drinker," he indulged in sporadic sprees. He would form sudden and enthusiastic friendships, cooling off almost as rapidly. This is no unusual character portrait. The important factor to his role in pottery was the fact that Christopher Webber Fenton was very good at sketching. He could sketch small objects, shapes, and ornaments, such as had not been attempted by any other American potter. Thus, in a brief span of years, C. W. Fenton became the Wedgwood of America. The products of his United States Pottery were endless in their variety and ornamental ingenuity. Even when he was still in partnership with business-man Julius Norton they had begun to produce not only ordinary stoneware, but yellow and white ware; Rockingham ware, which is usually a brown glazed ware, mottled, with manganese as its essential coloring agent, and many other variants on the usual types of American pottery.

Another of Fenton's gifts was the ability to choose talented men to work for him. He had an uncanny eye for the right man for the right job. Modellers, designers, throwers, furnace men, flocked to Fenton from all over the world. Outstanding among these was Daniel Greatbach, who came to Bennington in 1852. A modeller and designer, he was the son of William Greatbach who had modelled and designed for Wedgwood.

Cow-shaped creamers, Dachshund-handled water pitchers, ornamental lions with spinach-like manes; no verbal description could give any impression of the variety and imaginative quality of their work.

Technically speaking, the greater part of their production was of three types: Rockingham, flint, and scroddle-ware. Rockingham has already been described.

Scroddle-ware, sometimes called agate, or lava-ware, is made by using alternate thin layers of different colored clay, piling these up like a thin layer-cake, pressing them together, then rolling them up and cutting the resultant cylinder into slices with a fine wire. The final ware was then molded from these slices. The resultant pottery is composed of labyrinthine intertwinements of varied color. This is sometimes confused with the process known as "combing," wherein an object is covered with a thin slip of different color and the whole is worked over with metal combs, in the manner of artificial "graining" on woodwork. Close inspection will show that on the surface of the latter type of work one color will be very slightly raised above the other.

As to the flint-ware, or flint enamel ware, this is generally a pottery with a siliceous glaze, but Fenton had patented a special process of coloring it. This was simply to sprinkle a mixture of metallic oxides onto the object after it had been painted with the glaze mixture, before the final firing. The result of this was a beautiful intermixture of orange, green, and blue throughout the lustrous, opaque glaze.

All three types of ware abovementioned should be easily recognized by the amateur collector. They are all interesting. Only the third was made exclusively at Bennington. The others might have been made anywhere, but this does not detract from their value if they are well or unusually made. Less than half of the ware made at Bennington is stamped with a trademark.

The United States Pottery failed because of the same element that had made it great: the excessive aims of Christopher Webber Fenton. His Company was phenomenal in its produc-

112-117. Specimens of Pennsylvania—German Slip-Ware, Sgraffito Decoration. Note piece by the well known Potter, Samuel Troxel, molded cistern by Solomon Bell, Waynesboro, Pa., and combed plate.

Metropolitan Museum

118. Jar by Thomas Commeraw.

119. Snuff Canister. Pennsylvania.

121. Jug From Maine.

120. Connecticut Mower's Ring. Made to be worn over shoulder, as a drinking bottle, while working in field.

23. CUP FRAGMENT. Showing patriotic design popular after the Revolution.

124. TEAPOT, BENNINGTON, IN THE MANNER OF FENTON.

Metropolitan Museum

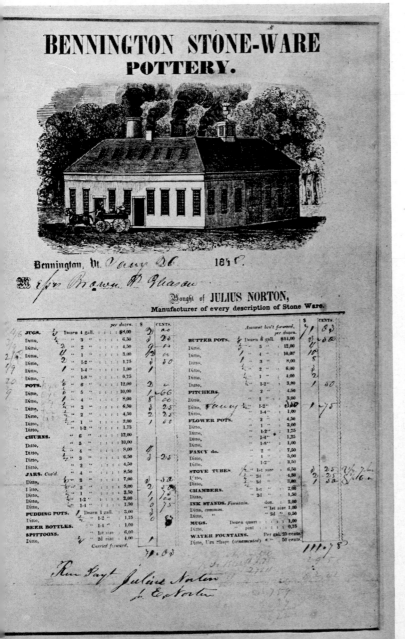

122. BILL HEAD OF JULIUS NORTON, BENNINGTON.

N. Y. Historical Society
Bella C. Landauer Collection

125. PARIAN PITCHER. Possibly Norton.

Metropolitan Museum

126. The "Throwing Wheel." Early stage in the making of a vase.

127. The Same Vase. A later stage.

The Rookwood Pottery Co..

The Rookwood Pottery Co.

129. FIRING THE KILN.

128. LOADING THE KILN. Note the earthenware trays, or seggars.

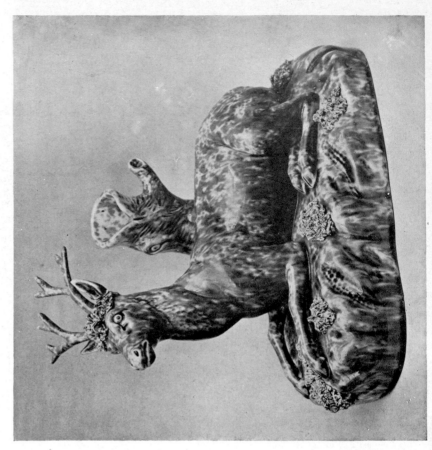

131. BEAN POTS, BENNINGTON.

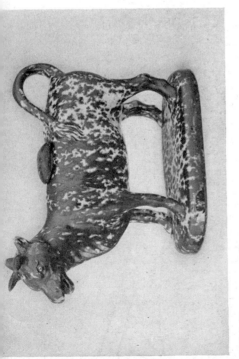

130. CREAMER BY FENTON.

Metropolitan Museum

4. POTTERY BOTTLES BY FENTON.

Metropolitan Museum

135. CHRISTOPHER WEBBER FENTON. From an old Daguerreotype.

Antiques

136. CAST, OR MOLDED WARE BEING FINISHED UPON WHEELS.

The Rookwood Pottery Co.

137. DRINKING JUG, REVOLUTIONARY
PERIOD. Decoration shows Fort.
One figure is climbing flag pole
saying "Damn the Reblels (sic) I
will give them some trouble." The
other says "Slush it well Johnny."

138. GROTESQUE DRINKING JUG.

Metropolitan Museum

139. DECORATING POTTERY BEFORE GLAZING.

The Rookwood Pottery Co.

140. POTTER'S TRADE CARD.

Metropolitan Muse

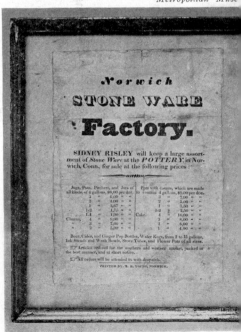

tion and in its sales, but unfortunately was even more phenomenal in its overhead. This incongruity brought it to ruin in May,
1858.

AMERICAN CHARACTERISTICS

The favorite pottery of early America was stoneware. Probably hardly a single home was without one or more pieces of it.
It was put to every practical use: crocks, jugs, jars, wine-vats,
churns, water-coolers, flasks, bottles, pudding dishes, milk pans,
mugs, and so on. Yet its makers strove toward, and its buyers
demanded, work that was decorative in form as well as in surface ornamentation. The pottery itself was usually some shade
of grey or tan, covered with a transparent salt-glaze. The ornamentation was most often a cobalt blue slip. In the earlier work
this is incised on the body of the stoneware, but later it was
merely applied by means of a stencil or brush.

During the 18th century the decorations took the shape of
formalized loops, flowers, animals, fish, birds, and butterflies.
These formalized designs gradually became more naturalistic
and more elaborate. They began to include domestic items, such
as chickens, and also various political symbols, such as the American Eagle, bearing the national shield. The designs do not appear to have been incised after 1820, and at this time the element
of brushwork becomes visible. Then, about 1860, the figures
again tend toward formalization, but in a way that suggests the
use of stencils rather than the crude free-hand manner of the
18th century.

Stoneware was probably first manufactured in this country
in the second quarter of the 18th century. It spread rapidly
throughout the colonies. Most often the potters tried to establish
their works on the banks of rivers, to facilitate transportation,

although generally speaking, stoneware was primarily made for local use.

Pottery is one of the few crafts possessing a directly literary interest. The substance and technique of the craft invite inscription. Everyone has a homily, a religious rhyme or two, or at least a humorous toast in the back of his mind. If not, there are always the realms of personal malice, political sentiment, or occupational aggrandizement.

There is, oddly enough, a strictly American aspect to certain English pottery of the 18th century. This is the British work inscribed with invectives against America and Americans. Thomas Paine, probably because of his embarrassing brilliance as a spokesman, seems to have been a particular target. One of their jugs shows Paine, seated on the back of a pig, addressing a crowd of other pigs. The inscription reads:

> Ye pigs who never went to college
> You must not pass for pigs of knowledge.

A white mug of the same period is inscribed:

> Prithee, Tom Paine, why wilt thou meddling be
> In other business which concerns not thee.
> For while thereon thou dost extend thy cares,
> Thou dost at home neglect thy own affairs,
>   God Save the King!

Another piece adds to the above:

> Observe the wicked and malicious man
> Projecting all the mischief that he can.

In actual American pottery, the real master-poets were the Pennsylvania-Germans. The innumerable curious rhymes that have been found on their slip- and sgraffito-ware, along with their taciturn nature-designs and the ubiquitous tulip, form a real chapter of American folk-lore.

Such rhymes were no doubt most often the spontaneous conceptions of half-literate potters or, occasionally, of the person for whom the piece was designed. They touch upon many subjects and opposing points of view. Thus:

> In the dish on the table
> Merry he who yet is single
> Sad is he who is engaged.

Contrasted to:

> All the young women in the world
> Would willingly become wives.

One item suggests some of the fleeting little poems of the Chinese:

> I like fine things
> Even when they are not mine
> And cannot become mine
> I still enjoy them.

A sage note is struck with:

> If loving were unhealthy
> Surely the doctor would avoid it
> And if it would hurt the wives
> Surely they would not allow it.

Excessive and dour personal rebellion would seem to be indicated in the owner of the piece inscribed:

> To consume everything in gluttony
> And intemperance before my end
> Makes a fitting enough testament for me.

The humor of American potters occasionally manifested itself on the practical side. Sometimes this took the form of realistically modelled and colored frogs fastened to the bottoms of beer mugs. Occasionally some trickster would make a puzzle-jug. This would be a drinking jug with a concealed opening, allowing the potion to flow out of the handle or some equally inappropriate place to the confusion of the unwary drinker. One such deceitful container bore the challenge:

> From Mother earth I claim my birth
> I'm made a joke for man,
> But now I'm here, filled with good cheer,
> Come taste me if you can.

The record of Pennsylvania-German slip-ware drolleries is well climaxed with the baffling stanza:

> There are no birds, there are no fish,
> No cuckoo knows what it is.
> To dedicate a flower
> Is to pass away the time, 1793.

This was inscribed on a pie-plate decorated with fuchsias and may well bring sleepless nights to the more rational students of American ceramics.

CHAPTER 6

MAKERS OF GLASS

GLASS, more than any other substance used by man, has qualities that verge upon the miraculous. The miracle of glass begins in the fact that such dead substances as sand, soda, and potash, when heated together, can suddenly metamorphose into a material that is gleaming, transparent, lustrous, and beautiful. The continuation of the miracle lies in the almost infinite workability of glass in the molten state. When highly fluid it can be cast; when viscous it can be rolled like dough, blown into a bubble so thin that it will float on air, or drawn into a thread fine enough to be woven into a textile; not only can it be poured into molds when in the fluid state, but when viscous it can be blown in, or forced with a mechanical plunger; with various simple tools it can be worked into almost any conceivable shape or design. By the addition of drab metallic-oxides it can be made to assume the most luminous and varied colors.

Glass is not a primitive necessity, as urgent to the settlers of America as the products of the house builder, the cabinetmaker, and the potter. Yet paradoxically enough, the first real manufacturing venture in America was a glassworks at Jamestown, in 1609. Following the course of American glass manufacture, and the personalities of the craftsmen and speculators involved in it, will lead us through one of the most extraordinary stories of early America, peopled with some of its most singular figures.

The celebrated Captain John Smith, of the Virginia settlers, returned to Europe after his first American visit and wrote a book in a rather highly imaginative manner. He was in the position of a real-estate promoter whose claims cannot be verified, at least for some time. The book was read by many persons, and it so inspired a group of young English aristocrats that they formed a company, "The London Company," got together several ships and set sail for Virginia. They called the voyage, with simple candor, "the venture of the purse." In 1606 they arrived and planted themselves about fifty miles from the mouth of the Chesapeake Bay, calling the spot James Towne, in honor of the reigning King.

This was an enterprise of gentlemen, and it had a tragic fate. Fully equipped with jewelled swords, lace collars, velvet breeches, silver buckles, and plumed hats, they found themselves hopelessly inadequate. They had leisure class manners and habits, with a thorough contempt for labor. They had come to pick up the gold they supposed to abound in forest and glade. Unfortunately the gold proved to be mica, and these fine-feathered Englishmen were unwilling to soil their hands in tapping the gold of the real resources lying all around them. Rather than degrade themselves through manual effort, they traded their guns to the Indians, ate the available food, caught dysentery, and starved to death pitiably like dumb but elegant beasts. Within two months their number was reduced from 105 to 39.

In 1608 a second company of seventy was sent over from England. In this group there were four bankrupt English jewelers and goldsmiths, eight Dutch and Polish glass blowers, and two women.

Although glass was still a rarity in England, enterprising

business men were beginning to be aware of its possibilities. One of the main problems in its manufacture was fuel. This was before the use of coal, and covered glass-pots, so that huge quantities of wood were required to furnish the tremendous and prolonged heat. Thus it seemed that America, with its limitless forests, was an ideal spot for a glassworks.

The Dutch and Polish immigrants set to work at once, put together some sort of a furnace, and began to make glass. How much, for how long, and of what quality is not known. Some of it was shipped back to England, the first industrial export of America.

But there was still a preponderance of gentlemen among the settlers. The glassworks, along with the rest of the Colony, failed to prosper. There were eight skilled glassmen, but no one to fell trees, dig sand, or saw wood.

In 1620 the London Company launched a promotion scheme. They organized three "rolls" and invited subscription to them. One "roll" was the project of shipping a large number of English girls, pure and uncorrupt, to the Colony. Another was for the "Guest House," and a third was for the "Glass House." The girls were "sold" to the Colonists for from 100 to 200 pounds of tobacco each. The six Venetian glass blowers of the third "roll" set to work to found a new glass industry.

This time there was really a perspicacious scheme behind the attempt. It had occurred to the London Company that by means of scintillating and brightly colored glass beads the Indians could be limitlessly cheated out of land and furs. It was a part of their idea to keep these products sufficiently scarce, however, to preserve their trade value. With this in mind the six Italians set about the manufacture of all manner of little pieces of pierced glass. The same year brought the first shipload of

African slaves. Also, an iron furnace was started and, in general, things began to prosper.

The end of the second Jamestown glassworks is not known. Some historians believe it was destroyed in the great Massacre of 1622, when Chief Opechancanough killed 350 Colonists in his first surprise attack. Indian graves still reveal an occasional glass bead with a strong Venetian influence in design.

In 1641 the first northern glass-house was built at Salem, years before that town went on its famous and ghastly spree of witch-burning. This was the period when manufacturing was forbidden to the Colonies by the Companies who had promoted them, and by the home government. The Colonists had already begun to be angered at the exorbitant prices of imported goods and the arrogant prohibition of their own endeavors. They stubbornly set about a variety of manufactures, as often as not receiving the support of their local governors.

In the beginning, the form of American manufacture most dreaded by the home government was that of textiles. Arms and gunpowder probably ranked second, with liquors running a close third. The glass industry in Europe did not amount to much at this time. Also glass was too fragile, took up too much space, and was too definitely in the luxury class to be a profitable export to the hard-driven Colonists. Therefore there was not much opposition to the glass industry. In the case of Jamestown, the ill-fated glass industry had been a Company-managed project.

The chief difficulties of the American glass manufacturers arose, not so much from political opposition, as from practical local causes: lack of proper clays, sands, and alkalis, and, above all, the lack of skilled workers.

The Salem glassworks was founded by Lawrence Southwick

and Obadiah Holmes, who later took into partnership Ananias Concklin (or Caukdayne). They were beset by financial difficulties at the outset, received a certain amount of subsidy in the form of a public loan, but nevertheless failed completely in a very few years.

The failure was tragic in more than a commercial sense, for one of the members of the original partnership was meted out a cruel and ironic reward for his efforts. This was Lawrence Southwick, a Quaker, and a man of infinite gentleness. In the dead of winter, without food or any kind of supplies, he was banished to a barren island off the coast and left to starve and freeze to death; all because of his Quaker faith in a Puritan stronghold.

In the growing port of New Amsterdam, three Director-Generals had betrayed their Company in a greater or lesser degree, when the one-legged Stuyvesant arrived in 1647. He was a man after the Company's own heart and successfully defended the Colony against the Colonists until 1664, when the arrival of a British fleet relieved him of this responsibility.

It is not certain in what year Johannes Smedes came over. He had probably been here quite a while when, in 1654, he was allotted an area of land on which he erected a glassworks. The bordering path soon became known as Glass-makers Street, so it is probable that there were enterprises other than Smedes'. After a few years in America, Johannes simplified his name, becoming Jan Smedes. He retired from the glass business in the same year that Peter Stuyvesant "retired" from the Governship. He probably made "bulls-eyes," of which we shall hear more later, for the Dutch windows and doors, as well as bottles for Dutch brews and all the customary hollow ware for the tidy Dutch homes.

Glass-makers Street eventually became Smee Street, then Smith Street, and is now William Street. Jan Smedes continued to be a leading citizen, under English rule, and in 1670, a year before his death, was appointed Road Commissioner. Cornelius Dircksen and one Jansen, who had been previously apprenticed to Smedes, started glassworks of their own. How they prospered is not known.

Evert Duycking, who came to America in 1638, made window glass in New Amsterdam and was a leading citizen. Duycking was a general artisan and was succeeded in 1674 by one of his assistants, Jacob Melyer, whose progeny are said to have made glass "unto the third and fourth generation."

Little is known of the glassworks apparently located on Chester Creek, in Delaware County, Pennsylvania, in 1638.

Caspar Wistar, son of the electoral huntsman to Carl Theodore of Bavaria, came to this country in 1717 and commenced the successful manufacture of brass buttons. He married Quakeress, Catherine Jansen, and himself became a Quaker. In 1739, with the aid of four Belgian glass blowers whom he had imported, he launched a glassworks near Allowaystown, New Jersey. His son Richard, born in 1727, learned the business from the ground up. But the effects of the Revolution, the loss of skilled workmen, and the fact that glass was still more or less a luxury product, was too much for the Wistar enterprise and it failed in 1780.

The Wistars were responsible for the special type of early American glass known as "South Jersey." This is distinguished generally by being wide and generous in form. It is the most truly "American" glass made prior to the 19th century.

One of the characteristic types of decoration identifying these graceful bulbous forms was the superimposing of a layer of glass, usually of the same color. The finished object was dipped into molten glass to a depth of about one third. Then, while still malleable, this was cleverly dragged up at various points thus forming an uneven additional thickness which began at the bottom. The winding of spiral threads around the necks of carafes was also characteristic of the South Jersey glass.

The Wistars at one time employed several members of the Stanger family. The Stangers later launched a glassworks at Glassboro, New Jersey, in which nine members of the family were employed.

Glass enterprises were attempted, during the 18th century, near the towns of Quincy, Lee, and Braintree, and other locations in Massachusetts, all of which were unsuccessful. Robert Hewes made a glassmaking attempt at Temple, New Hampshire, in 1780. There were others, before the second quarter of the 19th century, in New Hampshire, New York, New Jersey, Vermont, Massachusetts, Connecticut, Pennsylvania, Maryland, and Ohio.

Among all the early American glassmakers, three stand out as cases so extraordinary as to repay detailed investigation.

The Retirement of Lodewyck Bamper

In Holland, Lodewyck Bamper had amassed a fortune as a merchant and ship owner. His career had been one of daring enterprise and continual success. He had married well and lived well. In middle age, he was persuaded by his friends to retire. The conventional move, expected of him, was to settle down in his Amsterdam mansion and be a leading citizen. But Bamper had original ideas. Though willing to retire, he determined to do so in the New World, rather than the old.

Sometime between 1720 and 1730, Lodewyck Bamper embarked for America in one of his own ships. It was manned by

African slaves and carried a cargo of luxuries such as the New World had never seen before: silver plate, in every shape; gold plate; paintings and tapestries; exquisite needlework; silks; laces; linens; carpets; jewelry and unmounted jewels; pottery and fragile porcelain from East to West. In addition to these things he brought the finest mares and stallions for breeding purposes; tulips from Holland; rare plants from the tropics; curious bulbs; shrubs; and trees from everywhere; parrots, parrakeets, monkeys, and other exotic birds and beasts; and a large pipe-organ with pewter pipes.

His particular megalomania is revealed in the names of the four Negresses who served his household: Europe, Asia, Africa, and America.

Soon after arrival he erected a brick house with a fifty-foot facade in the finest style of the day. The beams and panels of the various rooms were carved with complex patterns designed by Bamper himself. In common with other outstanding figures of these early times, he was not merely an employer of craftsmen, but was himself a master craftsman with an inspired imagination. The large gardens extending behind the house quickly flourished into exotic beauty, and for these Bamper designed a great many life-size figures carved from wood, painted and gilded. These figures, cleverly arranged at the turnings of the many paths and sometimes half-hidden behind foliage, were of Grenadiers in full uniform, and occasionally of their wives and children. The pewter pipe-organ was installed at one end of the high-ceilinged dining-room and Bamper had brought a valet-musician with him to play it.

The very fact that he chose to "retire" in the crass and violent New World should have been sufficient indication to astute observers that Lodewyck Bamper was not the retiring type. Try as he would to be a member of the leisure class, Bamper soon found himself sending ships scurrying hither and yon. An acute need for additional peacocks for his own garden would somehow develop into an extensive trading enterprise. Then, to his astonishment, he found that he was opening shops all over New York City, speculating in real estate, and before he knew it he was launched in the glass business.

In 1752, Lodewyck Bamper, Samuel Bayard, Matthew Earnest, Christian Hertell, and a professional glass-man, John Martin Greiner of Saxe-Weimar, Germany, entered into partnership and organized the Glass House Company of New York. Its first glassworks was built far out in a location which would now fall between 34th and 40th Streets, and 8th and 11th Avenues of the present city. This distant location was then known as New Found Land, to which stage coach excursions were arranged for adventurous citizens of New York.

Two years later, in 1754, an advertisement appeared in a New York paper:

"Notice is Hereby Given, That there is to be sold by Thomas Lepper, Store-Keeper to the Glass House Company, living at their store on the late Sir Peter Warren's Dock, at the North River, near Mr. Peter Mesiers, all sort of Bottles from 1 Quart to 3 Gallons and upwards as also a Variety of other Glass Ware too tedious to mention, all at reasonable rates: and all Gentlemen that wants Bottles of any size with their Names on them, or any Chymical Glasses, or any other sort of Glass Ware, may by applying to said Lepper, have them with all Expedition. N. B.: Said Lepper Gives ready Money for ashes and old Window Glass."

In addition to the glassworks at New Found Land, the Glass House Company built another furnace further up the Hudson River near the town of New Windsor, and ambitiously operated both at the same time. The Manhattan works failed in 1767, while the New Windsor manufactory probably continued to operate for some eighteen years longer.

None of this glass has been identified, and little is known of the techniques employed. Considering the attributes of Lodewyck Bamper, and the general background of the enterprise, it may be inferred that they turned out an excellent and artistic product. It is quite possible that a certain amount of the glass variously attributed to other makers may have come from the Glass House Company of New York.

"BARON" STIEGEL

In 1750 Heinrich Wilhelm Stiegel, later known as Henry William Stiegel, still later known as Baron Heinrich von Stiegel, arrived in the city of Philadelphia. He came aboard the *Nancy,* with his mother, and his younger brother, Anthony, his father having died some nine years earlier.

Taking the oath of allegiance to the Crown of England and to William Penn, he settled his mother and brother in Schaeferstown, among their fellow-immigrants from Germany, while he himself went off to scout around the countryside in search of golden opportunity. He found his chance in a baser metal, which proved as good.

Pennsylvania, at this time, had the most productive iron mines, forges, furnaces, and consequently the most affluent, ironmasters in the country. One of these was Jacob Huber, of Brickerville. It was to Huber's iron works that young Stiegel found his way. He appeared there sometime in 1752 and got a job, probably keeping the books. He proceeded to work himself to the top by the simplest possible expedient. In November, 1752, he married his employer's daughter, Elizabeth Huber. The furnace at Brickerville was called Elizabeth Furnace, whether before or after Henry's alliance is not certain.

Stiegel was a remarkable fellow, as soon became apparent. After his marriage to Huber's daughter he was made general manager of the works and at once began to make changes in the iron business. The main product of the Elizabeth Furnace was stoves. In those days it was customary among the Pennsylvania-Germans to decorate their stove-plates with Biblical scenes and pious quotations. Stiegel put an end to this waste of good advertising space. Some of his first stove-plates were cast with the following inscription, honoring his father-in-law:

> Jacob Huber ist der erste Deutsche Mann
> Der das Eisen werk vollfuren kann.

> Jacob Huber is the first German
> Who knows how to make iron work.

Later, when his hold upon the establishment had become more secure, this rhyme was exchanged for:

> Baron Stiegel ist der Mann
> Der die ofen machen kann.

> Baron Stiegel is the man
> Who knows how to make stoves.

After five years he bought the Elizabeth Furnace outright, tore it down, and built a larger one. He manufactured Franklin stoves, and a large, ten-plate stove with increasing success. The ironmaster's daughter bore him two children, Barbara and Elizabeth, and then, after six years of marriage, she died.

So far as any evidence is concerned, Stiegel's title of "Baron" was wholly spurious. Probably someone called him "Baron," half in sarcasm, half in admiration. Stiegel apparently liked and affected the title. This is psychologically understandable, particularly in the case of our man. The pride of many a titled man in dropping his title in America was counter-balanced by the pride of many commoners from Europe who seized the occasion to adopt bogus titles. America was a place for dropping inhibitions. It offered the opportunity for being autocratic as well as democratic.

Six months after Elizabeth Huber died, the Baron married Elizabeth Holtz. His son by her was named Jacob, after his first wife's father.

At about this time he began developing a pipeless stove designed to fit into the jamb of the kitchen stove. By 1760 he was one of the most prosperous ironmasters in America. He employed about 75 men and built 25 tenant houses near the furnace. It was in this same year, probably, that he purchased Charming Forge, near Womeldorf, Berks County, Pennsylvania. At this establishment only bar iron was made, and much of it was used to manufacture the finished products at Elizabeth Furnace.

An adjunct of Stiegel's business was the manufacture of apparatus for refining molasses. Large quantities of such machinery were shipped from Elizabeth Furnace to the West Indies. At this period Stiegel summed up his assets thus:

Elizabeth Furnace	4000	Pounds
Charming Forge	3088	"
Other lands	540	"
Retinue	208	"
Musical instruments	375	"
Store	870	"
Furniture	483	"
Clothing	260	"
Negro Cyrus	80	"
Cellar stores	49	"
Sundry accts	2028	"

141. The Duke's Plan of New Amsterdam in 1661. The dotted line indicates Glassmakers Street, later Smee Street, Smith Street, and now William Street. Jan Smedes' Shop was located here.

142, 143. TWO SOUTH JERSEY PITCHERS IN GREEN GLASS. Note the additional bottom thickness "dragged" up for decoration.

144. BOWL WITH BALL COVER, SOUTH JERSEY. Note bubbles and also crude severance of ball from blowpipe.

145. SOUTH JERSEY CANDLESTICKS IN LIGHT GREEN GLASS. Note spiral at base of sockets.

146. MORTAR AND PESTLE, SOUTH JERSEY, AMBER AND
      GREEN GLASS. Probably by the Wistars.

147. AMBER BOWL, SOUTH JERSEY. Probably by the
      Wistars.

148. EARLY PITCHER. Maker unknown.

149. EARLY MUG. Maker unknown.

151. STIEGEL GLASS. SALTCELLAR AND CREAM JUG.

150. DYOTTVILLE FLASK, PATTERN MOLDED.
     "Winter-Summer" design.

153. STIEGEL. ENGRAVED WINE GLASSES.

152. DYOTTVILLE FLASKS.

STIEGEL. ENGRAVED BOWL.

155. STIEGEL. ENGRAVED FLIP GLASS.

STIEGEL. BLUE FLINT GLASS VASE.

157. DYOTTVILLE FLASKS.

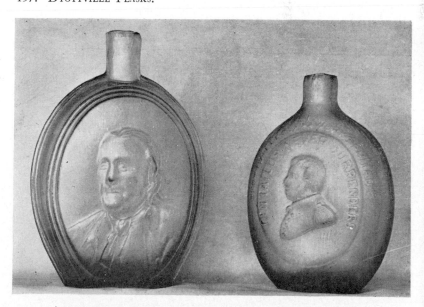

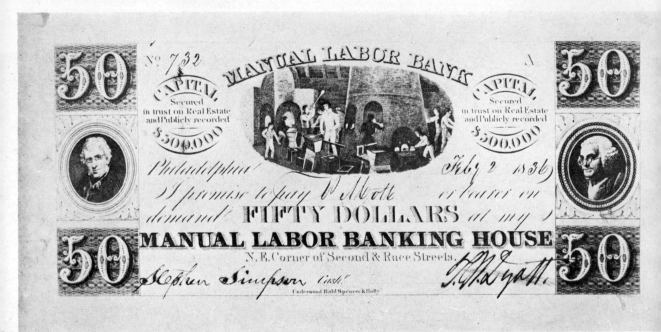

158. MONEY ISSUED BY DYOTT'S ILL-OMENED BANK. Note picture of Dyott at left, and at right, picture of Franklin, of course, had nothing to do with the bank.

159. BASKET, BLOWN IN A THREE-SECTION, HINGED MOLD.

160. MUG, BLOWN IN A THREE-SECTION H MOLD.

w of the Glass Works of T.W. DYOTT *at Kensington on the Delaware n.ͬ Philad*

161. FROM AN OLD PRINT.

162. BLOWING IN A ONE PIECE MOLD.

NEW YORK STATE

Locations of Glass Factories

1. BERNARDS BAY, OSWEGO CO. 1852–19thCen.
2. BINGHAMTON, BROOME CO. 1880–?
3. BRISTOL, ULSTER CO. c.1810–?
4. BUFFALO, ERIE CO. Late 19th Cen.
5. CLEVELAND, OSWEGO CO. 1840–1899
6. CLYDE, WAYNE CO. 1820–1880
7. CORNING, STEUBEN CO. 1868–Present
8. DUNBARTON, ONEIDA CO. 1802–19thCen.
9. DURHAMVILLE, ONEIDA CO. 1845– 19thCen.
10. ELLENVILLE, ULSTER CO. 1836
11. GENEVA, ONTARIO CO. 1810
12. GREENPOINT, KINGS CO. 1860–c.1867
13. GUILDERLAND T'SHIP, ALBANY CO. 1785–1815

15. LANCASTER, ERIE CO. 1849–1907
16. LOCKPORT, NIAGARA CO. 1840 19thCen.
17. MT. MORRIS, LIVINGSTON CO. 1841–1848
18. NEWBURGH, ORANGE CO. Mid-19th Cen.
19. NEW LEBANON, COLUMBIA CO. 1873–1876
20. NEW WINDSOR, ORANGE CO. 1753–1785
21. NEW YORK CITY, N.Y. CO. 1698 19thCen.
22. PETERBORO, MADISON CO. 1804–1830
23. REDFORD, CLINTON CO. 1831–c.1852
24. REDWOOD, JEFFERSON CO. 1833–1860
25. SANDLAKE T'SHIP, RENSSELAER CO. 1806–1853
26. SARATOGA, SARATOGA CO. 1844–1890
27. UTICA, ONEIDA CO. c.1809–1822

163. Map of New York State, Showing Locations of Glass Works, Early and Modern.

Antique

164. GLASSMAKING TOOLS.
Note blowpipes, calipers,
shears, pucellas, mold,
ladle, etc.

165. "GATHERING" GLASS FROM THE FURNACE.

166. THE WORKMAN HAS BLOWN A GOBLET AND
SHAPED ITS STEM. He now takes an additional
"gather" from a "servitor," to shape the foot.

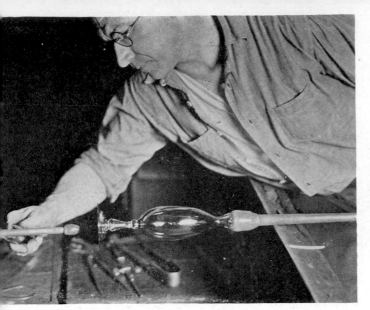

167. HAVING SHAPED THE FOOT HE ATTACHES IT TO A PONTIL BY A SMALL GATHER AND CUTS IT FROM BLOWPIPE.

168. NOW HE CLIPS OPEN THE END OF THE BULB SO THAT IT MAY BE SHAPED.

169. THE GOBLET BOWL IS SHAPED WITH THE PUCELLAS.

170. THE FINISHED GOBLET IS BROKEN FROM THE PONTIL AND TAKEN TO THE ANNEALING OVEN.

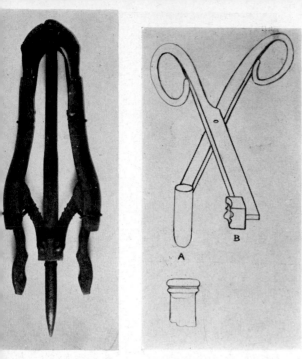

171, 172. IMPLEMENTS FOR SHAPING BOTTLE NECKS.
Antiques

173. BOTTLE BLOWING IN AN AMERICAN FACTORY, C. 1860.
Antiqu

174. CANDLESTICKS, SANDWICH PRESSED
GLASS.

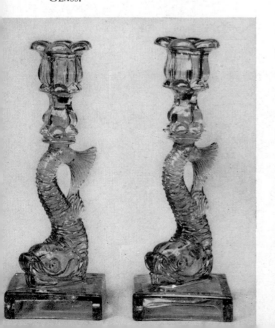

176. FILIGREE FLASK. Blown, and de
rated with alternately white a
colored twisted ribbons. This is
"off hand" piece by Nich
Lutz, Boston and Sandwich G
Co.

175. PRESENTATION CHALICE. A
blown by Nicholas Lutz. The
tions of colored glass in the st
must have been built up in se
rate gathers in the shaping proc

Metropolitan Museum

177. SUGAR BOWL WITH COVER. Sandwich glass. "Princess Feather" Pattern. Blue and white pressed glass.

178. PITCHER. Attributed to new England Glass Co.

180. TIN LANTERN WITH GREEN BULL'S EYE LENS.

179. WINDOW PANE OF BULLS EYE, OR CROWN GLASS.

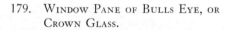

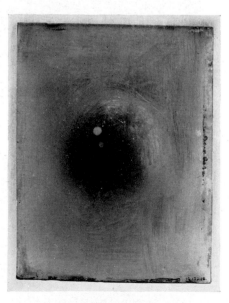

81. SANDWICH PRESSED GLASS CUP PLATES. Note famous design of "The Wedding Day and three weeks after." Tu
picture upside down for effect.

182. CAMEO GLASS BOWL. White on red ground. 19th Century.

183. "AGNUS DEI." Engraved vase designed by Sidney Waugh and executed by Steuben Glass, 1902.

185. GOBLET WITH COVER.
CLEAR, ENGRAVED GLASS.
Made at the New Bremen
(Maryland) Glass Manu-
factory, John Frederick
Amelung, Proprietor. C.
1784.

184. ENGRAVED GLASS GOBLET,
BEARING COAT OF ARMS OF
THE STATE OF PENNSYL-
VANIA. Said to have been
presented to Gov. Thomas
Mifflin, of Pa., in 1791.
Made by Amelung.

186, 187. THE BOSTON AND SANDWICH GLASS FACTORY AND ONE OF THE GLASS-PRESSING MACHINES, AS THEY ARE TODAY.

188. ENGRAVED GLASS BOWL WITH ZODIAC PATTERN. Designed by Sidney Waugh, executed by Steuben Glass, 1904.

Metropolitan Museum

This adds up to £11,981, or approximately $59,905. In buying power at that time this sum was equivalent to about $150,000 today, constituting quite a fortune.

Stiegel's next venture was real estate promotion. In 1762, in partnership with Charles and Alexander Stedman, he purchased 729 acres of land on the north bank of Chiquaesalunga Creek in Lancaster County, Pennsylvania. There were two log cabins on this property at the time. But among the Baron's many accomplishments was that of surveying, and he soon laid out a pattern of streets and alleys and landmarks in this section of wilderness and named it Manheim. He and his partners then began to build houses which they planned to sell outright while charging rental for the property on which they stood. The boom was successful, and soon Manheim was a flourishing Pennsylvania-German town.

On a choice intersection of his town the Baron had built for himself a mansion of English brick. It took two years to build, and possessed many unusual features. It was luxuriously furnished. The walls of the great parlor were hung with tapestries of hunting scenes, the doors and wainscoting were heavily panelled, and the mantels were set with blue Delft tiles. A full half of the second floor was taken up by an arched chapel, fully equipped with pulpit and pews. Here he instituted the custom of gathering his workmen into his chapel and delivering sermons to them in the best Lutheran tradition. On the roof was a bandstand.

On a hill near Schaeferstown, between Elizabeth Furnace and Charming Forge, the Baron built his Thurm Berg. This was a strange tower, built of heavy wood in the shape of a truncated pyramid, and painted red. It was 50 feet square at the bottom, 10 feet square at the top, and 75 feet high. The interior was divided into vast banquet halls and guest chambers. On its summit were mounted brass cannon which are said to have fired a 24 round salute whenever the Baron approached, and a 12 round salute for the approach of distinguished guests, such as George Washington, who reputedly visited there.

Stiegel drove about the country at breakneck speed in a coach drawn by six white horses, with wigged and uniformed outriders. There were other cannon at his Manheim mansion to boom his approach. This was a signal for all the townspeople to gather in the streets to cheer his entry, and for his bandsmen to drop their regular work, don their fancy outfits, grab their instruments, rush to the platform on Stiegel's roof, and blast out with a stirring German march. All in all it was no mean affair when Baron Henry Stiegel came to town.

Perhaps it was inevitable that Stiegel should have come to the making of glass. To the early manufacturer the production of glass had an adventuresome and speculative aspect tempting to the gambler, in its probability of failure, its obscurities of formulae, and the fabulous beauty of its finished output.

Just as Stiegel had a good knowledge of the ironworker's craft, of surveying, building, music, bookkeeping, theology and polemics, he probably knew a good deal of the craft of glassmaking. His first efforts were at Elizabeth Furnace where he made window glass and bottles on a small scale, employing five blowers as early as 1763.

As soon as he had determined to begin the manufacture of glass on a large scale he made a trip to Europe and brought back a group of workmen whom he had secretly recruited in Germany and England. Then, at an expense which would be equivalent today to about $20,000, he erected a glassworks at Manheim.

Tradition says that the glass-house was 90 feet high, and that a four-horse team could be driven through its doorway, turned around, and driven out.

He began operations with only five blowers. On April 14, 1766, he wrote, "This evening the Glass House ended the season, the men being worn out." His first year's efforts had brought in $3005.

By 1769 he was going full speed and employing thirty-five glass blowers. He soon had his own wholesale and retail distributors in Philadelphia, Baltimore, New York, and Boston. He bought out the Stedmans' interest in the town of Manheim.

The decline and fall of Baron Stiegel was abrupt and significant. Like many another, he had become associated with men who were less imaginative, had less of the Grand Manner, were more cautious, less generous, and infinitely more cunning than himself. Such men are capable of waiting for a long time for a man of Steigel's type to fall into a trap. They waited, and Stiegel fell. He extended his credit to the breaking-point with constant re-investments and expansions. Then, when the shadow of impending revolution stilled the activity of commerce, and creditors rushed to draw back their money, Stiegel had everything but cash. On October 15th, 1774, he pawned his wife's gold watch. No mercy was shown to him by men who had long envied him. He was thrown into a debtors' prison.

There was something extremely fragile about his nature, for all his bombast. In prison he wrote pitiable letters to people whom he hoped would help him. He composed prayers of really fine literary quality. Finally, "an act for the relief of Henry William Stiegel languishing prisoner in the gaol of Lancaster County with respect to the imprisonment of his own person. . . . ." was passed by the legislature and he was released.

Baron Henry William Stiegel somehow did not have the

resilience to recover. He had lived a fantasy, and in this one abrupt failure he had lost the thread of it forever. He tried to live in the old house at Elizabeth Furnace, and the owners, whom he thought were his best friends, did not like it. The letters he wrote to them are full of apologies that stand in bitter contrast to the romantic splendor of a few years past.

He tried teaching school and was for a while foreman of Elizabeth Furnace, where he had begun his American career. But he was beaten, and at forty-eight he was a thin, bent old man. Michael Quigley, who met him at that time, wrote in his diary, "He appeared terribly dejected. He had laid aside his fine wig; his round skull was nearly bald, his eyesight had become dim."

In the period of his helplessness he witnessed the rise to power of the nation whose industry and art he had greatly stimulated. On January 10th, 1785, he died.

THOMAS DYOTT

One of the many poor boys who came to America near the end of the 18th century was Thomas W. Dyott. He began his efforts in Philadelphia as a bootblack. He differed from the average bootblack in that he manufactured his own blacking. From this highly successful chemical endeavor it proved but a stone's throw to "Dyott's Patent Medicine Ware House; No. 57 South Second Street."

Shortly thereafter, just as Henry Stiegel had decided that he was a Baron, Thomas Dyott made up his mind that he was a Doctor of Medicine and appended the requisite M.D. He announced that his products were "celebrated for most of the diseases to which the human body is liable." His offerings included:

Stomack Elixir of Health
Vegetable Nervous Cordial
Celebrated Gout Drops
Stomachic Bitters
Infallible Worm Destroying Lozenges
Patent Itch Ointment
Infallible Toothache Drops
Anti Bilious Pills
Ointment for the Cure of Tetter, Ring Worm, etc.
Embrocation for the Rheumatism
Balm of Iberia (for the complexion)
The Circassian Dye Water
The Restorative Dentifrice

He was selling such huge quantities of these salubrious remedies to the new American public that he decided to manufacture his own containers, and in 1833 bought the Kensington Glass Works, which had been founded in 1772 by James Leacock and Robert Towers.

Under his management this establishment rapidly expanded. He soon had five furnaces in operation, but shortly thereafter he began to suffer from what many another glass manufacturer had encountered; the drunkenness of his glass blowers. Whereupon, despite the fact that one of his main productions was whiskey flasks, of which many are the most prized by antiquarians, he began an experiment in prohibition and in the general moral direction of his laborers. His effort was the first large-scale example of "Paternalism" in American industry.

Despite the manufacture of whiskey flasks and balms of life he discovered within himself, as occasion required, unsuspected depths of piety. Out of these depths he evolved *The System of Moral and Mental Labor Established at the Glass Factory of Dyottville, in the County of Philadelphia.*

His brochure is a masterpiece of empty eloquence combined

with the cunning moral justification of bad labor practices. "It is too much the propensity of our nature, to run after Fortune with intoxicating ardour, without considering how many human hearts we may crush in the heat of the pursuit; or without paying very punctilious regard to the means by which we accomplish profit. The passion for gain is often too powerful to be modulated by Reason, arrested by Judgement, or qualified by Justice. It is perhaps to this point that we are to refer the hitherto neglected point of combining mental and moral with manual labor. . . ."

So keen was the social conscience of Dr. Dyott that he decided to put little children, six years of age, to work in his factory: "I projected the plan of instructing boys in the art of Glass Blowing, taking them at so tender an age that their pliant natures could be molded into habits of temperance, industry, docility, piety, and perfect moral decorum, under a system of instruction within the walls of the Factory, fully adequate to develop all these moral and intellectual faculties, which make the happy man, the good citizen, and the valuable operative."

He employed about 400 persons at one time. 130 of these were boys of 10 to 16 years, who were apprentice glass blowers. The still younger children were employed in sifting clay and in weaving baskets for wrapping around flasks (which Dyott claimed was one of the most moral of all endeavors). He confessed that having all these young persons, most of whom were orphans of the poor, under his tutelage, imposed ". . . the most serious duties upon the proprietor, as to the best means of shedding light on the benighted understanding, and reforming the evil passions of the vicious heart."

He was the first glass manufacturer in America to work his men twelve months per year, in defiance of all previous tradition. As regards the supposed strenuousness of glass blowing, the Doctor writes, "The mere act of blowing does not cause an exertion of the lungs . . . and habit soon renders the heat imperceptible." In fact, he adds later, ". . . the exertion of blowing glass, by giving a slight and healthy expansion to the chest and lungs, adds vigor and energy to the whole frame."

He employed his men and children not only throughout the year but eleven hours per day. His moral and mental instruction took place between the hours of 7 and 8 P.M., and inasmuch as this period opened and closed with singing and prayer it seems questionable whether a great deal in the way of culture was conveyed to the orphan boys concerning whose welfare Dr. Dyott felt so deeply.

The clothes of the apprenticed boys were dispensed to them one suit at a time, without consulting their taste, again under the guise of moral welfare, for they were thus saved from ". . . the temptation to sell their garments, or to elope; as they never have a single change in their own possession . . ."

Thomas W. Dyott was seventy years of age when he became too deeply involved in the intricacies of his Manual Labor Bank, in Philadelphia, and was convicted of "criminal insolvency." He lived nearly a quarter of a century longer, but his glassworks had been closed and he was never able to launch another enterprise. When he died in 1861 America bid farewell to one of its most energetic and unscrupulous fakers.

THE GLASSMAKER'S CRAFT

There are several special circumstances that should be kept in mind in thinking of the early American glass industry. The only item on the favorable side of the ledger was an abundant fuel supply. Against this there stood the painful lack of skilled labor. Glassmaking and glass-blowing are not crafts which a man may step into through some natural aptitude. They require a complexity of traditional information and a variety of technical skills that can result only from long and disciplined training. The failure of the guild system in America, and the impotence even of the simple apprentice system, hardly made for an abundance of this type of craftsman. Other nations, well aware of their value, passed laws against the emigration of glass-men. Those who came to America were smuggled from their homelands.

These smuggled glass workers were jealous of their skill and, despite agreements to the contrary, they were not too anxious to convey this skill to native novitiates. Also, recognizing their rarity and consequent independence, they were inclined to be arrogant, and generally speaking, to take advantage of their importance in a very human way.

Indeed, glass men held a very superior rank in the general order of craftsmen. There had been a time in Venice when all glass blowers had been made Burgesses and it was even permissible for noblemen to marry their daughters and have noble issue! Later, in France, the exclusive right to make glass was assigned by the King to various noble families in this and that province and was considered one of the most valuable concessions. In such cases it was not a question of mere ownership or management, but of actual practice. Says a writer of the time: "The gentlemen work only twelve hours, but without resting, and always standing and naked. . . ."

It should be remembered that glass-blowing is such an arduous and health-destroying labor that it was customary, except at the establishment of Doctor Dyott, to work only six to nine months out of every year.

A 17th century commentator observes: "It must be owned those great and continual heats, which those gentlemen are exposed to from their furnaces, are prejudicial to their health; for coming in at their mouths, it attacks their lungs and dries them up, whence most are pale and short-lived by reason of diseases of the heart and breast, which the fire causes; which makes Libarius say . . . 'they were of weak and infirm bodies, thirsty and easily made drunk' . . ."

In addition to drunkenness and general unreliability of the workmen, there were the Salamanders to be considered. These were horrendous creatures which made their abode in the flame of the furnace itself. The frequent disappearance of glass-blowers, even those who were under contract, was sometimes attributed to these supernatural beasts which often, when no one was looking, reached out and snatched a luckless craftsman and cruelly devoured him within their roaring sanctuary, to the considerable regret of his employer. At any rate so the tale was told when itinerant glassworkers disappeared without notice.

The types of glass most commonly used in Colonial times were flint, crown, common window, bottle, and plate.

Flint glass, or crystal glass, was an English discovery and quickly surpassed in popularity the Venetian and Bohemian glass which had previously dominated the market. It is made by adding a high percentage of lead to the elements of the glass. Lead gives lustre, heightens refractory power, increases weight and fusibility.

A common formula for flint glass was: "one half sand, one third red lead or litharge, one sixth potash, and a little saltpeter, manganese and arsenic to improve the color." To this mixture about one fourth by weight of "cullet" was added; that is, broken glass of the same type.

Today glass is usually melted in metal vats, but up until about 1863 it was necessary to use earthenware pots. Thus the potter was a very necessary man around the glassworks, and every glassworks had its pot-room. This is another aspect of the travail of early glassmaking. The manufacture of these pots was no simple matter. They had to be made of a very special clay in order to resist the intense and prolonged heat, and the chemical action of the glass matrix. In the early days of America the best clay for this purpose, that of Stourbridge, in England, had to be shipped to this country at high prices. This was a slate clay, usually brown. Suitable clay was discovered in Delaware and Missouri early in the 19th century, but until well into the third quarter of that century most of it was still imported from Europe.

Once the necessary clay for the melting pots was obtained and pulverized into a fine dust, it had to be exposed to the elements and allowed to "ripen" for about a year. Then a quantity of broken pots, called "potsherds," equivalent to the "cullet" in the glass mixture, was cleaned and ground and mixed with the ripened clay to the amount of about one fifth by weight. Water was added, to make a thick paste, which was "worked" with the bare feet, "bugging," to the consistency of putty. The resulting substance was again put away, for more ripening, for as long as half a year. Then the pot was carefully built up and shaped by hand, taking several more weeks. A third ripening of from six months to a year was then necessary. At last came the actual baking and annealing. To top it all, if the pot was a success and had a clear ring while at high temperature in the furious flame of the glass oven, its average life was less than two months! From this it may be seen that the glass industry was not a venture to be taken up light-heartedly. As a matter of distressing fact, the greater number of glass-men were financial failures until the advent of the machine age, when the pressing-machine greatly curtailed the romantic craft of glass-blowing and took glass out of the luxury class.

The construction of the furnaces and of the glass-room itself depended upon the type of glass being made. In the case of flint glass, a round or elliptical furnace was used, in a room usually large and square with a high ceiling. In the case of bottle glass the furnace was usually oblong or square, and the room was often oblong.

In addition to his pots and furnace, the necessary tools of the early glassman were: the blowpipe, a hollow tapering tube from four to seven feet long; the pontil, (pronounced "punty"), an iron rod somewhat shorter than the blowpipe; the marver, a polished, cast-iron plate; the pucelas, a pair of tongs with dull wooden blades fastened together with a flexible metal bow; large and small shears for cutting off excess glass. Also, various pincers, compasses, rulers, blocks and paddles of wood and metal. In spite of the advent of machine-made glass, the tools and processes of fine, hand-made glass have not changed or modified appreciably for centuries.

In the making of a piece of blown glass, the batch of glass was cooked for the required length of time, (ranging anywhere from sixteen hours to three days, depending on the type of glass), at a temperature as high as 12,000 degrees Fahrenheit. Then an assistant to the boss-blower dipped the heated nose of the blowpipe into the crucible until a sufficient quantity of the hot glass, called "parison," adhered to it. He then rolled this lump of viscous glass on the marver, to give it a regular shape. Next the loaded blowpipe was presented to the boss-blower who, by reason of his uncanny skill, was the Number One man of the glassworks. As the boss-blower blew the glass shape expanded, and as he swung his blowpipe the shape lengthened. When he was satisfied, the long iron rod, the pontil, was brought with a small blob of glass on the end of it. This enabled it to adhere to the end of the blown bulb opposite the blowpipe. Then the "wetter off," by means of a piece of iron dipped in cold water, broke the blown glass bubble off from the blowpipe so that it was now handled by the pontil. This was handed to the "chair-man" who rolled it back and forth on the arm of his chair and gave it its final shape by means of the various simple tools, such as paddles and pincers. Finally the shaped piece was broken off from the pontil and carried on a tray to the leer, or annealing oven, where it was subjected to a long and slowly decreasing heat to assure its resistance to varying temperatures.

When the pontil has been broken away from the shaped piece a rough spot, called the "pontil mark," is left on the base. This is the characteristic identifying mark of all hand-made, blown glass, early or modern, for it remains in one form or another, even if it has been to some degree smoothed off by reheating, or ground away, leaving a slight hollow.

The most extraordinary of the early blowing processes was that described for the manufacture of "crown glass," that is, the "bulls-eye" type of window glass. All early window glass was blown. The processes of "plate glass," made by simply pouring it onto flat iron or copper tables, was a later development. The ordinary early window glass was blown into cylinders, then split and flattened. Not so with crown glass.

The formula for this required ". . . . kelp and white sand . . . . in proportions of eleven of kelp to seven of sand." The kelp, or seaweed, had of course been subjected to a lengthy burning process to reduce it to a mineral ash. In time, carbonate of soda replaced the kelp and produced a clearer glass.

After this had been cooked from sixteen to twenty hours, a proper sized "gather" was taken onto the end of the blowpipe and blown into a large, thin sphere. A pontil was attached to the side opposite the blowpipe and the blowpipe detached, leaving an aperture of from one-and-a-half to two inches. The sphere was then re-introduced into the furnace and rapidly whirled by the craftsman who held it by the pontil. As the sphere began to soften in the furnace heat the artisan whirled it faster and faster, until through centrifugal force the opening opposite the pontil began to expand. Judging the operation carefully, he kept on whirling the glass bubble until, in the words of an eye-witness, ". . . . the aperture suddenly flies open with a loud ruffling noise, which has been aptly compared to the unfurling of a flag in a strong breeze; and the glass becomes a circular plane or sheet of from four to four-and-a-half feet in diameter, of equal thickness throughout, except at the point called bullion or bulls-eye . . . ." where the pontil is attached. The craftsman continued the whirling in order that the circular glass plate might maintain its shape, and gradually withdrew it from the fire. After annealing it was cut to the proper shape and size.

That this extraordinary process was responsible for many of the windows of early American buildings demands a special tribute to the craftsmen who were able to master it.

Sometimes a mold was used in order that a pattern of some sort might be raised or impressed on the surface of the article. In this case the process was simply to do the blowing inside the mold. The molds were made of brass, iron, and occasionally of very hard woods. The designs were usually cut intaglio so that the patterns on the finished glass were raised. The molds were usually made in two, three, or four parts. A two part mold, commonly used, was opened and closed by a foot pedal operated by the blower.

One part molds were also used and required a special technique of blowing. They were made in miniature. The "gathering" of glass was blown into them, then contracted by means of an inhalation of the breath, and removed from the mold. It was then blown out to full size, the pattern expanding uniformly with the glass. Work of this kind was, of course, seamless, while objects made in the two, three, or four part molds showed seams where the parts were joined unless the piece were thoroughly "flashed," (reheated), or unless the seams were cleverly made to coincide with some element of the pattern.

The models for molds were usually carved of mahogany and from them was made the "master mold," from which, in turn, were made the actual molds for the glass. Needless to say, much of the beauty of this type of early glass depended upon the artistry of the mold maker.

The liquor flask is one of the most interesting, as well as important items in American craft history. Covering its manufacture an early authority writes: "The common green or bottle glass is made of the coarsest materials; sand, lime, sometimes clay, any kind of alkali or alkaline ash, whose cheapness may recommend it to the manufacturer, and sometimes the vitreous slag produced from the fusion of iron ore. The mixture most commonly used is soap-makers' waste, in the proportion of three measures to one measure of sand. The green color of this glass is occasioned by the existence of a portion of iron in the sand, and it may be also, of the vegetable ashes of which it is composed. When castor-oil or champagne bottles are wanted, a portion of green glass cullet is added, to improve the color."

From this mixture, after it had been properly cooked and skimmed of impurities that had risen to the top, the flasks were blown in the manner described, but usually in a two section mold operated by the foot.

"The finisher then warms the bottle at the furnace, and taking a small quantity of the metal on what is termed a ring-iron, he turns it once around the mouth forming the ring seen at the mouth of bottles. He then employs the shears to give shape to the neck. One of the blades of the shears has a piece of brass in the center, tapered like a common cork, which forms the inside mouth; to the other is attached a piece of brass used to form the ring. The bottle is then lifted by the neck on a fork by a little fellow about ten years of age, and carried to the annealing arch. . . ."

CHARACTERISTICS AND IDENTIFICATIONS

Among the most interesting specimens of early American glass are those known as "off-hand" pieces. These were objects blown by the workmen for their own use, for their employers, or for local people; not for general sale. These pieces usually have an unconventionality about them, because the blower felt free to express his individual talents. Even in glassworks largely confined to the making of window-glass there was usually a "corner pot" from which off-hand pieces were blown.

Aside from the pontil mark, which we have already mentioned, blown glass may be generally recognized by its slight irregularities of shape and by the fact that if blown in a mold, the pattern in reverse will appear on the inside of the vessel, unless the glass is unusually thick.

Old glass also shows signs of wear, usually on its base, and of discoloration due to exposure to light.

The many early American liquor flasks extant are important collectors' items. These flasks were made in many shapes and with various patterns. Most common is the Eagle, with George Washington as a runner-up. But there are great numbers of formal as well as historical patterns: scrolls, statesmen, cornucopias, etc., etc. These have been well catalogued in various books and are readily identifiable by reference.

Another identifiable form of American glass is the cup-plate.

This sprang from a widespread American habit of drinking tea from the saucer, particularly prevalent in the early 19th century. Naturally when one elegantly poured one's tea into the saucer the question arose, where to put the cup while drinking from the saucer? The obvious answer was, ". . . on a cup-plate!" These flat dishes were made for this homely purpose.

The cup-plate came in with pressed glass, in 1827, and the most precious are those of Sandwich. They are from two and three quarters, to three and three quarter inches in diameter and should not be confused with similar flat dishes, such as toddy or honey dishes, which are of different sizes. Like the flasks, they were given to historical as well as formal patterns: famous steamboats, Henry Clay, log cabins, and so on. Most of them can be dated and constitute a lure to the collector. Some are rare, others common. Once sold for five cents each, certain ones now command high prices and the ebullient enthusiasm of collectors.

The "industrialization" of glass manufacture began with the advent of the glass-pressing process. This greatly curtailed the traditional methods of glasswork and relegated blown glass more or less permanently to the status of a luxury product. On the other hand, it made a marked contribution of its own, introducing certain new aspects of glass craftsmanship.

Deming Jarves, an enterprising young citizen of Boston, after an unsuccessful attempt to subsist as a pottery retailer, procured a job with the New England Glass Company in 1819. The company had been founded two years earlier. Five years later Jarves left the organization and started a glassworks of his own, which he called the Boston and Sandwich Glass Factory. He had originally intended this to be a small craft endeavor. An over-zealous purchasing agent, however, loaded him with more land than he could support, thus forcing him into expansion, and a consequent world fame. He took some former members of the New England Glass Works into partnership and they were incorporated with a capital investment of $300,000.

Deming Jarves says in his *Reminiscences,* that the glass-pressing machine was not invented in America, basing the statement on his claim to have seen early pressed glass "salts" of European origin. It is a blurred point, for there was a good bit of confusion among early commentators in regard to blown-mold glass and pressed glass. As the case may be, pressed glass was not used extensively until a workman by the name of Robinson invented a glass-pressing machine at the New England Glass Works.

The machine was quickly taken up by the Boston and Sandwich Glass Factory and achieved a rapid perfection. Jarves immediately saw that the new method made possible decorations of much finer detail and complexity than could formerly be achieved in glass. He promptly employed the most brilliant mold-makers in the world. These men cut their designs in wood, from which iron or brass molds were subsequently made.

Thus it can be seen that the mold-makers were the great craftsmen of Sandwich Glass. Clement Bossett, a New Englander, and Newell Hoxie, a Quaker, were most notable among these creative carvers. The Sandwich works produced a "lace glass" the like of which has never been seen before or since, so fine are the lines, so perfect the balance of ornament.

The Sandwich glassworks, in contrast to Dr. Dyott's venture, was one of the rare examples of *successful* industrial paternalism which occurred during the 19th century. Practically every member of the community of workers that grew up around the factory was as passionately interested in Sandwich Glass as was Deming Jarves himself. There were several reasons for this. The policy of Jarves was to pay his men well, for the times, and not to decrease production or salaries during depressions. As a business man, Jarves had learned that to work his enterprises at anything below full capacity meant increased cost of production. To work at full speed was aways cheaper in actual production cost, even though he continued to pay pre-depression wages. He merely stored his output, when selling declined, and was later able to sell his product for less than his more cautious competitors. Certainty of employment, therefore, must have contributed greatly to the morale of his workers.

Moreover, it was a rule of the glassworks that employees could make whatever pieces they wanted for their own use at no cost. Even the youngest apprentice boys were encouraged to experiment as freely as they chose. In later years a charge was made for the glass by weight, but at a price so low that it was of no individual consequence.

Deming Jarves knew how to capitalize upon the spirit-of-craftsmanship which exists in all people. Two of Jarves' workmen, Frank Kern and Joseph Marsh, had miniature glass-furnaces in the cellars of their own homes where they could experiment during their spare time. Both of them were intensely interested in experiments with glass and were amply rewarded for their discoveries by Jarves. One of his best known workmen was the blower, Nicholas Lutz. Not a little of Jarves' success at this stimulating of enthusiasm was due to the fact that he was extremely interested in glass himself, rather than merely in the profits to be derived therefrom.

Weekly wages at the early Sandwich works were high for the period. The scale was $17 for blowers, $14 for servitors, $6 for footmakers, and $3 for boys. The work was ten hours per day in broken shifts of five hours each. But this was only for four days per week, thus making a forty-hour week. The week-end began Thursday night and ended Monday morning.

The whole town became passionately interested in the making of better and better Sandwich glass. The result was, that for variety of pattern, perfection of material, and general ingenuity of workmanship Sandwich glass has never been surpassed. It flourished from 1825 to 1888.

Patterns of Sandwich-ware of particular American significance were the Eagle, Bunker Hill, American ships, George Washington, Henry Clay, William Henry Harrison, and the log cabins which were adopted as the symbol of Harrison.

It is not to be supposed that all items of pressed glass are works of art. The technique has its run-of-the-mill output and the pressing process remains the basis of the modern glass industry.

CHAPTER 7

AMERICAN SILVERSMITHS

SILVERSMITHING is a craft in which we may well expect to find pride of workmanship and permanent value of the finished object at their highest. Two factors in his work set the silversmith apart from all other craftsmen. These were the value of his material, and the artistic requirements of his craft. The silversmith had to be a man in whom everyone had absolute confidence. He was the social equivalent of the small town banker. We shall find in him none of the Bohemianism of the carpenters and none of the flamboyance of the glassmakers. Such qualities were not conducive to investment.

And investment was, in an oblique way, the business of the silversmith. In the 17th and 18th centuries each piece of silver was made to order for an individual. The customer gathered together enough silver coin for the purpose, handed it in a sack to his chosen silversmith and said, "One porringer . . . three caudle-cups . . . one tankard . . ." or anything else he might desire.

This was the same as putting money in the bank. The skill of the craftsmanship in the finished product added a certain amount to the actual value of the silver, comparable to interest. The buyer's investment was thus a good one in which he gambled only with the slight margin of the craftsman's skill. He felt the silver objects to be slightly safer from thievery than the coin would have been, being unidentifiable, and paper currency was most uncertain. Silver was his gilt-edged security.

In the 17th century the English standard for silver coin (sterling), and hence for plate, was 925 parts of silver to each 1000 parts of metal. In case the coins given him were not all sterling the silversmith's first step was to remove the base metal and bring the finished piece up to standard. The opportunities for cheating were manifestly great. The entire proceeding would be virtually impossible today, first because all our metal coins are largely alloy, and also because it would now be a violation of the law to destroy or deface United States currency.

Only about 1750 did it become common for the silversmith to furnish his own silver and be paid for this in addition to his workmanship. But he still continued to acquire his silver in the form of coin, much of which came from the Spanish colonies in South America. Silver was not successfully mined in the United States until 1852.

The silversmith had to establish himself by means of personal contact, whereas most other craftsmen could merely hang out a shingle and start to work. He was probably one of the first Americans to fraternize in the interests of business. He held office wherever he could, joined every club, the most affluent church, and was active in politics. After all, a fellow assemblyman might order a tea-set from him. A reputation for honesty was one of his major assets. Part back-slapper, part banker, part artist, part worker; the early American silversmith was a wily and versatile man indeed!

The earliest known American silversmith came from London to Boston in 1634. His name was John Mansfield. Unfortunately no specimen of his work has been found.

One of the earliest smiths whose work survives was John

Hull (1624-1683). A Boston man, he has the distinction of probably having been the first silversmith to learn his craft in America. He was the son of a blacksmith and was apprenticed to his half-brother, Richard Storer, who had formerly been a member of the London Goldsmiths' Guild.

Hull apparently flourished and in 1652 he was selected by the Massachusetts Assembly to be the head of their new and illegal mint. For this work he took, as partner, his friend Robert Sanderson, who had come to this country as a full-fledged goldsmith in 1638. This partnership, though created originally to supply coins for the Massachusetts Bay Colony, extended into all branches of silversmithing so that *Hull & Sanderson* became one of the commonest marks on early American silver. Hull became wealthy and held many political offices in addition to that of Mint-Master.

Hull had an apprentice, Jeremiah Dummer (1645-1718), an excellent silversmith who subsequently became as successful as his former master, holding the positions of County Treasurer, Judge, Selectman, etc. in the customary manner of silversmiths. In addition to these accomplishments, Dummer was one of our foremost early painters. He left us a self-portait, together with portraits of many of his contemporaries. Dummer's son, William, later became Lieutenant-Governor of Massachusetts.

We can already begin to see that nearly all American silversmiths, within a given region, were related to one another either by blood, marriage, or apprenticeship.

John Coney (1655-1722) was the brother-in-law of Jeremiah Dummer and was probably apprenticed to him. Coney, in turn, had as apprentice a Frenchman by the name of Appollos De Rivoire, whom we shall have occasion to consider later. John Coney was not only a silversmith but a good engraver. He made the plates for the first paper money of America, that of Massachusetts Bay, in 1690. He also made the Seal of Harvard College.

When Coney died the Reverend T. Foxcroft, a relative by marriage, delivered his funeral oration. Fragments from this eulogy are worth repeating:

"I have often heard him speak of Christ with expressions of Love and Esteem; of Sin, with Tears; of earthly Enjoyments with a just Contempt; and of Heavenly Things with much Concern and Affection.

"The lying Tongue, the false Ballance, all deceitful Working, & subtil tricks, criminal Postponing of Payments, ec. was an abomination to him.

"His moral Defects I have not mentioned; for there are only such as are consistent with a good Estate, and small in Comparison of his Virtues: and therefore to be charitably covered in sacred Silence."

John Coney was, in truth, an excellent craftsman, who taught his art well to those who were to follow him.

Timothy Dwight (1634-1691), another prominent New England silversmith, is known to have lived with John Hull and was probably apprenticed to him. Edward Winslow (1669-1753), who produced a great quantity of silver work, was the grandson of trouble-making Anne Hutchinson of religious fame. He held even more political offices than was usual among his fellow smiths.

David Jesse (1670-1705), John Allen (1671- ?), and John Edwards (1671-1746) were well known artisans. John Hurd did good work, and so did his son, Nathaniel. In regard to the latter some of his account books bring out an interesting fact. Nathaniel Hurd was a true artist-craftsman, and also one of America's great early copperplate engravers. Yet his books show that he mended pots and did other similar tasks. Thus it is seen, and evidenced by records of other American silversmiths, that these aristocrats of craftsmanship were by no means above the most humble task within their skill. Such was hardly the case in England, where a prominent silversmith would not stoop to anything beneath his position.

Newport, Rhode Island, was a center of silversmithing. Among its silver workers are prominent names in American silver annals: Samuel Vernon (1683-1737), Benjamin Benton (1659-1749), John Tanner (1713-1785), John Coddington (1690-1743), Thomas Arnold (1739-1828), Daniel Rogers (1753-1792), and Jonathan Otis (1723-1791), who practiced the latter part of his career in Middletown, Connecticut.

In the center of Rhode Island's anomalous Narragansett region, where a society closely resembling the rich Southern feudalism grew into being, there existed the hilltop town of Little Rest, now Kingston. In this town flourished a number of silversmiths, in spite of the fact that this is not a craft usually occurring in a country town.

The "Narragansett Planters" were tremendously rich, and although they probably ordered much of their plate from the famous craftsmen of Boston, or Newport, there was still enough demand to support a group of local artisans.

One of this group, Samuel Casey, has on record one of the more speckled careers in American silversmithing. He was the son of one Thomas Casey, supposedly the only survivor of the Irish Massacre of 1641. Thomas subsequently fled to America, to the town of Newport, where his son was born.

Samuel Casey was made a freeman in Exeter, R. I., in 1745. Nearby he acquired a home and practiced the craft of silversmithing. Where he learned it is not known. He prospered. His work is much more imaginative than that of most of his con-

189, 190. PINE TREE SHILLINGS. Made for the Massachusetts Colony by Hull and Sanderson, 1663-1683.

Metropolitan Museum

191. TANKARD. By Jeremiah Dum c. 1675.

192. SELF PORTRAIT. By Jeremiah Dummer, Boston Silversmith.

Owned by the late Paul M. Hamlen, Direct Descendant of Dummer.

193. CRAFTSMAN PAINTS CRAFTSMAN. Portrait of John Coney, Boston Silversmith, by Jeremiah Dummer.

S. W. Sleeper

194. TEAPOT. By John Coney.

Metropolitan Museum

195. TANKARD. By John Coney.

Metropolitan Museum

196. PORRINGER. By Samuel Vernon of Newport, R. I.

197. PORRINGER. By Samuel Casey of Little Rest, R. I.

198. PITCHER. By Samuel Casey.

199. CHOCOLATE POT. By Edward Winslow, of Boston.

Metropolitan Museum

200. CHALICE. By James Boelen, of New York.

203. TANKARD. By Henricus Boelen, New York.

204. BOWL. By Jacob Boelen, New York.

CANDLESTICKS. By Jacob Hurd.

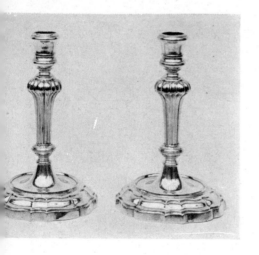

205. BOWL. By Cornelius Kierstede, New York.

MUG. Koenrat Ten Eyck.

206. TRENCHER SALT. By Jacob Ten Eyck.

Metropolitan Museum

7. Portrait of Nathaniel Hurd, Silversmith. By John Singleton Copley.

208. PORTRAIT OF PAUL REVERE, SILVERSMITH. By Gilbert Stuart.

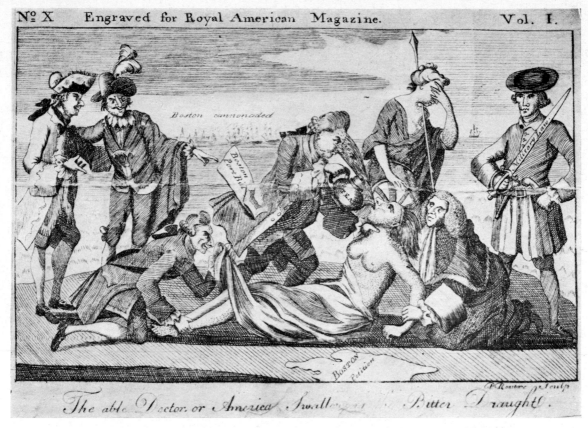

The able Doctor. or America Swallowing the Bitter Draught.

209.   COPPERPLATE ENGRAVING. By Paul Revere. This is a forebear of the modern political cartoon.

PITCHER AND SUGAR BOWL. By Paul Revere.

211.   TEAPOT. By Paul Revere. These pieces are in his characteristic and highly individual style.

Metropolitan Museum

213. TANKARD. By Paul Revere. Note Pine
Cone Finial as in Teapot.

Metropolitan Museum

212. PORRINGER. By Paul Revere, Senior.

4, 215. TRADE CARDS, REVERE AND SON.

temporaries. He engraved naked ladies straddling large fish, and other skilful and intricate designs. Then, on a windy September night, his house caught fire and burned to the ground. His entire fortune, of about five thousand pounds, was invested in the house, its luxurious furniture, and the implements of his craft.

After this catastrophe he moved to Little Rest and took over the "Helme House," a large gambrel-roofed building with a capacious garret. In Little Rest, in point of fact in this very garret, Casey forsook the strict probity which we have cited as characteristic of American silversmiths. It must be remembered, in justice to Casey, that an ironic fate had directed a craftsman of his superlative skill to a small town that was not willing or able sufficiently to patronize him. In addition to this, he was apparently supported by the community in his misdemeanors.

The fact is that Samuel Casey took to what was then called "Money Making," but would now be called counterfeiting. He was in league with certain local merchants and his strong young apprentice-relative worked the press which was located in the attic. There was much hiding of dies under stone piles and concealment of false metal in "great chambers." There was obscure talk, and the burying of false Spanish Dollars in local salt-water lagoons.

In some way Casey was exposed. Anticipating trouble he asked one of his relatives to take the dies, press, and other apparatus to a nearby lagoon and sink them out of reach; which was done.

When arrested, Casey at first broke down and told all, then regretted and pleaded Not Guilty. The jury, composed of his fellow townsmen, brought in a verdict of Not Guilty. They were severely chastised by the Magistrates and sent back into the jury-room to think the case over at greater length. After more painful thought the harassed Jury returned to the court-room with the Gilbertian verdict that ". . . if in the opinion of yr Honors the written confession of the Deft. be considered lawful evidence, then we find the Deft. Guilty; otherwise Not Guilty."

The irate Magistrates lost no time in deciding that the defendant's written confession was quite legal and condemned Samuel Casey to be hanged by the neck until dead.

On the night before Casey was to be hanged a large mob of towns-people painted their faces black and attacked the jail. It is not recorded that they met with any resistance. They broke down the doors and set Casey free. He rode hurriedly South-ward and no more is known of him. It seems likely that he prac-ticed his craft in some other colony under another name.

Other men in Little Rest who struggled against the almost insurmountable odds of metropolitan competition were Samuel's relative, Gideon, and his apprentice, John Waite. Waite, while by no means the equal of Samuel Casey, earned a considerable reputation. He was Justice of the Peace and held various Judge-ships and other offices. He engraved bills for the State of Rhode Island and also practiced the humbler trade of locksmithing. When the Revolution came John Waite organized a Militia Company which called itself the Kingston Reds (*sic*). Under Waite's leadership this company distinguished itself against the British.

Waite's brother, William, combined silversmithing with the calling of a Baptist Minister. Another silversmith of the period, Joseph Perkins, was also a gunsmith. The city council com-manded him to go to New York City to purchase one hundred firearms with which to resist the British, then immediately decided to save money by ordering the arms by mail. Perkins served for one year in the Kingston Reds, under John Waite.

Then he concentrated on becoming a successful manufacturer of silver buckles and buttons which he distributed, with a perspicacity ahead of his time, through retailers at a commission of 7%. He prospered, notwithstanding the fact that he became exceedingly intemperate before his death. When he was buried his respectable family changed his profession, engraving upon his tombstone, "Joseph Perkins, Merchant, died 1789. . . ."

Nathaniel Helme was another excellent craftsman of Little Rest. He is an instance of a silversmith springing from a wealthy and cultured family. His father, Judge James Helme, had built the house occupied by Samuel Casey.

There were some fine smiths in Connecticut: Captain Robert Fairchild (1703-1794), Ebenezer Chittenden (1726-1812), John Gardiner (1734-1776), Peter Quintard (1700- ?), Cornelius Kierstede (1675-1757), and others. The two last named were New York City silversmiths who practiced in their later years in Connecticut.

The silversmiths of New York City numbered several prolific families. One of these was the family of Boelen. Jacob and Hendrick were brothers. Henricus was the son of Jacob, father of another Jacob, and cousin of Koenrat Ten Eyck. This spans nearly three quarters of a century of silversmithing.

New York City had a custom of bestowing the honorary status of freeman upon persons who had no possible use for it. The first of these was given to Provincial Governor Cornbury in 1702. It was decided that the document should be enclosed in a gold box and "Alderman Boelen (the first of the Jacobs) is directed to make the said box."

Bartholomew Le Roux, one of the many Huguenot refugees in New York, afterwards made a number of these boxes, as did one Samuel Johnson. Le Roux, in common with the majority of his fellow French immigrants, was violently anti-French and was a leader in insisting that the city should guard itself against French attack. He married a Dutch girl and his son Charles was later official silversmith of New York City and made the greatest number of the famous "freeman boxes."

Peter Van Dyck, who was probably apprenticed to his father-in-law, Batholomew Le Roux, became the most prolific of early New York silversmiths. Myer Myers, a Jewish silversmith (1723-1795), was also outstanding among them.

In Philadelphia the earliest record is of one Cesare Ghiselin, another Huguenot, being paid for a piece of silver work by William Penn in 1701.

John Nys, still another immigrant Frenchman, practiced in the Quaker City at about the same time. Phillip Syng Sr. (1676-1739), an Irishman, founded one of the numerous silversmithing families there. There were two sons, Daniel and John, and two grandsons, both "Phillip," all good silversmiths.

Francis Richardson (1681-1729), of the same city, also sired a brood of smiths. He was succeeded by sons, Joseph and John, and grandsons, Joseph and Nathaniel. This family engaged in active smithing up until 1827, when Nathaniel died.

A few silversmiths struggled against great odds in Charleston, South Carolina. They could not flourish for it was the consistent habit of the southern gentry to send to Europe for their luxuries.

In discussing Boston we mentioned John Coney's French apprentice, Appollos De Rivoire. This Appollos was born in France and was taken, as a child, by his fleeing Huguenot family, to the Island of Guernsey. While still a boy he was sent, alone, to Boston, there to be apprenticed to the famous Coney.

He was well supplied with money and his apprenticeship was strictly for educational purposes. John Coney died before the expiration of Appollos' apprenticeship and so the boy served out the rest of his time under some smith whose name is not known. By 1723 Appollos De Rivoire had changed his name to Paul Revere and was well established in his own business.

Of this name-changing, his son later wrote: "Appollos made this alteration merely on account the Bumpkins could pronounce it easier . . ." Revere married a Boston girl and begat several children, of whom Longfellow's night-riding hero was the third, (1735).

With no implied disparagement of his father, the second Paul Revere was one of the most excellent and versatile of early American craftsmen. The bottom rung of his talents is revealed through an advertisement, printed in 1770:

"ARTIFICIAL TEETH. PAUL REVERE takes this method of returning his most sincere Thanks to the Gentlemen and Ladies who have employed him in the care of their Teeth . . . he still continues the business of a Dentist, and flatters himself that from the experience he has had these Two Years, (in which time he has fixt some hundreds of Teeth), that he can fix them as well as any Surgeon Dentist who ever came from London . . ."

He adds further that he also cleans teeth and will do so in any Lady's or Gentleman's apartment.

Even in this ad his anti-Royalist proclivities are apparent. He was a powerful influence among the Revolutionary element of Boston. He engraved, printed, and sold many virulent caricatures and bombastic allegories of patriotism. Most famous, perhaps, is his engraving of the Boston Massacre. His copper-plate engraving, it must be added, was bad. As he had had no training this was a fact rather more to his credit than otherwise.

Revere was a man who would tackle anything. To the question "Can you do it?" he had only one answer. He would clean his neighbor's teeth or attempt a view of the City of Boston in copperplate with equal alacrity. His engravings were published in the magazines of that day on the strength of his name and his effrontery rather than on their merit. He was also the author of quite a bit of undistinguished verse, largely on political and revolutionary themes.

Revere was a leading organizer of the Sons of Liberty. His personality commanded respect from both workers and merchants. He was an excellent horseman and hence was employed as messenger by the Committee of Safety. He took part in the Boston Tea Party. He was forty years old when he made his famous midnight ride. William Dawes started ahead of him, by a different route, with the same message, warning Hancock and Adams that the British had placed a price on their heads and were about to raid ammunition hide-outs. Revere arrived first, and hence gets the credit. On the way he was ambushed and pursued by British horsemen, but out-rode them, arousing the Minute Men as he galloped through the countryside. On the following day was fired the "shot heard round the world" and the war was definitely under way.

Revere manufactured gunpowder, repaired spiked cannon, and became a Lieutenant-Colonel. On the mismanaged expedition to Maine in 1779 Revere, who was in charge of the artillery, became insubordinate and was subsequently arrested. This probably unjust consequence spoiled his chances of securing a high post in the Federal Government, for it was not until 1782 that he was acquitted by an adequate Court-Martial.

He had married Sarah Orne, in 1757, and she had borne him eight children. Five months after her death, in 1773, he married Rachel Walker. The second marriage was childless.

Typical of Revere's versatility and his willingness to tackle anything is the fact that when, in 1775, the Continental Congress authorized him to issue the first national paper money he not only engraved the plates but constructed the presses on which he printed it. He was, in all, in addition to being a silversmith, dentist, engraver, powder manufacturer, printer, brass-founder, maker and merchant of hardware and jewelry, bell-founder, iron-founder, seal maker, picture-frame carver, and it is even said that he occasionally shod horses. He ventured into ship-building and made copper sheathing for the hulls of boats. His contributions toward design for speed helped pave the way for the later Yankee Clippers. His son, the third Paul, followed him in all these trades and was proficient.

As a silversmith he had virtually perfect taste and endless skill, both in his forms and ornaments. The high price of Paul Revere's silver today, of which a relatively large quantity exists, is by no means entirely due to his Midnight Ride. He stands without need of apology in the top rank of American craftsmen. He died in 1817, leaving a fortune of $31,000.

The silversmith's craft is difficult and intricate. He works with a vast assortment of odd-named and baffling tools. Possibly one of the simplest ways to roughly itemize these would be to take bodily a list found in the last will and testament of one John Burt, silversmith, of Boston, in the year 1745:

"2 Show Glasses . . . pair of Chapes and tongs . . . 11 files . . . a pair of large and small bellows . . . a large Forgin anvil . . . one small ditto . . . 9 raising anvils . . . planishing Teaster . . . 2 Spoon Teasters . . . planishing ditto . . . 3 bench vises . . . 9 small vises . . . 2 beak irons . . . 40 hammers . . . pr. hammer . . . 2 Melting Skillets . . . 37 bottom stakes and punches . . .

a drawing bench & tongs . . . Drawing irons . . . 10 pairs of shears . . . 2 brass Hollowin stamps . . . a pair of brass Salt punches . . . 1 thimble stamp . . . 6 pair of molds for casting . . . 15 pairs of tongs & plyers . . . a pair of large scales and weights . . . pewter and lead molds . . . 36 old files . . . 12 strainers . . . 1 oyl stove . . . 3 small saws . . . 4 boreax boxes . . . 3 burnishes . . . 1 Triblet . . . 2 boiling pans . . . a parcel of punches . . . 1 Touch Stone. . . ."

For the uses of these implements, so far as we can penetrate them, let us try to follow some of the silversmith's processes after he had received his instructions and a bag of silver coin from one of his customers.

The first thing he did was to melt the coin and remove any excess base metal by means of chemical processes. As a rule this refining would not be necessary and all he would have to do, after melting, would be to cast the silver into a plate of the requisite size, thickness, and shape. As often as not it was cast in the form of a round "skillet."

Then came the process called "raising." This meant hammering the flat sheet of metal into the required form. This basic shape might be like a pear, large at the bottom, narrower at the top, yet it was hammered from a single piece, without seams of any kind. The tools used in this process were simply a number of variously shaped anvils and hammers. Silver becomes hard and brittle under prolonged beating. This was remedied by frequently "annealing" the piece, re-heating it to a temperature just below the melting point.

Sometimes the silver must be "dragged" or drawn, into the desired shape. The "dragging" process involved manifold difficulties. The metal tends *not* to spread evenly, but to thin out in one direction under stress. The successful culmination of the

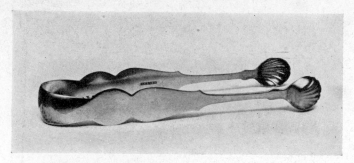

216. TONGS. By Paul Revere 3rd.

217. SALTCELLARS. By Charles Le Roux, New York.

218. BOWL. By Myer Myers, New York.

Metropolitan Museum

The Bloody Massacre perpetrated in King — Street Boston on March 5th 1770 by a party of the 29th Regt.

Engrav'd Printed & Sold by Paul Revere Boston

Unhappy Boston! see thy Sons deplore,
Thy hallow'd Walks besmear'd with guiltless Gore:
While faithless P—n and his savage Bands,
With murd'rous Rancour stretch their bloody Hands;
Like fierce Barbarians grinning o'er their Prey,
Approve the Carnage and enjoy the Day.

If scalding drops from Rage from Anguish Wrung,
If speechless Sorrows lab'ring for a Tongue,
Or if a weeping World can ought appease
The plaintive Ghosts of Victims such as these:
The Patriot's copious Tears for each are shed.
A glorious Tribute which embalms the Dead.

But know, Fate summons to that awful Goal.
Where Justice strips the Murd'rer of his Soul.
Should venal C—ts the scandal of the Land,
Snatch the relentless Villain from her Hand.
Keen Execrations on this Plate inscrib'd,
Shall reach a Judge who never can be brib'd.

The unhappy Sufferers were Messrs. Saml. Gray, Saml. Maverick, Jams. Caldwell, Crispus Attucks & Patk. Carr
Killed. Six wounded; two of them (Christr. Monk & John Clark) Mortally

219. COPPERPLATE ENGRAVING, "THE BOSTON MASSACRE." By Paul Revere. Note the specimen of his patriotic verse.

process requires a profound intimacy between the craftsman and his material.

Of course the "dragging" of the main form is only the first step. Soldering in those days was an awkward process: there was no blow-pipe or soldering iron. The direct heat of a charcoal fire had to be applied to the required joint.

Ornamentation was embossed, engraved, or separately cut. The first of these methods consists of forming a raised design. In early times, if the piece were hollow ware, making it difficult to work from the reverse side of the design, the first thing was to fill it with pitch. Then the design was lightly hammered in outline from the outside with small, dull chisels. This is known as "flat chasing" and sometimes constituted the sole decoration.

If the embossing, also known as *repoussé,* continued the pitch was taken out and "snarling irons" were used. The snarling irons were so named because of the sound they made when struck. They were pieces of iron with curved ends in various shapes. They were fastened in a vise and the curved end placed inside the silver piece at the point which was to be pushed outward. Then the snarling iron was struck with a hammer and conveyed the impact to the point of its contact with the silver, pushing the metal outward. In this manner many free-hand ornamentations were raised on early silver; the outlines were usually afterward sharpened by being gone over again with small, dull chisels.

In the process of engraving the metal is simply cut away in thin lines. At first this was done in unbroken lines but later the custom of engraving in short, almost microscopic gauges became generally accepted. The craft of engraving on silver is so similar to the fine art of engraving on copperplate for printing, that this accounts for the number of silversmiths who practiced both arts.

The third method of decorating pieces of silver was to *cast* silver ornaments and then solder them on. In casting, the ornament was usually first carved of wood. From this model an impression was made in the two halves of a sand mold, in which the silver was then cast and subsequently finished with small files. A less common practice was to make the model of wax. This, when baked in a sand mold, caused the wax model to melt and drain off, leaving the space for the silver to enter. Under this method a model could only be used once.

Another mode of decoration had a brief vogue between about 1690 and 1710. It was known as the "cut-card." In this method a sheet of thin silver was cut to the desired shape and then soldered or welded onto the main body.

AMERICAN SILVER STYLES

The styles of early American silverware were dominated by New England. New England styles, in turn, were an imitation of the prevailing modes of the mother country, the more so inasmuch as silver is essentially a luxury item. In order to follow the style trends of Colonial silver design it is sometimes necessary to look at the influences shaping English taste.

By the time New England's colonists had time to turn their attention to the accumulation of silverware, a Puritan had mastered the England from which they had fled. Cromwell's Commonwealth (1649-1660) brought a new set of churchly oppressors to England. To English and Colonial decoration it brought a certain reticence of form and ornament. The relatively austere style of silverware resulting found ready acceptance and extension among New England's early silversmiths. During this era forms were uncomplex. Simple flat-chasing was most common.

When the Stuarts returned to power in 1660, in the person of Charles the Second, a reaction occurred in England. Silverwork was suddenly enriched with a luxuriance of new ornament. The revived trend toward ornament continued in the reign of William and Mary. *Repoussé* work and a variety of cast ornaments were popular.

In 1697 England experienced a shortage of coin-silver which produced a new silver law. Whereas, by the Sterling standard, each twelve ounces of coin had to contain eleven ounces, two hundredweight of pure silver, each twelve ounces of silver-plate had to have eleven ounces, ten hundredweight of pure silver.

The law was intended to discourage the making and accumulation of silver-plate so that silver coinage would be more plentiful. In practice it apparently had the opposite effect. It meant that the silver used by the smiths had to be of a much harder alloy, for silver of the new standard was of an impractical softness. It was necessary to make silverware thicker, increasing the cost of the individual pieces. This was hardly calculated to discourage the investment in silver-plate as a form of personal wealth. The result was a new period of austerity in design, influenced by a somewhat different cause than Puritanism.

In all considerations of style we must remember that silver pieces were distinctly for display purposes. They were lined up in elegant array upon sideboards and mantels. Under this circumstance ornament of too delicate or subtle a nature possessed little value, which explains the predominance of *repoussé* and cast ornament over engraving. When engraving is found on early silver the chances are that it was done largely for identification. Usually such engraving was heraldic, or the plebeian substitute for heraldry, called "Cyphers," a form of complex, reversed monogram.

Fluting achieved its greatest excellence in about 1700, during the thin-plate era. It was at first a simple, vertical *repoussé* work and then took a spiral form.

Between 1725 and 1750 the rococo style had its hey-day in England. In America it extended until 1770. Then the classic revival, which dominated furniture and architecture at this period, made itself felt in silver as well. The classic revival in terms of American silver, meant a period of lightness, elegance, formality, and upright, structural lines. This was an era of expansion, manifesting itself in beautifully formalized tea-pots, coffee-pots, chocolate-pots and punch bowls.

Much of the early silver has been preserved through the custom, on the part of pious parishioners, of presenting or willing pieces of plate to their churches. Often, though not always, such plate was intended for use in the various ceremonies attendant upon worship. Catholic, Lutheran, Puritan, and Quaker churches possessed silver. There is a record of some early silver made for a New York Synagogue by Myer Myers, a superb silversmith, then acting head of the Gold and Silversmith's Society of New York City.

Many of the products of the early silversmiths were objects no longer made or used today. The various tankards for ale or mead were notable items. Supposedly these tankards or beakers were modifications of the drinking horn of Viking fame. The assumption is probably a little too general as such utensils appear to have many possible origins and backgrounds other than the horn.

Two early English-American drinks claiming special vessels were caudle and posset. Caudle was a mixture of warm wine or ale with sugar, breadcrumbs, spices, and occasional eggs. Posset was the same thing with the addition of curdled milk. Both were served in small two-handled cups, still known as "caudle-cups."

The porringer, another familiar item of early silver, is a small bowl with a single, flat, horizontal handle. It was probably used largely as a serving dish.

The tankard is a large container for the drinking of ale. It has one handle, and a cover which opens by means of a thumb-piece. For some reason it was made in Scandinavia, Germany, and England, but not in Holland. The silversmiths of New Amsterdam adopted it from the English colonists, giving it a new, sturdy form. The early tankards of Massachusetts were from five-and-a-half, to six-and-a-quarter inches high, with flat covers. As time passed they were made taller and slimmer, their covers became domed and were ornamented with finials.

Cups without handles were called beakers. Standing-cups were stemmed drinking cups, or goblets. These were not used for household purposes after 1700, being relegated largely to sacramental purposes.

Spout cups were novelties; cups with spouts, like tea-pots, for giving drinks to children or invalids.

While salt was still a luxury, and hence the object of much ceremony, the great-salt, or standing-salt, was an important object. It was placed between the right-elbow of the host and the left-elbow of the guest of honor. The cheapening of salt brought the individual salt-and-peppers. These came in the late 18th century and were frequently in sets including sugar and at least two kinds of pepper.

Spoons were, of course, basic implements; but the fork, an Italian notion, did not come into general use until after 1700.

INDUSTRY ENCROACHES UPON SILVER

The first hint of industrialization in silversmithing was the discovery of the process of silver-plating. Thomas Boulsover, a cutler of Sheffield, England, accidentally discovered, while repairing a knife, that a thin sheet of silver could be made to adhere to a thicker sheet of copper by employing the right amount of heat, and that thereafter the two could be hammered and otherwise treated as a single metal. This was about 1742, but it was many years before other men took full advantage of it. Boulsover himself had used it solely for the manufacture of buttons. By the 19th century, however, the manufacture of Sheffield plate was well under way. Not only was it decidedly cheaper than solid silver, but it could even achieve certain more slender and elegant forms due to the greater hardness of copper.

Thus the advent of Sheffield plate, along with the more reliable banking conditions, contributed to the complete relegation of solid sterling silverware to a luxury status. Finally, in 1860, the Sheffield plate, which had so far been a craft product, was displaced by the still cheaper, thoroughly "industrial" technique of electroplating.

CHAPTER 8

WEAVING

THE weaving of textiles is another of the more ancient crafts of mankind, and another of those essential to a pioneer society. Its origins are lost, along with those of many other crafts, in the deep shadow of Time.

Simple fabrics are made by weaving threads in and out across a layer of other threads at a right angle. An obscurity has fallen over the details of this once common process today when the average person has little or no contact with the means by which his cloth is manufactured. Also, it is a far cry from the miraculous efficiencies of industrial weaving to the simple methods of the hand loom. Yet the mysteries of warp and woof, heddle and shuttle, are not very profound and may be easily understood.

The *warp* is the lengthwise threads. These must be the strongest and are usually of a better type or grade of thread than the crosswise threads, called the *woof,* or *weft.*

A loom is a frame upon which the warp threads are vertically stretched. These threads are passed, at top and bottom, through tiny loops of string or wire on small pieces of wood, called *heddles,* which resemble minute piano keys. At the top of the loom every other heddle is attached to one crossbar, while the intervening ones are attached to another. Thus, when one crossbar is pushed out every other thread is separated from its neighbor. When the other crossbar is pushed out the action is reversed. In weaving this permits the easy separation of every other warp thread so that the woof thread, attached to a shuttle, has merely to be tossed through the intervening space, after which the separation of the warp threads is reversed and the shuttle is passed back again. The above process is for the weaving of simple, unpatterned textiles. When patterns are desired, more than two sets of heddles are necessary, for threads of different colors. The foot-loom, with various pedals to work the crossbars, thus leaving both hands free to manipulate the shuttle, came in the early 17th or late 16th centuries. To produce still more intricate patterns the draw-loom was invented. This was a method whereby the many sets of heddles were operated by cords which were pulled by a skilful small boy who had to swing about precariously, monkey-fashion, atop the large loom.

In 1733 John Kay, an Englishman, invented the flying shuttle; a means of making the shuttle pass back and forth by the pulling of cords instead of by hand to hand tossing. But this invention did not find ready acceptance.

Then in 1784 Edmund Cartwright invented the power loom, which performed all the operations of moving the heddles and the shuttle in any manner desired. Cartwright was an English clergyman with no knowledge of weaving and practically none of mechanics. He is an outstanding example of the frequency with which amateurs in the crafts and sciences make great discoveries, possibly because they are uninhibited by any knowledge of the "real difficulties" involved in their ideas. The superhuman weaving machinery of today's textile mills is essentially based on the principle of the simple loom of antiquity.

It was really not until almost the 18th century that Great Britain became frightened at the possibility of American manu-

220. "Candlewick" Embroidered Bedspread. Patriotic Pattern.

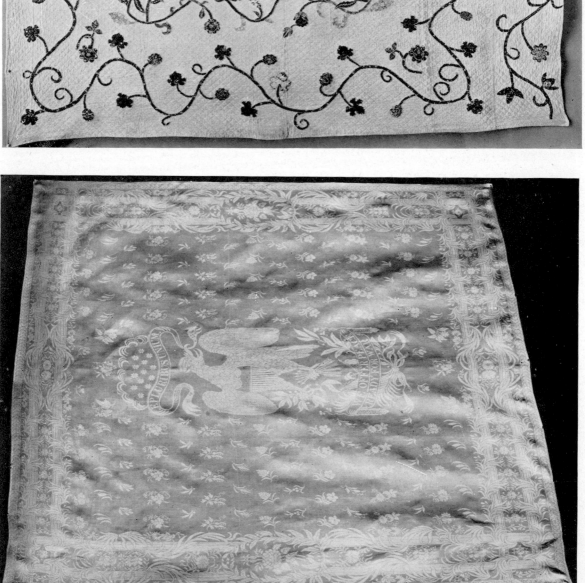

222. Coverlet. Attributed to Eliza Armstead Miller, Richmond, Va. 18th Century.

221. Damask Tablecloth, Hand Woven. Patriotic Pattern.

Antiques

224. COVERLET FROM VIRGINIA. 19TH CENTURY.

226. SAMPLER, MADE BY MARY E. BULGER. 19TH CENTURY.

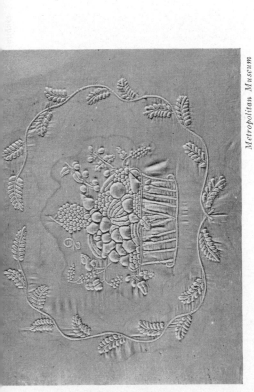

223. QUILTED AND PADDED COVER. 19TH CENTURY.

225. HANDKERCHIEF WITH PATRIOTIC PRINT.

227. PATCHWORK QUILT. VERMONT.

228. Quilt With Eagle Pattern. *c.* 1850.

Mr D Lambert died without any previous illness, at Stamford, whither he had gone with an intent to exhibit himself at the races. He was in his 40th year, and upon being placed upon the famous Caledonian balance, a few days before his death, he weighed 52 stone 11 pounds, 14 lbs to the stone, which is 10 stone 11 lbs more than the famous Mr Bright. His coffin was 6 feet 4 inches long 4 feet 4 inches wide 2 feet 4 inches deep being 112 superficial feet of elm, it was built on two axletrees and four clog wheels, and upon these his remains were rolled to thegrave A regular descent was made by cutting away the earth slopingly for some distance. The window and wall of the roomin which he died, were taken down to allow the removal of the corpse _ he died the 28th of June 1809 ~~~~~~~ Worked by Elizabeth Gerrish in her 8th year

229. Sampler.

AH Few and full of Sorrow are the Days Of miserable Man His Life decays dies
Like that frail Flower which with the Suns uprise Her Bud unfolds and with the Evening
He like an empty Shadow glides away And all his Life is but a Winters Day

Sarah Watt Her Work 1767

30. SAMPLER, 1767. Note the lugubrious text.

232. Sampler, Bristol, R. I., *c.* 1795.

231. Embroidered Mourning Piece, *c.* 1887.

234. PORTRAIT OF MISTRESS ANN GALLOWAY, A QUAKERESS, BY GUSTAVUS HESSELIUS. Note the use of rich materials in the "plain" dress.

233. EMBROIDERED VEST.

235. VEST EMBROIDERED WITH PROFILE OF LAFAYETTE.

236. PORTRAIT OF ROGER SHERMAN, BY RALPH EARL, SHOWING TYPICAL PURITAN COSTUME.

factures making the Colonies economically independent. The London Company had sent weavers, among innumerable other craftsmen, to Jamestown in 1620. There was no 17th century British resistance to cloth manufacture in New England.

The Pilgrims landed at Plymouth in 1620 and the Puritans came to Massachusetts Bay in 1630, and although their hardships were terrible their success was sufficient to induce large numbers of other persons, mostly with similar religious persuasions, to follow them to New England.

Almost all Colonial families sowed flax and hemp. The "hemp" was not really hemp but a species of bark, *Apocynum Cannabinum,* used by the American Indians. Although cotton was indigenous to the American continent, the only cotton available to the early American Colonists was imported from the Barbados.

A great deal of weaving was carried on by journeymen. These were travelling craftsmen. Their title, however, does not come from the fact that they travelled but from the fact that originally the term "journey" meant a day's work. In other words, they were craftsmen who worked by the day. They were active not only in weaving, but in a greater or lesser degree, in pottery, carpentry, tailoring, and various other crafts. Sometimes, in the later frontier days, they were on their way to a permanent home. Sometimes they simply liked to travel. They were an enlivening influence throughout the Colonies and were depended upon for vivid gossip and tall tales of other places.

Weaving was, in earliest America, for the most part a household industry. Most housewives could perform its simple operations but it did have a professional craft aspect. There were some families having looms but not knowing how to use them adequately. It was for such as these that the journeymen travelled from home to home, weaving various fabrics.

Puritan Governor Bradford was himself a fustian weaver from Austerfield, England, which probably did a good deal for tolerant laws toward weavers in the Massachusetts Bay Colony. The warp, in those days, could not be made from cotton for the technique of spinning a sufficiently strong cotton thread had not yet been developed. The commonest fabrics of the period were a mixture of linen and cotton which was variously called "fustian," "dimity," etc.

Weavers who established themselves in a fixed locale were accustomed, according to J. L. Bishop in his *History of American Manufactures,* ". . . to provide themselves with the linen warp and the new cotton each on his own account. It was then carded and spun by their wives and children and afterward woven by the head of the family. The weaver plied his loom during a part of the day, the remainder being employed in gardening or other affairs." The cloth was then carried to the nearest market for sale. During these times when the Colonial government was so concerned about the home manufacture of textiles, bounties were paid for the growing of fibres and for the weaving of fabrics.

The method of non-itinerant weaving, just described, was made tremendously more efficient about 1740 by a completely new system. Textile merchants sent their agents throughout the country to supply household weavers with linen yarn and raw cotton at stated intervals and received their woven cloth in return.

Thus, by approximately 1767, there were three kinds of American textile manufacture. The greatest amount was probably amateur activity. Most early American housewives could weave as well as spin. They wove fabrics for the family needs and sold any excess in the city markets. Second, were the homes that had looms but did not know how, or did not wish to use them. These were serviced by the journeymen weavers who were paid ten to twelve pence for each yard of a half-yard width of material. Third were the non-itinerant weavers, supplied with threads by central distributors, working, in effect, by consignment.

About 1700, when the population of the English Colonies in America had reached 250,000, the British suddenly became aware of the danger of American manufacturing enterprise and began to fight it with intolerable laws. After they had lost the Revolutionary War thus precipitated they continued to struggle in the purely economic field by selling British goods in America for as much as 25% less than the price in London.

When craftsman-inventor Eli Whitney invented his cotton gin in 1783, he influenced the course of American history, for the first three quarters of the 19th century. Before the cotton gin there had been a stronger "abolition" sentiment in the South than in the North, due to the increasing unprofitableness of slave-holding. This vanished with Whitney's invention, for when the negroes could be used for extensive cultivation and picking, their maintenance became practical. Still more important, the slave-owning plantation owners were no longer confined to the Tidewater areas for they could now use the short-fibred upland cotton which had not previously been satisfactory. With this impetus the Southern cotton interests rose rapidly to a national domination and to a conflict with Northern economy which was only terminated, and not altogether justly, by the Civil War.

Eli Whitney's little machine increased cotton production in America one hundred fold in the first seven years of its existence, and made cotton one of the essential determinants of world situations unto this present day.

Silk worms were nurtured in Georgia as early as 1734, but it was not until 1810 that the first American silk mill was successfully operated in Mansfield, Connecticut.

One of the variations on plain weaving in early Colonial times was the making of coach-lace, which was not lace at all but was a woven strip with ornamental braid in floral or geometric patterns.

As in England, the printing of cotton in this country was early inspired by the beauty of India prints. American cotton prints were at first done in simple colors from rectangular wooden blocks on which the design was either raised, or cut intaglio. That some of these blocks were carved by real artists or craftsmen is indicated in the advertisement of Francis Dewing in Boston, 1716, who claimed that he ". . . engraveth and printeth Copper Plates, likewise cuts neatly in wood and Painteth Calicoes." American cotton printers in general imitated the patterns of India Prints, but after the Revolution eagles and other patriotic symbols came into fashion.

In the process of printing the fabric was fastened to the floor or to a large table. The block was "inked" by pressing it onto a color pad, in the manner of a rubber stamp. The block was then applied to the material. For greater "fastness" the dye was sometimes mixed with glue.

Perhaps the greatest of all American non-professional crafts was that of weaving coverlets. Rural women wove these of coarse yarns from early Colonial times far into the 19th century. They are a truly American expression. The patterns, sometimes recorded on paper, were called "drafts" and were passed around from family to family, town to town, county to county. These patterns, like folk-stories and folk-music, were gradually added-to by the more creative persons who used them until they changed beyond recognition. Each had an obscure evolution of its own.

Some of the patterns have commonplace, realistic names, such as "Sunrise," "Cat Tracks," "Dog Tracks," and so on. Others are direct expressions of Americanism, such as the one called "E pluribus unum," and another known as the "Declaration of Independence." This latter one has a formal floral pattern in its central area, but the border is composed of columns, stars, and eagles holding bunches of arrows in both feet, instead of only the left as in the Seal of the United States. Also, on the coverlet, the eagles have the national shield apparently tattooed on their lower bellies instead of being borne on their breasts. On one such cover is woven: "American Independence. Declared July 4, 1776. Wove in 1839. J. A. Getty."

Other patriotic "drafts" are George Washington, and Anthony Wayne. Masonic emblems were also common.

But the majority of these coverlet patterns are rather obscure abstractions entitled, variously: Governor's Garden, Rich Man's Fancy, Bonaparte's Retreat, Winding Leaves and Folding Windows, Queen of England, Youth and Beauty, Muscadine Hulls, Ladies' Delight, Frenchman's Fancy, Tennessee Trouble, and Missouri Trouble.

Next in prominence to the coverlet are the familiar American "samplers." These are embroidered pictures and words done on a background of coarse linen or canvas. Technically speaking they are not samplers unless they are signed and dated, but are merely embroidered pictures.

In the beginning samplers were highly intricate displays of embroidering virtuosity. It was in the 19th century that they became primers for the female young. One of the earliest and most excellent specimens, still in existence, was made by Miles Standish's daughter, Lora, in 1623.

In the 19th century the sampler had become largely a device for keeping young girls out of trouble! The young ladies were handed squares of linen, needles, and colored threads and directed to work out pictures of animals, houses, and flowers, combined with religious, filial, and moral sentiments. When the family could not think of any pious sentiment the girls were often instructed to embroider the alphabet, which thousands dutifully did, sometimes in both capital and small letters. Maps were occasionally embroidered as an instruction in geography, and in the second quarter of the 19th century there occurred the celebrated morbid era when the deaths of illustrious persons or relatives were the subject of such art work. Tombs and winged angels of death poured from the needles of all the industrious maidens.

The sampler was also used as a genealogical record, in the manner of the Family Bible. Deaths, births, and marriages were recorded in various appropriate colors whenever an occasion arose.

The final addition to the list of characteristic American household textile crafts is the art of richly-colored and vari-patterned quilt-making as it has been practiced by rural housewives from earliest times to the present. These manifold aspects of folk-art and handicraft constitute one of the richest seams of our national cultural heritage.

What the Colonists Wore

As the products of the spinning wheels and looms we can consider the costume styles of early America. To a large degree, even though American made, these were imitations of the prevailing English styles on the various class levels.

The gentlemen of Jamestown wore "Elizabethan" clothing. It was a style which the English had derived from the Spanish, and is generally described as "Spanish bombast." The word "bombast," incidentally, originally meant cotton, or other stuffing, used in costume to pad out and improve the male figure.

These first Virginia gentlemen wore corsets, called busks, laced extremely tight. The main garment of upper clothing was the doublet. This was a tight-fitting jacket, with plenty of bombast stuffed under it between the linen shirt and the corset. It usually extended a little below the waist, and produced an extremely rigid form. Sleeves were separate garments and were attached by lacing to the doublet, the splice being concealed by a special roll of decorative material. The doublet, as well as the sleeves, was often slit to reveal the fine linen shirt worn beneath.

Ruffs of various sizes were worn for dress occasions. These were thickly starched and reinforced with wire. For informal wear lie-down collars of linen were worn. Sleeves had cuffs turned back to match the ruffs or collars. A leather jerkin, a sort of second doublet, was sometimes worn for additional warmth or protection. It was primarily a military garment.

Breeches were short and bulky. At about the time of the Virginia colonization the awkward "pumpkin" style was just going out and the new "knee-breeches" were coming in. Cloaks of all length were worn; the hip-length Spanish cloak being the most popular among the Southern gentlemen. One of the genuinely "American" phenomena of the period was the copying of European cloth styles in the handy fur of the colonies.

Beneath the short breeches those who could afford them wore silk hose usually extending up the full length of the thigh. Silk hose for men continued in style until the 19th century.

An additional pair of shorter, coarser stockings, called "boot hose," was worn to protect the silk hose from the friction of the boots. Boots were made of very soft leather and extended up to mid-thigh but could be rolled down to any desired height. A common affectation of the early Colonial dandy was to wear one boot nearly hip-high and the other rolled down below the knee.

A variety of hats were in vogue; high and low crowned, wide and narrow brimmed, plumed and unplumed. All immigrants to Virginia were advised to bring with them a *Monmouth Cap*. This was a knitted sort of skull cap, tight around the brim, but with plenty of loose material above. It was decorated with a tassel and somewhat resembled the caps now worn by skiers. This practical head-gear was favored less by the gentlemen than by the craftsmen and hard-working men of other colonies.

The ninety-two "chaste and uncorrupt" women who were shipped to Jamestown by the Virginia Company were from the lower classes of England, and were accordingly not lavishly arrayed. Their fabrics were not of a costly variety.

They wore a low-waisted bodice, with low neck and a stiff lace collar standing up behind. Tight sleeves had linen cuffs turned back to match the collars. Their skirts hung to within a few inches of the ground, were very full and were usually split in front to reveal the contrastingly colored underskirt. Probably few of these women were wealthy enough to wear the fashionable farthingale, or hooped underskirt. Their capes, hats and gloves were rather similar to those of the men. They wore shawls, which substituted for the standing collars among the poorer girls, and small muffs. They used paint, powder, and "beauty spots" in moderation and had small mirrors dangling from their waists.

By 1730 these essentially Jacobean costumes had given way

237. Cotton Quilt With Portrait Print of the First Seven Presidents, Washington to Jackson. Made probably shortly after 1829.

240, 241. Cast Iron Stove Plates By "Baron Stiegel, of Glassmaking Fame.

238. A Link of the Great Hudson River Chain Used at West Point During the Revolution.

N. Y. Historical Society

242. Cast Iron Indian. Said to have bee used as a protective sign for hous on land purchased from the Indian

239. Andirons. "Hessian Soldiers." 18th Century.

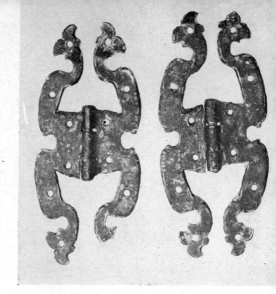

245. Cock's Head Hinges, Wrought Iron.

Metropolitan Museum

From a Drawing by A. H. Sonn, in "Early American Wrought Iron."

243. Old Wrought Iron Weathervanes.

44. Wrought Iron Door Handles.

Metropolitan Museum

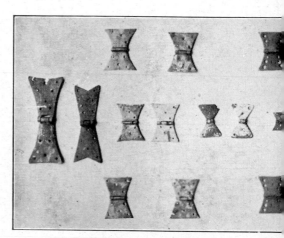

246. Butterfly Hinges.

Early Am. Ind. Assn

247. Franklin Stove, Cast Iron. Much reduced in scale.

Metropolitan Museum

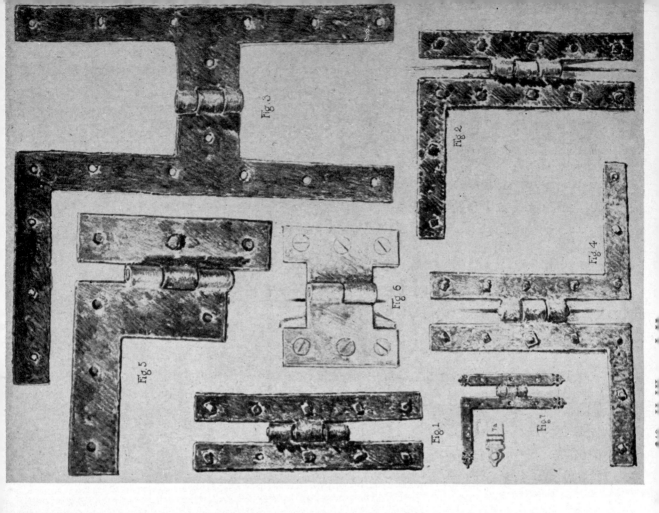

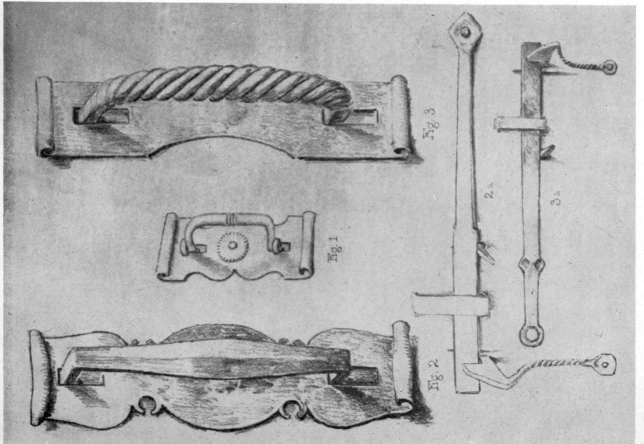

248. Wrought Iron Latches, Escutcheon Type.

to the Cavalier trends from the court of Charles the First. The
doublet and breeches, which were now all knee-length, were no
longer padded with bombast. The doublet was full skirted and
the jerkin had become the more important garment. Lie-down
collars were entirely the vogue, and the doublet was fashionably
left unbuttoned below the sternum to reveal a greater area of
pleated linen shirt. Sleeves were slit for the same purpose but
had many buttons which could be fastened in cold weather.
Silk stockings were still worn beneath the knee breeches, but
shoes had generally replaced boots. Each shoe was decorated
with a pompom called a "shoe rose" and there was no distinction
in form between left and right shoes.

In the settlement of New England the Pilgrims of 1620 were
not a great influence. They were poor and of no power. Accordingly they were more or less absorbed by the later immigration
of Puritans in the Massachusetts Bay Colony, in 1630.

Of the 102 Pilgrims who had arrived on the celebrated *Mayflower*, thirty-five had first migrated to Holland, where they had
absorbed certain Dutch mannerisms. They had all mortgaged
themselves to a company in London and their lot was miserable.
Their religious convictions, eschewing frips and furbelows,
affected costume largely in a matter of degree. Thus we find that
the apparel of the New Englander was much the same as that
of the Virginian in form, but was stripped of decoration and
accoutrement and lacked gay color. Sermons against fancy
dress were virulent and laws were passed to regulate the expense
of costume. The stiff broad-brimmed hat found general acceptance.

It must be pointed out that by the middle of the 17th century less than one-fifth of the population of New England
belonged to the Puritan church. Others were not enfranchised.

Those who did belong were under the thumbs of a group of eccentric and misanthropic zealots. It is the severe costume of this group which has come to be known as the Puritan costume. The majority of New England inhabitants imitated the costume of contemporary England, with only such degree of restraint as was more or less inevitably imposed by the proximity of their fanatical neighbors.

The Puritan women did not wear the farthingale or the stand-up collar. They wore the lie-down collar of linen, or simply a shawl draped in a similar manner. Their hair, usually knotted behind, was most often covered by a hood which was part of their cloak.

The craftsmen of this era, throughout the colonies, worked in a waistcoat, or short doublet, and shirt sleeves. They wore coarse woolen stockings beneath their knee-breeches, usually a Monmouth Cap, often a crudely shaped leather apron with a handkerchief fastened around the neck to absorb rolling sweat.

The colonists of New Amsterdam wore similar garments, except that they adopted a squarer cut. They were fonder of color than any of the English colonists and used contrasting shades of many brilliant hues.

The Quakers of Pennsylvania imposed upon themselves much the same denial of ornament adopted by the Puritans. Their motive, however, was less a hatred of gaiety than an awareness of the functional. They did not condemn rich fabrics, or other materials, as did the Puritans, but only useless ornateness of design.

The Pennsylvania-Germans, the Swedes, the Scotch and Irish, the Spanish and French settlers brought their own costumes with them, which were not tremendously different due to the close correspondence between the European courts.

About 1670 male costume altered and revealed the beginnings of the coat and vest. In Western Europe, England and
America the coat and waistcoat came into use. The coat was
evolved from the cassock, a loose, knee-length coat with buttons
all the way down the front. This, in turn, had evolved from the
military jerkin. The waistcoat, which eventually became the
vest, was first merely an inner coat several inches shorter than
the outer garment. It was often ornately brocaded. By the time
of the American Revolution it was shorter and the wide-
lapeled, double-breasted outer coats were cut away in front to
display the attractions of the waistcoat.

Both coat and waistcoat grew shorter as they evolved toward
our present costume. Then, suddenly, in the 19th century, the
pants descended to cover the entire leg. For a while they remained tight, to reveal the attractions of the well-molded leg,
but rapidly became looser until they achieved more or less their
present form.

Women's clothes moved toward greater convenience. By
the seventeen-nineties there was actually a vogue of bobbed-hair.
The style was known as *á la victime,* and was a by-product of
the French Revolution. The hair was cut short and combed forward, a few strands dangling over the fashionably squinted eyes.
Hats became an anarchic free-for-all.

All these prominent modes of costume in the original colonies were, as we have said, essentially European. Little American creativeness went into them. But as Americans began to
push westward the new American personality, the *frontiersman,*
had little contact with and no desire to imitate Europe. The
people of the frontier lived constantly in dangerous and difficult
circumstances. They had to match the Indians at their own
game, (whatever it might be at any given time), and function as
fur-traders, farmers, explorers, and ambassadors, all at once.

Their log cabins, adopted from the Swedes of Delaware, were little fortresses. Their gardens yielded meagre provender at the best.

The frontiersman wisely imitated the Indian in his costume. The most important item was the hunting shirt. This was a loose, smock-like tunic, pulled on over the head. It was usually made of buckskin. The seams were decorated with fringes. Sleeves were tight but not too tight for action. Sometimes there was a short slit at the throat laced with buckskin thongs. The tunic usually extended to just above the knees, and had a wide collar, covering the shoulders like a short cape. Edges, like seams, were decorated with fringe. No breeches were worn, but buckskin leggings extended the full length of the legs, and an Indian "breech-clout" was worn around the loins. Soft Indian moccasins replaced shoes. The close forest necessitated a small hat, and thus the tight coonskin cap, associated with Daniel Boone, evolved.

This was essentially the costume of the early, backwoods riflemen who were the deadliest marksmen of the Revolution. The Buckskin wearers became so well known for their deadliness that Washington once recommended the buckskin costume to the Continental Army at large purely for its demoralizing value.

The frontier women had few, if any, of the fancy items of civilization. They usually wore a loose bodice. In place of a collar they used a brief shawl or merely a kerchief. Hats were not worn. Skirts, for utilitarian reasons, were shorter than those of the women in the eastern communities. For "formal" occasions these girls and women wore moccasins, but when not travelling they frequently went barefooted.

CHAPTER 9

IRONMASTERS

SIR WALTER RALEIGH'S expedition reported the presence of iron ore on Roanoke Island, in 1585. Bog-iron was shipped from Jamestown to England in 1608 and references to "bog-iron" occur in all early American documents relating to ironwork. It was a soft iron ore found in marshes. Iron salts, dissolved from the soil and washed into the marsh, are precipitated by the carbonic acid given off by decaying vegetable matter and form spongy strata quite common in swampy regions. Wherever bog-iron was found throughout the early Colonies attempts at iron production were launched, most of which were failures.

Joseph Jenks is supposed to have operated an iron and brass foundry at Lynn, Massachusetts, for a brief time in 1645.

The first really successful American ironworks seems to have been at Saugus Center, near Lynn, about 1685. The organization was granted the right to make ironware "on condition that the inhabitants of this jurisdiction shall be furnished with all sorts of barr iron for their use, not exceeding 20 per ton." The clause about "barr iron" seems to indicate the presence of a great number of blacksmiths without iron, for bar iron is not a substance which even the most versatile average colonist could have used to advantage. The meaning becomes clearer when we reflect that the earliest blacksmiths apparently had to work with expensive,

133

imported iron. And there was a large number of blacksmiths in America before 1685, as Colonial registers amply testify.

But though one of the most useful, iron is also the most difficult of metals to separate from its ore. Hence it was not until about 1750 that a securely established iron industry existed throughout the Colonies. Once under way, however, it flourished rapidly, with Pennsylvania as one of its most notable centers. We have already seen one aspect of iron manufacture in Pennsylvania in the case of the versatile Baron Henry Stiegel, and the Biblical cast-iron stove-plates of the Pennsylvania-Germans.

These stove-plates were the most interesting aspect of cast-iron work. We are now concerned largely with forged iron; that is, objects hammered from bar iron.

The blacksmith executed nearly all early ironwork. He was then no mere shoer of horses. The blacksmith made all forged, or wrought, ironwork: latches, hinges, gates, fences, andirons, and similar objects. He was also the general maker of tools. An interesting aspect of collecting ancient tools lies in the fact that some of them were undoubtedly made to order by blacksmiths for a certain function, never duplicated, and never formally named.

Again England attempted, unsuccessfully, a great deal of prohibitive legislation to prevent the growth of the American iron industry. They were especially opposed to the manufacture of iron, for iron means, aside from industrial uses, swords, guns, and cannon. Because of the restrictive measures the industry had its ups and downs. In 1748 both New York and Connecticut were shipping iron to England. Then new prohibitions were enacted. Nevertheless, when the American Revolution occurred, the American forges were amply able to supply the needs of the Continental Army.

No service of ironworkers to the cause of American Independence is more fascinating than the history of the construction of the great chain across the Hudson River at West Point. The necessity for a variety of river obstructions, to hinder the British navy from ranging unchecked up the Hudson River as far as Albany, was early seen. Familiar devices, such as the sinking of vessels and other obstructions at certain points, were adopted. But the West Point chain was an imaginative *tour de force*.

It apparently originated in the minds of the Board of War of the Continental Congress. In 1778 this body called Peter Townsend, ironmaster, before them and asked him if, in his opinion, it would be possible to construct a giant chain which could be hung across the Hudson at the narrows of West Point, to hinder naval action.

Townsend gave it as his opinion that the thing could be done. He returned to his Forge, at Sterling, New York, traditionally in a blinding snow-storm and accompanied by the War Board whose members wished to see the thing begun. The chain was to be forged with a swivel to every hundred feet, a clevis to every thousand feet. Twelve tons of anchors were required, in addition.

Sixty men were furloughed from the army to assist in the construction. Working day and night, at full capacity, they completed the chain in *six weeks!* Teamsters hauled it to West Point in separate sections of ten links each, as they were completed. Their weight was enormous and over the rough, nearly impassable winter roads the going was hard indeed, making a formidable task.

The sections were assembled at West Point and floated out across the Hudson on a log boom, with the anchors to fix it in place. Plans for coping with this chain were part of Benedict Arnold's plan for the betrayal of West Point. That it was a job well done is evidenced by the fact that the chain was never broken, either by the enemy or the elements, but was broken up and removed at the close of the war.

The blacksmith was frequently an armorer. In the case of one William Cheesebrough, who settled in the early days at Wequetequok, Connecticut, the local magistrates ordered him to move into the town of New London for fear he would repair guns for the Indians.

By the time the early American blacksmith was well established his most common product, after tools, was probably door and furniture hardware. Latches and hinges were the most important.

As we have discovered with other crafts, no new forms and ornaments necessarily sprang into being in America. The Colonial blacksmith, in common with his fellow craftsmen, imitated the familiar forms of his homeland and added only a slight touch of his own here and there. This, of course, was coupled with the general tendency toward simplification and directness which was partly the result of limited resources and partly of the unaffected nature of the adventurer-colonist-craftsman himself.

The first models of door hardware were whittled of wood. This was distinctly American and due entirely to the lack of iron. These wooden pieces were whittled as nearly as possible to conform with the colonists' memory of iron objects in the Old World. It was during this period that the wooden latch was in use, operated by a string, which was thrust out through a hole when the householders were at home. From this comes the phrase, "our latch string is out."

As soon as iron latchmaking was feasible, the four types of latch used at the time in Europe came into use. These have become known as the Suffolk, Norfolk, and Knocker Latch, and the Escutcheon Lift.

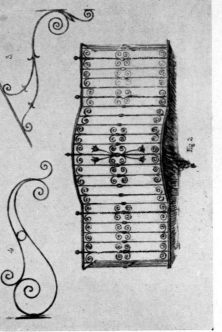

253. Wrought Iron Gate and Balcony.

From a Drawing by A. H. Sonn, in "Early American Wrought Iron."

250. "Squatting Ladies." Andirons.

251, 252. Early American Iron Pots and Kettles.

Metropolitan Museum

254, 5, & 6. WROUGHT IRON GATE AND BALCONY DETAILS. NEW ORLEANS.

Antiques

257, 8, & 9.   Wrought Iron Balcony and Balcony Details.   New Orleans.

260, 1, & 2. WROUGHT IRON GATEWAYS AND DOORWAY
AND BALCONY DETAIL.

From Drawings by A. H. Sonn, in
"Early American Wrought Iron."

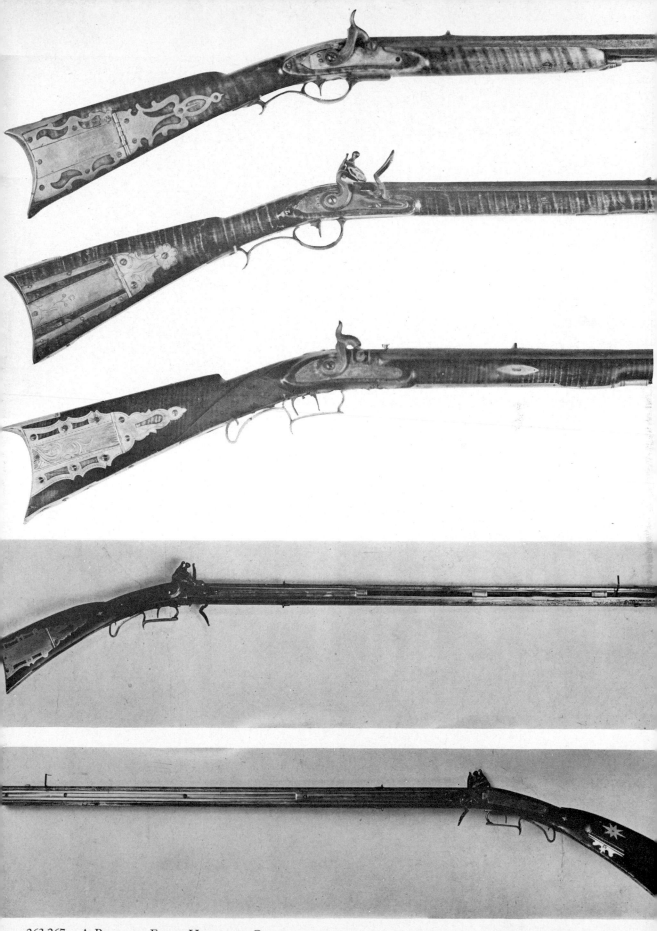

263-267.   A Panel of Early Handmade Guns.

268. INTERIOR OF THE OLD HENRY RIFLE WORKS, AT BOULTON, PA., showing the grinding wheel and belt wheel.

269. AN EARLY RIFLE SHOP IN EASTERN TENNESSEE, showing dam and flume. Grinding was done here for individual ill-equipped smiths.

From "The Kentucky Rifle" by Captain J. G. W. Dillin

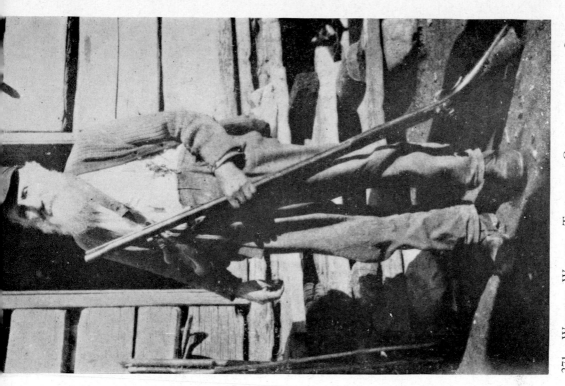

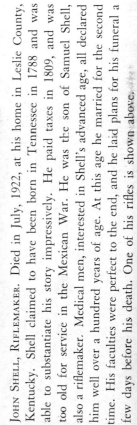

271. WILLIAM WALKER, TENNESSEE GUNSMITH OF THE LATE-FLINT-LOCK EARLY PERCUSSION PERIOD. One of the most famous hunters and riflemen of his day. His exploits are fabulous. Walker was born in 1838 and died in 1919, youthful by Shell's standard.

From "The Kentucky Rifle"
by Captain J. G. W. Dillin

270. JOHN SHELL, RIFLEMAKER. Died in July, 1922, at his home in Leslie County, Kentucky. Shell claimed to have been born in Tennessee in 1788 and was able to substantiate his story impressively. He paid taxes in 1809, and was too old for service in the Mexican War. He was the son of Samuel Shell, also a riflemaker. Medical men, interested in Shell's advanced age, all declared him well over a hundred years of age. At this age he married for the second time. His faculties were perfect to the end, and he laid plans for his funeral a few days before his death. One of his rifles is shown above.

272. ANOTHER CASE OF CRAFTSMAN PAINTING CRAFTSMAN. Portrait of Eli Whitney, of cotton gin and gunmaking fame, painted by Samuel F. B. Morse, inventor of the telegraph.

Yale Univ. Art Gallery

The Suffolk Latch was the most popular. In this type the handle was attached to two separate cusps, or plates, usually of similar design. The design of the plates was the main decorative feature of the latch. The most popular designs were those of the arrowhead, bean, ball, spear, swordfish, tulip, and heart. The door was opened by means of a thumb-press above the handle. Occasionally, in the Suffolk Latch, there was no lower cusp, that end of the handle being pointed and pounded through the wood of the door. Paradoxically this lack of a lower plate was more popular in Europe than in America, where one might have expected such an economy to be welcomed.

Between 1815 and 1820 the Norfolk Latch, which had long been in use, succeeded the Suffolk in popularity. This was a latch in which the handle, or grasp, was attached to a single metal plate called an "escutcheon." The shape of the escutcheon became the main decorative feature of this latch.

The other two types of early latch fell into the gadget class and were not so generally used. The knocker latch is made in such a way that the knocker, when twisted, lifts the latch. The Escutcheon Lift is arranged so that sliding up the escutcheon plate of an otherwise ordinary Norfolk type lifts the latch. The Norfolk style remained the most popular until William Blake's invention of the cast-iron latch, in 1840.

There were also four popular types of hinge: the dufttails, (dovetails), cross-garnet, and side-hinge, and the super-simplified strap-hinge of America. The latter was, of course, the first American hinge. The dovetail was later known as the "butterfly," which it more closely resembles. The side-hinge was a vertical device, the opposite of the horizontal strap-hinge. The cross-garnet was a combination of the slightly decorated strap-hinge, on the door, and side-hinge, on the frame. In addition, H-L, H, and L hinges were also used and were of the shape indicated by those letters.

The simple early American strap-hinges were often made from wagon-tires, their edges chamfered. (Pounding was not considered a decorative method until the era of our present-day antique dealers). The European hinges of this day achieved an extreme ornateness; but not those of America. The difference is so great that it hardly seems entirely attributable to lack of resources or ability. The fact is that the generally hardy American did not care as much for the intricate lacework of life in general as did the Europeans. This is again and again made evident.

What is called "chest hardware," hinges, latches, bindings for chests, naturally achieved a greater intricacy than door-hardware. This was because it was more distinctly an individual product for individual use, less directly utilitarian. Any personal feeling might find expression in this field.

The most famous type of American wrought ironwork is found in the grills, gates, fences, and balconies of the South. It is generally agreed that most of the exquisite ornamental ironwork of New Orleans was the work of negro slave blacksmiths. It was difficult to explain the peculiarly naive, yet vital translations from the Colonial pattern-books, of Spanish and French ironwork by any other conclusion.

Most of the fine New Orleans work is post-Revolutionary, due to the fire which almost entirely destroyed the city in 1780. But the exquisite freshness and freedom of its slave-made, wrought-iron fantasies are world famous.

The wrought-iron of Charleston, South Carolina, in some ways exceeds the quality of New Orleans work. It also offers many more examples of pre-Revolutionary work. But the finest work of Charleston dates after 1810, when the names of a few great smiths are actually recorded. These were the families Thibaut, Justi, Werner, McLeishe, and Ortman. Their flowing, imaginative curves are almost fluid in their quality of ease. These smiths worked their iron at white heat in accordance with the finest ancient tradition of the craft.

As the American frontier was pushed westward, the situation of the mid-western communities repeated that of the early seaboard colonies. In Ohio, for example, iron was first imported in bar form from the mills of Pennsylvania, Virginia, and Kentucky. The earliest mid-western blacksmiths imitated the forms of the eastern states just as the earliest American blacksmiths had imitated those of Europe.

Handwork in iron has naturally received a considerable setback from the industrialization of iron manufacture. Much modern ironwork, even when largely accomplished by hand, employs machinery in its various steps, and is performed upon cold iron. So far as the old tradition of iron craftsmanship is concerned, the Encyclopedia Britannica has stated the case with such succinctness as to make the quotation of an entire paragraph worthwhile.

"The interest and charm which the most unpractised observer must find in the work of the early craftsmen in iron is due to the fact that the metal was worked at a red or white heat. There was no time for measuring or copying a design save by the eye. Thus we get a spontaneity and a virility in forged work which expresses the life of the metal and gives the work its unexpected charm. These old craftsmen knew every branch of their work; they lavished as much skill and creative ability on a small handle as upon a great gate. No detail was overlooked, no matter how small or insignificant. This can be seen in various examples of their work, as in the fine old chests and boxes; the wonderful old locks, keys and other decorative hardware used in the great cathedrals. The sincere nature of craftsmanship and the proper use of materials for ends to which they are well adapted is little understood today. This is not because there is any lack of information on the subject, but because the perfection of the mechanical means of production at our disposal has blinded many to the simplicity of the means which produced the great works of the past."

GUNMAKING

The gun is a vitally important aspect of American craftsmanship. Because iron is its primary material and because the early gunsmith was often a specializing blacksmith, we can logically consider the gun in this chapter.

In its extremely primitive form, the match-lock, the gun appeared at the beginning of the 14th century. Germany, in the 16th century, produced the wheel-lock. This was a complicated weapon in which the explosion was produced by sparks struck by the revolving of a serrated wheel against a flint. The wheel was revolved by the trigger action. A more satisfactory form was the later flint-lock. It had fewer mechanical frailties. A flint was held by the hammer, which fell upon metal, striking the necessary spark in the priming pan. The flint-lock was the important gun through the period of the Revolution and until the development of the percussion gun using a fulminating charge.

One of the fundamental principles of the efficient firearm, a principle destined to be of great significance in American history, was the process of "rifling," from which the "rifle" takes its name. The problem of the early gunsmith was to make his bullet conform to the shape of the barrel. It was found that grooves within the barrel enabled the soft bullets to expand under the force of the explosion, and fit the barrel with a minimum of leakage. It was already known that a spiral movement to the right enhanced the accuracy and carrying-power of a projectile. These principles were combined, to the great improvement of firearms, by the Viennese, Gaspard Koller, early in the 15th century. The process of rifling was never employed to its full measure of efficiency until the advent of modern precision machinery.

The Colonial Americans largely used the prevailing types of smooth bore flint-lock musket. But the Pennsylvania-Germans were another story. They had brought with them the German rifles. These were none too accurate, as individual pieces, and, like the musket, had to be used in ranks for military effectiveness.

This did not fill the needs of peaceful settlers, who needed a reliable weapon with an accuracy adequate to the hunting of small and elusive game. Painstaking gunsmiths slenderized and lengthened the barrels and improved the rifling. The resultant weapon was known as the "Pennsylvania Rifle" and was, by a wide margin, the best gun in the world at the time. It contributed largely, both in use and in moral effect, to the American victory in the Revolution.

The Pennsylvania Rifle made possible the demoralizing guerrilla warfare in which hidden marksmen harried British ranks. The British recourse to Hessians, as mercenaries, was largely in the hope that their German rifles would offset the American guns. This hope was disappointed for the German guns were neither so skillfully made nor so well handled.

The Pennsylvania Rifle, however, was by no means the exclusive weapon of the Continentals. In terms of numbers, the chief gun of the American army was a smooth bore French weapon called the Charleville Musket. It was later manufactured by the Springfield Armory and became the first gun officially made by the United States Government for the use of its armies.

An American, Thomas Shaw, of Philadelphia, played a role in the development of percussion caps. But the true pioneer of fulminating powder was an Englishman, the Reverend Alexander John Forsyth, early in the 19th century. Another American, Jacob Snider, made one of the best early breech-loading rifles.

The first practical machine gun was an American creation. It was made by Gatling, in Chicago, and consisted of ten barrels, revolving around a cylindrical axis, coming into firing position in rapid succession. It fired 250 shots a minute and was successfully used in the Civil War, even though its heavy, cumbersome mechanism was a far cry from the up-to-date light machine gun.

But the two names which are of the greatest significance in American gunmaking are Eli Whitney and Samuel Colt. Eli Whitney was a latter-day craftsman, whose ambitions far outstripped any practical reliance on his own handiwork. Whitney represents one aspect of modern craft, as the man who creates, manually, a *first model,* relegating its duplication in mass to machine processes. His cotton gin, just such a case, brought him no profits due to the frenzied pirating of the device and the futility of the endless litigation in which he engaged, attempting to establish and enforce a patent.

Whitney came into his own as an arms-maker. In 1798 he undertook an unprecedented government contract for the manufacture of 10,000 "stand of arms," to be delivered in two years. He took eight years to fill the order. The government was tolerant, for in that time Whitney developed precision machine methods for the first manufacture of uniform arms with *completely interchangeable parts,* an impossibility for the most gifted hand craftsman. Subsequently, having established a fully equipped plant at Whitneyville, Connecticut, he undertook another government contract for 30,000 guns, which he fulfilled to the letter.

Samuel Colt was another craftsman contemptuous of his manual abilities beyond the point of initial demonstration. As a boy, on a single ill-relished voyage as a seaman, he whittled a wooden model of his famous six-shooter. The story of his years of struggle to manufacture and exploit this weapon is irrelevant here. The interesting fact is that Colt extended Whitney's principle. Where Whitney had begun uniform manufacture and division of labor, Colt actually applied the full-fledged assembly line, the fully developed industrial method with which Ford much later became popularly associated. Colt died, in 1862, at the relatively early age of forty-eight.

Although Americans have made other contributions in the field, arms-making, beyond the point here considered, becomes too specialized and too wholly a scientific machine process for us to pursue.

CHAPTER 10

PEWTER, AND OTHER METALS

PEWTER is an alloy of copper and tin. It is of considerable antiquity as a metal, probably having been discovered at about the same time as bronze, for the two metals are approximately the reverse in components. A good grade of bronze can be made from 90% copper and 10% tin, while an excellent grade of pewter can be made from 90% tin and 10% copper.

Although the major element of pewter is always tin it is sometimes alloyed with antimony and bismuth in addition to copper. Cheaper and more malleable varieties contain lead, and the formulae for pewter are nearly as numerous as pewterers.

Pewter ware, since antiquity, has developed its forms in direct imitation of pottery, bronze, wood, etc., having no special or distinctive forms of its own.

Pewter is cast, beaten, engraved, raised, turned, and planished. The latter method is that of hammering lightly to a smooth contour over a rounded surface. In mediaeval times it was always cast in smooth, perfectly finished, expensive brass molds. During the Renaissance, sand molds were used which involved a lengthy finishing process to smooth the pitted surface. During Colonial times both brass and sand molds were used, in addition to the more common mold of iron.

Perhaps no other popular substance in craft history has ever

Even faithfully Yours
Sam Colt

273. COLONEL SAMUEL COLT, Inventor of the Revolver and Pioneer of Industrial Method.

274. Experimental
Models of
the Colt
Revolver.

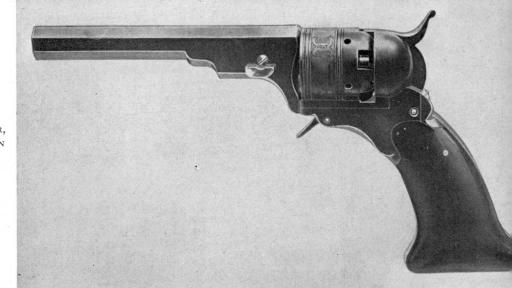

275. Colt Revolver,
Patterson
Model.

Walker Pistol

276. Colt Revolv-
er, Walker
Model.

Colt's Patent Firearms
Mfg. Co.

277.   PEWTERERS' FLAG.   Silk banner carried by the Society of Pewterers of New York City in the Federal Procession, July 23rd, 1788, by

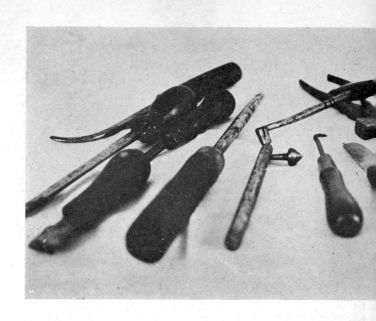

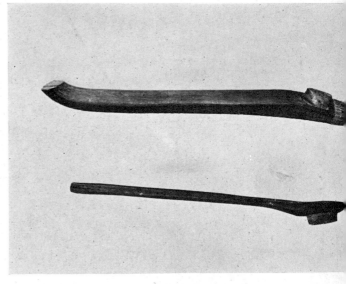

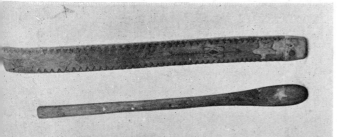

278-282. ISRAEL TRASK, PEWTERER, AND SOME OF THE
TOOLS OF HIS CRAFT.

Antiques

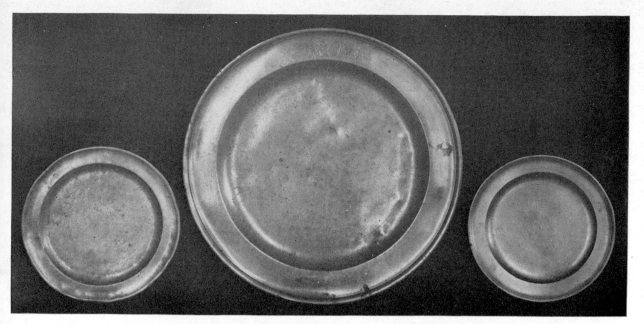

283. Two Eight Inch Plates and a Larger Plate By Thomas Badger. From the Kerfoot Collection.

284. Hallmarks of Boardman and Hall, Philadelphia Pewterers.

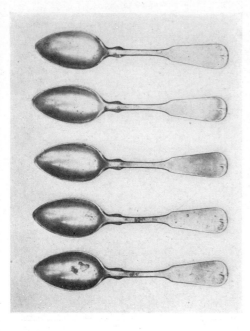

286. Fiddle-Back Teaspoons, Pewter.

289. Pitcher By Freeman Porter of Maine. c. 1825.

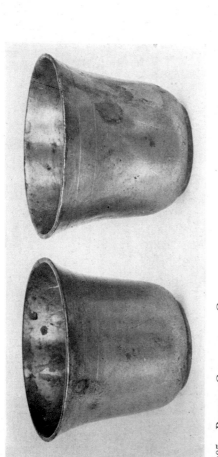

285. Pewter Communion Cups.

288. Teapot By George Richardson of Boston. c. 1810.

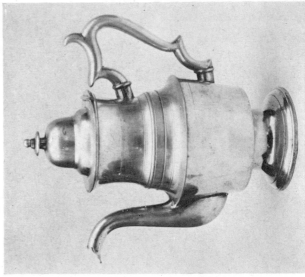

287. Soup Plate By B. Barnes of Philadelphia.

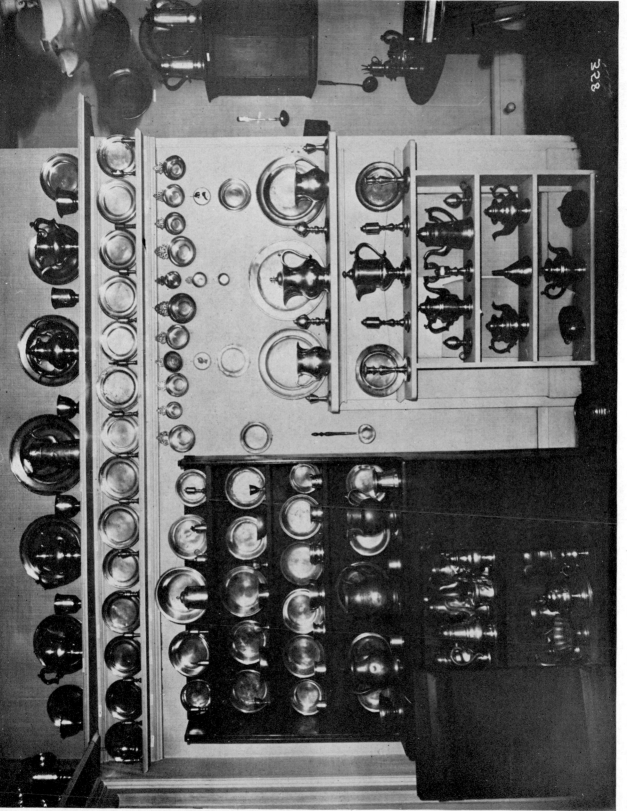

290. A Panel From the Famous Kerfoot Collection of American Pewter.

French and Co.

291. BRASS FURNITURE HARDWARE, 1650-1850.

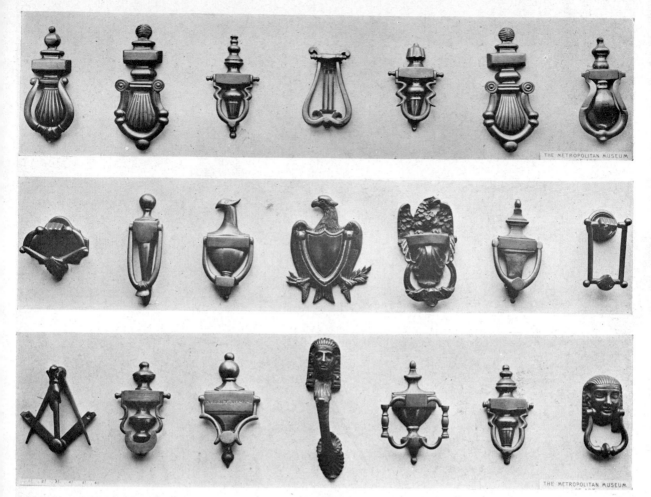

292, 3, & 4. BRASS DOOR KNOCKERS. Note Federal motif in the middle panel.

295. BRASS BUTTON WITH WASH-
INGTON'S INITIALS IN THE
CENTER. The border contains
the initials of the 13 original
States. *c.* 1789.

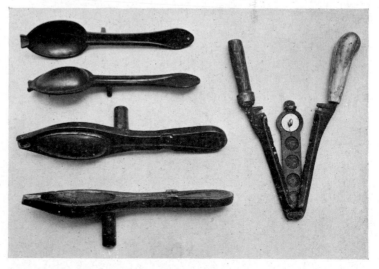

296. BRASS MOLDS FOR SPOONS AND BUTTONS.

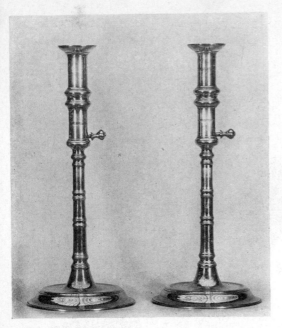

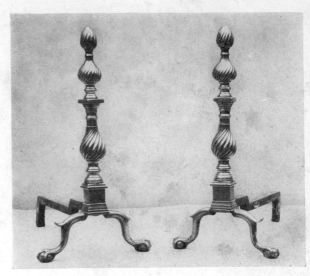

298. BRASS ANDIRONS MADE BY REVERE AND SON.

297. BRASS CANDLESTICKS. 1700-1750.

299. PIERCED BRASS FENDER, *c.* 1800. Note Federal motif.

300. BRASS WARMING PAN. Decorated with incised pattern. 1750-1800.

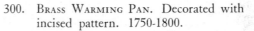

Metropolitan Museum

performed such a sudden and complete disappearance. The
third quarter of the 19th century abolished pewter almost as an
eraser wipes clean a slate. Cheap silverplate and the easy production of the false china, technically called "boneware," were
responsible.

In its hey-day, pewter was a commodity of the middle class,
for the very poor continued to use wood and the very rich used
silver. But even for the upper middle class it was a symbol of
elegance, and it was only well along in the 19th century that it
fell to the lowly position of being regarded as "kitchen ware."

Prior to 1750 the records give us the names of about 18
American pewterers. These men were located in the great commercial centers, New York, Philadelphia, Boston, and Salem.
Actually no really authentic piece of American pewter has been
found which may be attributed to this period.

The earliest lists of household possessions, and of things
which Colonial governors suggested new arrivals should bring
with them, do not mention pewter. Later lists begin to mention
pewter objects and it was probably at about this time that the
active making of pewter began in America. The manufactures
of this period consisted largely of salt cellars, spoons, trenchers,
platters, tankards, and porringers.

To those who study pewter, the period from 1750 to 1825 is
known as the "eight inch plate era." Simple, well-made, un-
decorated plates of that diameter made up one of the major
outputs of American pewterers at this time.

Some ninety or more pewterers are registered as of this
period. Of these, twenty-four were in New York City; sixteen
in Philadelphia; ten in Boston; six each in Baltimore, Maryland and Taunton, Massachusetts. Hartford, Connecticut and
Providence, Rhode Island had four apiece. There were others

in Bucks County and Germantown, Pennsylvania; Newport, Rhode Island; and New London, Norwich, Waterbury, and Rocky Hill, Connecticut.

There were no "great" pewterers. It was not only a humble craft but also one in which existed little possibility for innovation. A few names frequently mentioned in the "eight inch plate era" are William Will, of Philadelphia; Henry Will, of New York City; William Elsworth, "Pewterer and Coroner," of New York City; Frederick and Francis Bassett of the same place, and most especially, the Danforths of Connecticut. If any deserve the accolade of "great American pewterers," it is the Danforths. There were ten of them, in all, engaged in the making of pewter from before the American Revolution up until 1836.

The twilight of pewter, 1825 to 1845, is known as the "Coffee-pot era." The robust tankard and trencher were no more. Pewter had begun to imitate its expensive neighbor, silver. Pewter does not lend itself well to ornateness or delicacy of any kind. It is at its best in terms of solidity and simplicity. The simple pewter tankard is probably the most beautiful of all its forms.

In this final period, among other fancy articles including teapots and picture-frames, the big production of pewterers was the coffee-pot. A few men achieved a not unworthy rank through the wisdom of retaining in these more complex objects, the old ideals of simplicity, directness, and a decent respect for their material. Well conceived coffee-pots by such men as Israel Trask, (1825-1842), R. Dunham, and Henry Graves, of about the same time, deserve to take their places among the host of other vital American craft creations.

Little can be said of the American aspects of pewter, even as regards the usual quality of added simplicity. The pewterers of England and the Netherlands had long been distinguished throughout the world for their strict simplicity and avoidance of decorated surfaces. After the adoption of the nation shield, in 1789, many pewterers used various forms of the eagle as a part of their trade-mark.

BRASS, COPPER, TIN, AND LEAD

Although Mr. Joseph Jenks' ironworks near Saugus, Massachusetts, in 1645, is supposed also to have been a brass foundry, very little brass work, in proportion to other common metals, was done in America prior to the end of the 18th century. Brass is an alloy of copper with zinc, and zinc was not commercially mined in this country until 1837.

Brass work was usually cast, such as andirons, heavy pots, or door-hardware. An exception to this was the popular brass-button, upon which the fortunes of the glass-making Wistars of New Jersey had been originally based. These were most often made from old brass pots and other ware which the itinerant peddlers took in part payment for their goods and brought in for cash at the local foundries. These junked objects were first flattened into sheets and thereafter cut into buttons with sharp, steel dies, an anticipation of the role of craft in later industry in the person of the indispensable die-maker.

Copper was the next metal after iron to be successfully taken from its ore in America. This was first done at Cranby, Connecticut, in 1709. Therefore copper-ware became fairly common in early Colonial America.

Perhaps the most artistic copper and brass work was done in the making of warming pans. These were flat metal containers with long wooden handles. They were filled with coals and rubbed briskly over the cold sheets of one's bed. They were made of sheet-copper and brass and were decorated either by perforation or by engraving.

The use of copper for copperplate engraving has always been one of the most important utilitarian and artistic uses of the metal.

Tinware was at first imported, but by 1740, at which time the tinware firm of Edward and William Patterson began operations at Berlin, Connecticut, it had begun a rise which rapidly made it a major industry of America, particularly in New England.

Sheet tin was shaped into innumerable forms: candle-sticks, lanterns, sand-shakers, and boxes of all sizes and shapes. The sand-shakers were for spreading sand neatly on floors in lieu of carpets. The lanterns were tin cylinders, punctured by numerous holes, arranged in decorative patterns, with a candle-socket fixed inside.

Tinware was decorated with simple *repoussé* work, scalloped edges, fancy punch work and, less frequently, with attached ornaments, cut from sheet copper, as in the "cut-card" method of silversmiths. It was also painted and japanned.

Lead found a decorative purpose on early houses at the heads of drain pipes, for which purpose it was cast into appropriately ornamental forms. Cast lead was also used for details of classic revival architecture and furniture, in the forms of urns, drops, and finials.

CHAPTER 11

BOOKMAKING

SURELY there is no more enlightened and ennobling occupation than the combination of crafts and skills that go into the making of a book. Bookmaking is a craft-art of the purest order. The aspiration which it reflects is high. The impetus to make a book does not spring from the basic necessities underlying such crafts as carpentry, pottery, or weaving. It is free of the suspicion of ostentation which can so readily attach to silver or fine glass. It is one of the few art forms which actively propagates itself. Its product is a transmitter of democracy which must be banned or burned before a people can be enslaved in terms of ancient tyranny or modern totalitarianism. Its history in America is long and honorable, fraught with considerable richness of detail.

The initial craftsman, in bookmaking, is the author. His is a tangible craft and a technique. It can aspire to be more but cannot afford to be less, either in fiction or non-fiction. But by tradition, literary discussion falls more directly into the channels of criticism or art. It is, accordingly, the one basic aspect of bookmaking which we shall merely note in passing.

EARLY PRINTING

The story of the book in America begins with the printer. The first press in the English Colonies of North America was

149

established at Cambridge, Massachusetts in 1639. It is necessary to specify "English Colonies," for fine printing was being carried out by Spanish Priests in Mexico nearly a century before the first Cambridge Press was set up.

In 1638, an English clergyman, the Reverend Jose Glover, purchased a printing press and the necessary type, with the intent of taking them to America. What his underlying purpose may have been we don't know. It is fairly evident that he sincerely considered the value of the machine as a missionary instrument, as well as its general utility to the young Colonial Government. On the other hand, there is no reason to suppose that he was indifferent to the business opportunities of the venture. He engaged a former locksmith, Stephen Daye, as an operator, gathered up his own wife and children, and embarked for America on the ship the *John.* Unfortunately he died on the voyage.

Stephen Daye took over the enterprise and carried out the project of setting it up for business in the Massachusetts Colony. So far as we know, the *Freeman's Oath,* printed for the Government of Massachusetts by Stephen Daye's press, was the first matter printed in the colonies.

The earliest extant book, and presumably the first printed in America, is *The Whole Booke of Psalmes,* printed in 1640. A copy of this is in the New York City Public Library, but is not in its original binding.

Apparently the second press was set up, also in Cambridge, by one Marmaduke Johnson. Some time later, with the very grudging consent of the authorities, he moved his establishment to Boston. There is some significance in this for he was, in a measure, moving beyond the bounds of religious authority which had implicitly controlled and largely dominated the use of these American presses. To a degree, however mild, Johnson's move to Boston was an assertion of the freedom of the press.

Very shortly after his move, in 1675, Johnson died. His press was taken over and continued by John Foster. In 1677 Foster printed a *Narrative of the Troubles With the Indians in New-England.* The volume was illustrated with a map engraved by Foster, and was something of a landmark in American book illustration.

One of early America's largest publishing projects was born of missionary zeal. It was decided, by the Church Fathers, to expedite the work of conversion by printing the Bible in the Indian tongue. The first of several editions of the Indian Bible appeared in 1663, translated by John Eliot and printed by one Samuel Green.

It becomes difficult, beyond the earliest period, to trace the record of American printers. For this purpose the "genealogical table" of American printers, plate 308, is best used. In all, during the Colonial period of America, some one hundred or more master printers were at work, scattered in various towns.

In 1704 America's first "newspaper" came into being in the form of the *Boston News Letter,* a small sheet printed by one B. Green, the whole project headed by John Campbell, postmaster of Boston. The *News Letter* was printed regularly until 1776, when its career was apparently interrupted by the Revolution.

Another early figure in the field of newspaper publishing was James Franklin, brother of Benjamin. He printed the *New England Courant,* in Boston. Benjamin was "columnist" on his brother's paper, writing some dangerously trenchant political commentaries and satires. James Franklin was ultimately imprisoned for printing "seditious matter," which we can well suppose was of Benjamin's authorship. After his release he forsook Boston and established the first press in Rhode Island.

The first printing press in Philadelphia was established by William Bradford in 1685. The Quakers were none too pleased at this potentially dangerous instrument in their midst, especially in the hands of a non-conformist. In the very nature of the craft printers are and have always been great fosterers of dissension, since the "revolutionary" Gutenberg, who facilitated the Reformation. When Bradford took sides and printed pamphlets relative to developing schisms among the Quakers, the friction long latent between them grew to a sudden heat. Bradford finally gave up the battle, in 1693, and moved to New York, where he founded Bradford's *Gazette,* the first newspaper of the city. One of the important aspects of Bradford's sojourn in Philadelphia, however, had been the launching of a paper-manufacturing enterprise with William Rittenhouse. The business was the largest of its day and so flourished as to place Pennsylvania permanently at the head of the paper-making industry during the early period of America.

Benjamin Franklin fared better as a Philadelphia printer. He wrote and printed and sold *Poor Richard's Almanack* and a variety of other publications. His activities in American printing will be seen in a number of other instances.

The presses used in early America were, of course, those of Europe. They were of the old, slow-moving screw type, yet also of the styles beginning to employ newer and more efficient methods of leverage. Franklin tinkered with them. In a letter to a friend, ordering a press from London, Franklin begins, "If you can persuade your pressmaker to go out of his old road a little . . . ," and then proceeds to specify a number of detailed, technical improvements in the mechanism.

The first press-maker in America was Adam Ramage, who

302. TIN CHANDELIER. NEW ENGLAND. *c.* 1750.

301. COPPER KETTLE WITH COVER AND BRAZIER.
18TH CENTURY.

303. TIN LANTERNS. 18TH AND 19TH CENTURY.

304. TIN COFFEE POT, JAPANNED WITH PAINTE
DECORATIONS. EARLY 19TH CENTURY.

305. Franklin and the Lightning, Allegorical Portrait By Benjamin West.

THE

VVHOLE
BOOKE OF PSALMES
Faithfully
TRANSLATED into ENGLISH
Metre.

Whereunto is prefixed a difcourfe de-
claring not only the lawfullnes, but alfo
the neceffity of the heavenly Ordinance
of finging Scripture Palmes in
the Churches of
God.

Coll. III.
Let the word of God dwell plenteoufly in
you, in all wifdome, teaching and exhort-
ing one another in Pfalmes, Himnes, and
fpirituall Songs, finging to the Lord with
grace in your hearts.

Iames v.
If any be afflicted, let him pray, and if
any be merry let him fing pfalmes.

Imprinted
1640

306 & 307. STEPHEN DAYE'S PRESS AND THE TITLE PAGE OF THE FIRST BOOK
PRINTED UPON IT.

Vermont Historical Soc.
N. Y. Public Library

The Diffusion of Printing through the English Colonies, Louisiana, California, and New Mexico

BRITISH ISLES

Cambridge, Mass.
(*Stephen Daye*, 1639)

Boston, Mass.
(*Marmaduke Johnson*, 1674)
(*John Foster*, 1675)

Philadelphia, Pa.
(*William Bradford*, 1685)

Jamestown, Va.
(*William Nuthead*, 1682)

St. Mary's City, Md.
(*William Nuthead*, 1686)

Annapolis, Md.
(*Dinah Nuthead*, 1696)

Williamsburg, Va.
(*William Parks*, 1730)

Newbern, N. C.
(*James Davis*, 1749)

New York, N. Y.
(*William Bradford*, 1693)

Woodbridge, N. J.
(*James Parker*, 1754)

Charleston, S. C.
(*Thomas Whitemarsh*, 1731
Lewis Timothy, 1733)

Baltimore, Md.
(*Nicholas Hassel-
bach*, 1765)

Wilmington, Del.
(*James Adams*, 1761)

Charleston, S. C.
(*Eleazer Phillips, Jr.*, 1731)

Savannah, Ga.
(*James Johnston*, 1762)

Newport, R. I.
(*James Franklin*, 1727)

Portsmouth, N. H.
(*Daniel Fowle*, 1756)

Westminster, Vt.
(*Judah Padock Spooner and Timothy Green*, 1780)

New London, Conn.
(*Thomas Short*, 1709)

Dresden, Vt., now Hanover, N. H.
(*Alden and Judah Padock Spooner*, 1778)

FRANCE

New Orleans, La.
(*Denis Braud*, 1764)

MEXICO

Monterey, Cal.
(*Unknown printer*, 1833)
(*Agustin Vicente Zamorano*, 1834)

MEXICO ?

Santa Fé, New Mexico
(*Imprenta de Ramon Abreu á Cargo
de Jesus Maria Baca*, 1834)

308. CHART OF AMERICAN COLONIAL PRINTERS, COMPILED BY LAWRENCE C. WROTH.

The Southworth-Anthoensen Press, Portland, Maine

The Boston News-Letter

Published by Authority.

From **Monday** April 17. to **Monday** April 24. 1704.

London Flying-Post from Decemb. 2d. to 4th. 1703.

LEtters from *Scotland* bring us the Copy of a Sheet lately Printed there, Intituled, *A seasonable Alarm for Scotland. In a Letter from a Gentleman in the City, to his Friend in the Country, concerning the present Danger of the Kingdom and of the Protestant Religion.*

This Letter takes Notice, That Papists swarm in that Nation, that they traffick more avowedly than formerly, and that of late many Scores of Priests & Jesuites are come thither from *France*, and gone to the North, to the Highlands & other places of the Country. That the Ministers of the Highlands and North gave in large Lists of them to the Committee of the General Assembly, to be laid before the Privy-Council.

It likewise observes, that a great Number of other ill-affected persons are come over from *France*, under pretence of accepting her Majesty's Gracious Indemnity; but, in reality, to increase Divisions in the Nation, and to entertain a Correspondence with *France*: That their ill Intentions are evident from their talking big, their owning the Interest of the pretended King, *James* VIII. their secret Cabals, and their buying up of Arms and Ammunition, wherever they can find them.

To this he adds the late Writings and Actings of some disaffected persons, many of whom are such that Pretence; that several of them have declar'd they would rather embrace Popery than conform to the present Government; that they refuse to pray for the Queen, but use the ambiguous word Soveraign, and some of them pray in express Words for the King and Royal Family; and the charitable and generous Prince who has shew'd them so much Kindness. He likewise takes notice of Letters, not long ago found in Cypher, & directed to a Person lately come thither from St. *Germains*.

He says that the greatest Jacobites, who will not see themselves by taking the Oaths to Her Majesty do now with the Papists and their Companions from St. *Germains* set up for the Liberty of Subject, contrary to their own Principles, but only to keep up a Division in the Nation. He says, that they aggravate those things which the people complain of, as to *England's* refusing to allow them freedom of Trade, &c. and do all they can to foment Divisions betwixt the Nations, & to be Redress of those things complain'd of. The Jacobites, he says, do all they can to perswade the Nation that their pretended King is a Saint in his Heart, tho' he dares not declare it under the Power of *France*; that he is so with the Mistakes of his Father's Government, will govern us more according to Law; and set himself to his Subjects.

To magnifie the Strength of their own Party, the Weakness and Divisions of the other, in to facilitate and hasten their Undertaking; argue themselves out of their Fears, and into assurance of accomplishing their purpose.

From all this he infers, That they have notes of Assistance from *France*, otherwise they would never be so impudent; and he gives Reasons for his Apprehensions that the *French* King may send Troops thither this Winter, 1. Because the *English* & *Dutch* will not then be at Sea to oppose them. 2. He can then best spare them, the Season of Action beyond Sea being over. 3. The Expectation given him of a considerable number to joyn then, may incourage him to the undertaking with fewer Men, if he can but send over a sufficient number of Officers with Arms and Ammunition.

He endeavours in the rest of his Letters to answer the foolish Pretences of the Pretender's being a Protestant, and that he will govern us according to Law. He says, that being bred up in the Religion and Politicks of *France*, he is by Education a stated Enemy to our Liberty and Religion. That the Obligations which he and his Family owe to the *French* King, must necessarily make him to be wholly at his Devotion, and to follow his Example; that if he sit upon the Throne, the three Nations must be oblig'd to pay the Debt which he owes the *French* King for the Education of himself, and for Entertaining his supposed Father and his Family. And since the King must restore him by his Troops, if ever he be restored, he will see to secure his own Debt, before those Troops leave *Britain*. The Pretender being a good Proficient in the *French* and *Romish* Schools, he will never think himself sufficiently aveng'd, but by the utter Ruine of his Protestant Subjects, both as Hereticks and Traitors. The late Queen, his pretended Mother, who in cold Blood when she was Queen of *Britain*, advis'd to turn the West of *Scotland* into a hunting Field, will be then for doing so by the greatest part of the Nation; and, no doubt, is at Pains to have her pretended Son educated to her own Mind: Therefore, he says, it were a great Madness in the Nation to take a Prince bred up in the horrid School of Ingratitude, Persecution and Cruelty, and filled with Rage and Envy. The *Jacobites*, he says, both in *Scotland* and at St. *Germains*, are impatient under their present Straits, and knowing their Circumstances cannot be much worse than they are, at present, are the more inclinable to the Undertaking. He adds, That the *French* King knows there cannot be a more effectual way for himself to arrive at the Universal Monarchy, and to ruine the Protestant Interest, than by setting up the Pretender upon the Throne of Great *Britain*, he will in all probability attempt it; and tho' he should be perswaded that the Design would miscarry in the close, yet he cannot but reap some Advantage by imbroiling the three Nations.

From all this the Author concludes it to be the Interest of the Nation, to provide for Self defence; and says, that as many have already taken the Alarm, and are furnishing themselves with Arms and Ammunition, he hopes the Government will not only allow it, but encourage it, since the Nation ought all to appear as one Man in the Defence

[N° 3

THE
New-England Courant.

From MONDAY August 14. to MONDAY August 21. 1721.

Dr. Douglass

The History of Inoculation continued.
By a Society of Practitioners in Physick in
Boston.

Quis furor o Cives!

To the Author of the New England Courant.

SIR,

FINDING the *Infatuation* of in-
grafting the Small Pox *not altogether stisted*, we present the Town
with some Animadversions on a
late Advertisement, published by
the four inoculated Men; and a further
Dissuasive from that rash, sometimes hazar-
dous, and always dubious Practice.

This Advertisement, drawn up by ——
and signed by the four inoculated *Objects*,
were it more correct and not too tedious,
ought to supersede that *ancient Fable of the
Fox*, who by Misadventure loosing his Tail,
advises his fellow Citizens (or Foxes) to
part with their Tails; that the Calamity
being universal, he might no more be *houted*
at.

The long Advertisement runs in such a
silly indistinct Strain, with a *partial Repre-
sentation* of the matter, tho' under a Cloak
of Piety and Devotion, concluding with a
Quack Recommendation of the Operator; that
to give it any serious Answer or Animad-
version, would be debasing your Courant, and
imposing on your Readers, if this Affair were
not *countenanced by some*, whose proper Business is of another Nature.

They begin by insinuating, that the Town
may think this a *desperate Remedy*; the Small
Pox being a *very desperate Disease*, requires
no less. *The Small Pox in Boston* (say they)
*is a terrible Distemper, whereby many were se-
verely and dreadfully handled, and whereof so
many died, as gave an awful Prospect.* This
would better suit the *Plague* at *Marseilles*,
and is more than sufficient to occasion that
worst of Symptons in the small Pox, *Fear &
Dejection of Spirits:* And as a *false Rumour*
may tend to obstruct the Towns being supplied with Provisions from the Country, and
interrupt all Trade, Commerce and Com-
munication with our Neighbouring Colonys;
we reckon it our Duty to expose this as *im-
ulent*, and *notoriously false*. We find that
from the Arrival of the Small Pox here a-

bout the middle of *April* last, to the Date of
this Advertisement, the *Burials* in Town have
not *exceeded* those (*communibus annis*) of
other Years, for the same space of time.
Few *Epidemical* or Popular *Fevers* of any
Sort, have been more favourable. Notwithstanding of its spreading, it becomes *more
gentle*; the greatest Part of our Patients at
present having a *fair, large, distinct Sort*, and
many not requiring Confinement. The Burials in the Fall any Year are near double to
those of any other Season; if then for the
two or three following Months the Burials
should increase, we must not impute them
to the Small Pox as such, but as complicated
with common Fall Disorders.

How boldly do they tell the greatest Part
of the Town, that tho' many asserted Inoculation to be a Case of Conscience, &c. few
if any really believed it: This in plain English (pardon the Indecency of the Expression) is *calling the Town Lyer*. They say the
Experiment had been successfully tryed on
several amongst our Selves; tho' these were
only ——n's Child, and his own two Negroes, and with what Success has been formerly represented. They suffered only *something of a Fever*; witness old Mr. W——b's
Case. The Continuance of their running
Sores, is by them reckon'd a good Preventi-
on of Boyles, &c. with other such *Falsitys
and Absurditys* obvious to every Reader, require no other Answer than setting them in
a clear Light.

By Affidavit and Declarations lately published, we find that the Inconveniencys or
Diseases proceeding from Inoculation, are of
three Sorts. The First are the high Fevers,
and other dangerous Symptoms *immediately
attending the Inoculation*. M. *Desbonde* depo-
seth that some have died in that State. The
Town knows the violence of B——n's Son's
Inoculation-Fever, the narrow Escape of old
Mr. W——b, the heigth of C——s Fever, the great
Degree of Despair in Mr. H——r while ill;
these being four in ten of the Inoculated,
and three of the four Advertisers.

The other two Risques are what our *inoculated Objects* have still to *apprehend*, viz.
2*dly*, Impostumations and Ulcers in the Vis-
cera or Bowels, Groin, and other glandulous
Parts, Loss of the Use of their Limbs, Swel-
lings, &c. occasioning Death or miserable
Remnant

311. THE *Bay Psalm Book*. The earliest American-bound book. Printed and bound by Samuel Green, Cambridge, 1651.

THE AITKIN BIBLE. First English Bible in America, barring bootleg editions which cannot be verified.

313. ADVERTISEMENT OF SAMUEL TAYLOR, EARLY PHILA-
DELPHIA BOOKBINDER.

314. LABEL INSIDE COVER OF BOOK BOUND BY ANDREW BARCLAY, OF BOSTON.

began building American presses in 1800. In 1807 another American, John Clymer, made the Columbian Iron Press, a considerable improvement over the prevailing wooden presses, although not very drastically altered in mechanical principle. America contributed vastly to the rapid development of printing, and took it out of the status of a hand-craft once and for all, with the Hoe Revolving Cylindrical Press, in the first half of the 19th century.

Ink for the presses of early America was either imported from England, or mixed in the shop by the printer, using some convenient and simple formula. Benjamin Franklin was known as an expert ink-mixer and apparently supplied a good bit for the use of others as well as himself. (He simultaneously took a flier in lamp-black and related commodities.)

PAPERMAKING

The use of wood pulp in the making of paper had not been developed in Colonial times. Rags were the staple of the papermaker. Hand-made rag papers of widely varying quality were extensively produced in the colonies. Paper for the very best book printing was imported from England, where a more refined product was available.

The essential process of papermaking entails the reducing of the rag content to a pulp. The pulp is then pressed and molded in a variety of fine-meshed wire molds from which it derives its particular texture and pattern of "weave."

We have already spoken of the Bradford-Rittenhouse papermaking venture in Philadelphia. In 1696 John Holme, in a long, rambling poem called *True Relation of the Flourishing State of Pennsylvania,* notes Bradford's enterprise and also his enforced departure from Philadelphia.

Here dwelt a printer and I find
That he can both print books and bind;
He wants not paper, ink, nor skill
He's owner of a paper mill.
The paper mill is here hard by
And makes good paper frequently,
But the printer, as I here tell,
Is gone unto New York to dwell.
No doubt but he will lay up bags
If he can get good store of rags.
Kind friend, when thy old shift is rent
Let it to th' paper mill be sent.

This foreshadows the period of political tension between the colonies and the mother country, at which time a great scarcity of paper set in. Imports were curtailed and England was none too fond of the frequently seditious American press. A premium was set upon rags of every sort and a persistent campaign was launched for their conservation and collection. Generous sums were paid for old rags. The journals and general publications of the period abound in advertisements appealing for rags and offering inducements to their collection. The ads are most interesting and range in style from the matter-of-fact to the bombastic, the pleading, and the witty. A characteristic appeal was expressed in a poem, wittily chaffing the ladies about their many possible contributions to papermaking. It concludes with the lines:

Nice Delia's Smock, which, neat and whole,
No man durst finger for his Soul;
Turn'd to Gazette, now all the Town,
May take it up, or smooth it down.
Whilst Delia may with it dispence,
And no Affront to Innocence.

We find that Franklin, characteristically, was a notably successful rag-gatherer.

BOOKBINDING

Bookbinding is the "art of arranging the pages of a book in proper order, and confining them there by means of thread, glue, paste, pasteboard and leather." So said Edward Hazen of Philadelphia, very succinctly, in his *Panorama of Professions and Trades, or Every Man's Book,* 1837.

In the hand-binding process the printed sheets are folded into sections and the sections assembled into a complete book. They are then clamped into a *sewing frame* and sewn together. The book is then fastened in a vise and the back is rounded with a hammer. The next step is the *casing.*

The case consists of two "boards," (wood in the old days, cardboard in modern books), covered with cloth or leather. In the case of limp binding a sturdy, flexible leather may be used without boards. The case is fitted around the book and secured by additional sewing, or, in a less sturdy book, by pasting the end sheets of the first and last sections to the board of the cover. Any one of a number of additional touches may be added, such as the pleasing addition of a head band, edge-gilding, or marbling.

This is a very cursory survey of the process. There are a great many special techniques which vary the approach. *Flexible, hard, full, half, quarter,* or *check* are the names by which certain of the many processes are known.

One of the most important aspects of the binder's work is the decoration of the cover. This is done with a variety of stamps, dies, and other tools, set in wooden handles. The dies are engraved with various styles of lettering or with elements of design. They are heated and applied to the leather. Sometimes if a whole title is to be stamped, or a design of any type too large for efficient hand application, a large die, called a block, is used with the aid of a press. Long straight lines, as in borders, are impressed with a *filet,* a small wheel. Wider wheels, called *rolls,* with engraved patterns, are used for endless bands of design. The use of gold leaf, in tooling, is very common. On more sumptuous bindings other types of elaborate ornament, such as inlays of vari-colored leathers, or metal-work are sometimes used.

The earliest known American bookbinder was John Sanders, who took the Freeman's Oath in Boston in 1636. We note that he precedes by two years the first printer to come to the colonies. None of his work has been preserved.

The *Psalms, Hymns and Spiritual Songs,* popularly known as the Bay Psalm Book, was printed and probably bound by Samuel Green at Cambridge in 1651. It is really a second edition, as it were, of the *Whole Booke of Psalmes,* of 1640. The Bay Psalm Book is the earliest extant specimen of American bookbinding, and exists in a single copy, now in the possession of the New York City Public Library.

Some confusion ensues, in tracing early American binders, due to the fact that the art was fairly widely disseminated. Many persons known simply as printers or booksellers were also bookbinders and, as in the case of Green, above, it is often a matter of assumption that they bound the books they printed unless other binders are unmistakably identified with the work.

John Ratcliff was a bookseller and binder. He arrived in Boston about 1661, with the special commission of binding the Indian Bible. He has crept into history in the record of a petition to the Commissioners of the United Colonies, in 1664, protesting the meagre pay he was given for the large job.

Other bindings by Ratcliff were Increase Mather's *Call From Heaven,* in 1679; *Sewall's Commonplace Book,* in 1677;

and *The Book of the General Lawes and Libertyes Concerning the Massachusetts,* etc. about 1672. He was not a distinguished binder, in spite of the rather important items turned out by his hand. Authorities rank him as second rate and consider his work crude, even by the standards of contemporary Colonials.

Another bookseller-binder, Edmund Ranger, was Ratcliff's competitor. He was admitted to the status of Freeman in Boston in 1671. He practiced his craft actively until his death, in 1705. Increase Mather's *Practical Truths* is one of his best bindings. He may have been Ratcliff's nemesis, for many believe that Ratcliff's return to England was due to his inability to compete on any grounds with the younger Ranger's superior workmanship.

Isaiah Thomas was a practitioner of every aspect of the art of bookmaking, including authorship. He wrote a *History of Printing,* and operated the Columbian Press.

The Pennsylvania-Germans were not inactive in this field. An interesting specimen of the heavy style of metal-studded German binding is found in the *Gesang Buch,* bound by Christopher Sauer, in Germantown, in 1762.

Robert Aitkin came to Philadelphia in 1769 as a bookseller. He had been formerly apprenticed to a bookbinder in Edinburgh. He returned to England for a brief time, coming back in 1771. He published a short-lived *Pennsylvania Magazine* in 1775. In 1781 he printed the first English Bible in America. Isaiah Thomas, in his *History,* tells of an earlier "bootleg" Bible, printed in America under a London imprint. This cannot be verified.

The various journals of the Colonial period abound in the advertisements of bookbinders. Bradford's *Gazette,* of New York, affords several instances, including Bradford's own: "Printed and sold by William Bradford in New York where advertisements are taken in and where you may have old books, new Bound, either Plain or Gilt, and Money for Linen Rags."

In the *Gazette,* sometime in 1734, one Joseph Johnson proclaims that, "he is now set up Book-binding for himself as formerly, and lives in Dukes Street (commonly called Bayard St.) near the Old-Slip Market; (New York) where all persons in Town or Country, may have their Books carefully and neatly new Bound either Plain or Gilt reasonable."

The man generally conceded by authorities to be the greatest American bookbinder comes at a somewhat later period; William Matthews, 1822-1896. He was born in Scotland and served his apprenticeship to a London binder. In 1843 he came to New York, where, for some years, he was a journeyman binder before setting up an establishment for himself. In 1854, he took over the bindery of D. Appleton and Company, publishers, where he remained until his retirement in 1890.

With the rapid developments of machine printing and the consequent widening of book publishing and distribution, hand-bookbinding has been relegated solely to special editions, private hand-binderies, and amateur work. In this narrow sphere it still flourishes, while machines carry out most of the familiar processes in the mass production necessary to the modern publishing business.

The relative slowness of this development is interestingly demonstrated in the tone of an article written by W. G. Bowdoin, at the beginning of the present century, on *American Bookbinders and Their Work.* The article appeared in *The Independent,* issue of December 18, 1902. Bowdoin describes the fine work being done in several quarters, even in trade binderies, then adds: "Some binderies are kept so busy with commercial work that they neglect the field of special binding.

Commercial work is attractive to binders for the reason that it is speedily put through, and while the profit per volume is extremely small as compared with the returns from a specially bound book, yet the number that it is possible to execute more than makes good such a deficiency."

Private organizations have sometimes maintained "membership binderies" to serve the libraries of their members. Such activities have been naturally limited to the wealthy. A good example is found in the Rowfant Bindery, privately established by the Rowfant Club of Cleveland, in 1909. It imported several noted binders from England and France, some via New York, where they had been engaged by the Grolier Club. The bindery functioned until 1913, but ate up too much money to be maintained.

Fine bindings are still highly valued today. In some respects they may be said to have had a renaissance. We can see the effects in the immeasurably improved standards of commercial trade book binding as compared to such bindings ten, twenty, or thirty years ago. Some highly gifted amateurs are doing handwork in many parts of the country. Specimens of their work may frequently be seen in libraries or art galleries.

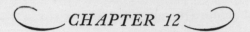

CHAPTER 12

SOME OTHER CRAFTS

AMERICA'S history of craftsmanship is not confined to those crafts in which staple products and basic necessities were provided, or from which great industries subsequently developed. There are, in addition to these, countless lesser crafts, variations or subdivisions of crafts, having their important and interesting ramifications. No single volume could readily list and hope to touch upon all of these. Definitions and dividing lines would be established only with difficulty.

Some of these crafts involve aspects of commercial enterprise; some may be called household activities; others may be regarded as full-fledged arts. Whatever the case, this cannot pretend to be an exhaustive research. Many crafts will necessarily be slighted or neglected altogether.

LAMPS

The problem of illumination is directly related to all the metal crafts and, in a lesser degree, to glass and pottery. As a problem it curiously failed to draw the attention of inventive genius for an astonishing number of centuries. The lamp of our founding forefathers was virtually the same as that of classic times: the cup-shaped device which many of us associate with the vestal virgins of the classic temple. In this country it was called a "Betty lamp." It was simply a dish to hold the oil, and a lip-groove in which the wick was placed, and a hook to hang it by. The fuel generally employed was the oil squeezed from the livers of the small fish abounding in the Atlantic Ocean. It was hardly a satisfactory fuel for it gave little light, caked the wicks, and produced a vile smell. A similar lamp, with the addition of a double dish to catch dripping oil, was known as the "Phoebe lamp."

At first such lamps were made of iron, which soon gave way to tin. About 1860 the practice of whaling gave rise to the use of whale oil as a fuel, giving a better luminosity and a less offensive smell. With the advent of whale oil certain marked mechanical improvements occurred in the lamps themselves. The wick was put into a central spout and glass chimneys and lenses were added. This paved the way for quick perfection of the kerosene lamp which came in with the extensive distillation of the latter fluid in about 1680.

Other early modes of lighting were the "rush-light" and "candlewood." Rush-lights consisted of the pith of reeds, such as the common cat-o'-nine-tails, dipped in fat and supported in special iron holders. The unburnt "wick" was rolled up and untwisted as it was needed.

Candlewood consisted of the most resinous sections of pine cut into straight sticks. These were stuck into the cracks of the fireplace, or wherever was convenient, and burned with a flickering and smoky light, dripping molten resin onto the floor or mantel.

When eventually, about the beginning of the 18th century, the colonists had enough cattle to begin to provide themselves with tallow the candle came into use. Far from being a truly primitive thing the candle in America was at first used only for highly ceremonial occasions, only gradually coming into general use. Sconces, candelabra, and candlesticks were made of nearly all the various metals, and later of pottery and glass. The ordinary candle-mold is probably one of the most familiar of all obsolete American household implements.

WALLPAPER

The history of wallpaper manufacture in America is a relatively unexplored subject. "Painted paper" is mentioned in a Boston inventory of 1700, but this was probably imported from France or England. Apparently the first manufacturer in this country was Plunket Fleeson, of Philadelphia, who announced in an advertisement in 1769, that he manufactured a product "not inferior to imported papers." The "paper makers and stainers division" of a parade in honor of Washington in 1789 carried a banner inscribed, "May the fair daughters of Columbia deck themselves and their walls with the products of our own manufactories." It seems probable, from this, that the marchers were giving a boost to the American textile craft in addition to their own.

By 1790 there were numerous manufacturers of wallpaper in New York, Boston, and Philadelphia. These included Ebenezer Clough, owner of the Boston Paper-Staining Manufactory, who issued the well-known Washington Memorial paper in 1800.

It is easier to find advertisements of paper manufacturers than to find examples of their work. Wallpaper is an essentially transitory and perishable medium of design. We can only conjecture, from the descriptions of their wares found in advertisements and from a few preserved fragments, what their product actually was like. All the early designs were hand-blocked in the technique of block-printing cotton fabrics, and many of the finest papers today are still made in this manner. In 1845

John Howell, of Philadelphia, imported the first color-printing machine. The process was essentially the same as that used in machine printing at the present time.

Early wallpaper was often used only as a border because of the impractically small size of the printed sheets. These were sold by the ream and were approximately sixteen by twelve inches. In about 1760, sheets were pasted together before printing and wallpaper was then sold in rolls of 24 sheets each. By 1799 a machine was invented for producing "endless" paper and wallpaper could then be sold in rolls of any desired length.

American designs began with simple geometric patterns in black and white. The ogee curve and strips were in popular use until about 1840. To these were added simple floral patterns in tones of gray or of one color.

Then came the more elaborate floral patterns, printed in many colors, which gradually became more realistic and brilliant of hue. As the 19th century advanced, floral paper came more and more to the fore, the wallpapers being a counterpart of the prevailing modes in chintz, with strong blossoms; peonies; large, full bright-colored roses; abundantly fruitful grapevines, often with brilliantly plumed birds perched on them. Large-scale textile patterns came back into their own, with a preference for heavy damasks and velvets. Small landscape medallions were current and from them evolved the popular 19th century landscape paper which often extended completely around a room without repeating a scene.

CLOCKS

When the Sons of Liberty dumped good British tea into the Boston Harbor in the celebrated "Boston Tea Party," two great American craftsman-patriots passed each other, probably without so much as a nod. These were Paul Revere and Thomas Harland.

Harland moved to Norwich, Connecticut and began making clocks. He had learned his craft in England. He first manufactured, or "assembled," a type of clock with brass works, imported from England.

Harland's clock, in common with most others of its period, had a one-second pendulum, approximately forty inches long. These clocks were usually in cases about six feet tall. The peddlers of the era often sold only the clock-works and the buyer had the case made to order by his local cabinetmaker. Sometimes, in the interests of economy, the purchaser did not order a case, merely fastening the bare works to the wall. These were called "wag-on-the-wall" clocks.

Among Harland's many apprentices was one Eli Terry, who subsequently, in about 1793, started business for himself in Northbury, Connecticut. Terry had also been apprenticed to Daniel Burnap, from whom he learned engraving. Burnap had worked in Andover, Massachusetts, and in Hartford, and East Windsor, Connecticut. Burnap's clocks were especially distinguished for their intricate calendar and moon attachments, and for their lack of spindrels.

Terry encountered considerable difficulty when he first started in business. He was forced to support himself and his large family by the repairing of clocks and watches. He also did engraving, and the repairing of spectacles, to scrape up extra money.

It was Terry, although the idea was not original with him, who undertook the first extensive manufacture of clocks with wooden works. These were much cheaper than those built with imported brass parts. For a certain combination of his wooden clock-works he took out what was probably the first clock patent in America, in 1797. Several times a year he went forth in his wagon to sell his clocks, while his two apprentices continued to make them. With their wooden works and various mechanical shortcuts, his clocks sold marvellously well. They were priced from $18 to $70. At this rate his business expanded so rapidly that he became the first to employ waterpower in the cutting of clock parts.

In 1807 he sold his original factory to an apprentice and bought an old mill where he began one of the earliest attempts at what may be called mass-production. He signed a contract with a retailing firm in Waterbury, Connecticut, undertaking to provide them with 4000 of his clocks, at $4.00 each, within a span of three years; the retailers to furnish the materials. This was an enormous contract, unprecedented in its time, but Eli Terry fulfilled it. Thereafter he again sold out, this time to two of his employees, Silas Hoadley and Seth Thomas. By that time the retail price of the average clock, without cabinet, had dropped to about five dollars.

Eli Terry never withdrew from one successful business without a tremendous scheme with which to begin the next. In this case it was a new clock-works which made possible the first cheap and practical shelf-clock. These could be vended by Yankee peddlers without benefit of local cabinetmakers, and were accepted with a fortune-making speed. Terry died in 1852, a wealthy man, at the age of eighty.

Seth Thomas and Silas Hoadley were two other examples of the early American self-made man. They represented the combination of craftsman, inventor, and business man, in whom all three elements seemed to balance without conflict and to produce an astonishingly capable and versatile personality.

Both Thomas and Hoadley had entered Terry's shop as humble joiners. Neither had any formal education; both came

from poor families, and had served their long apprenticeships
to learn the trade of joining. Yet in 1810, when Hoadley was
twenty-four and Thomas was twenty-five, they were able to buy
Terry's clock manufactory, which was the largest in America!

Seth Thomas founded a long line of clock makers, and a
firm which is still in business manufacturing one of the superior
clocks of America.

Silas Hoadley, after leaving the partnership with Thomas in
1814, prospered almost as well as his friend. He became a High
Mason, a Democratic State Assemblyman, and State Senator
before his death in 1870.

Another employee of Eli Terry, who rose to be a great American clockmaker, was Chauncey Jerome. The story of his life,
told in his *History of the American Clock Business,* was one of
courage, personal integrity, and ingenuity.

Competing with the clockmakers of Connecticut was another
group in Massachusetts. Outstanding among these was the Willard family. The first of the line, Benjamin Willard, advertised
in Boston in 1773 that he made clocks that "play a new tune
every day of the week and on Sunday a psalm tune."

Benjamin's two younger brothers were Simon and Aaron.
Simon was the better clockmaker, but Aaron the superior business man. Simon Willard invented the "banjo clock," so called
because of its shape. This new wall clock was an instant success
and in 1802 he had it patented.

About 1805 Simon gave up his previous peddling tours to
take care of his increasing business. In 1801 he made a magnificent clock for the United States Senate, for which he was
paid $770. It was destroyed when the British burned Washing-
ton in 1814.

Simon Willard is best remembered for the banjo clock,

which was quickly imitated despite his patent, and for his large public clocks, of which he made about thirteen. He retired in 1839, at the age of eighty-seven, but spent his remaining nine years puttering about the shop of his son, Simon, Junior, and that of a former apprentice, Elnathan Taber.

Simon's brother Aaron began business in 1780. (Curiously enough none of the Willards were ever partners.) His clocks were inferior to Simon's but, by dint of his business abilities, he made and sold more. Another Willard brother, Ephraim, was also in the clock business. Several of Simon's descendants carried on the tradition. The Willard clocks always had brass works and were more expensive than those of the Connecticut craftsmen.

It was the Connecticut group which was responsible for the unusually early industrialization of clockmaking. As a single group they transformed clockmaking from a simple local craft into a large-scale commercial activity.

LEATHER

All the varied aspects of leatherwork have their roots in the occupation of the Tanner. The shoemaker, the saddle and harnessmaker, the leather tooler, the upholsterer, the parchment maker and dozens of others need his product. In the narrowest sense tanning might be regarded as more of an industry than a craft. But since it has been largely a manual process, until the industrial era, it falls within our scope. Many other manual industries must necessarily be omitted. Leather takes its place because of the diversity of crafts which it supplied with a basic material.

The tanner is a long familiar figure. He has been immortalized by Shakespeare, in the grave-digger's scene of

Hamlet, for the dubious honor of outlasting other mortal remains in the grave.

Hamlet
How long will a man lie i' the earth ere he rot?

1st Gravedigger
Faith, if he be not rotten before he die,—as
we have many pocky corses now-a-days, that will
scarce hold the laying in,—he will last you some
eight year or nine year: a tanner will last you
nine year.

Hamlet
Why he more than another?

1st Gravedigger
Why, sir, his hide is so tanned with his trade
that he will keep out water a great while; and
your water is a sore decayer of your whoreson
dead body.

This is probably graphically true, as the processes of the tanner's trade will indicate. Shakespeare, the son of a tanner, was in a good position to know. The tanning process is the necessary step in the preparation of the skins or hides of animals for use. It entails the cleaning and preserving of the skins in order that they may be worked over by the currier whose task is the preparation of the leather for its subsequent specialized uses.

In the tanner's parlance *hides* are taken exclusively from cattle. *Skins* are taken from calves, or from smaller animals. The toughest and heaviest hides are known as *butts* and *backs*.

In the most primitive processes of leather preparation, preceding tanning, the skins were softened by being soaked in water for a long time, scraped, then treated with oil which was rubbed and pounded into the fibres of the material.

Tanning takes its name from the treatment of the hides with the chemical action of tannin, or *tannic* acid. Tannin is commonly obtained from the bark of trees, *tanbark*. Oak is favored, but willow and a large variety of other barks are also used, some of them adapted to the production of special leathers. The bark should be taken from trees at least thirty years old, and in the spring, when the sap has risen.

Tanbark is stripped from the tree with a tool called a *spud,* or *peeling iron.* It is laid out in slabs to dry and is then ground into a coarse powder to allow for the most efficient extraction of the tannin when it is mixed with water in the tanning pit.

In preparation for tanning, the hide is water soaked for several days, then scraped. It is next placed in a pit with lime and water for several days more. Sometimes it is hung up and smoked as an alternative to the latter process, in cases where the action of lime would be detrimental to the use for which the leather is ultimately destined. The smoking has the advantage of loosening the hair on the hide without the strong chemical action of the lime. Next the hair is scraped off with an *unhairing knife,* while the hide is stretched over a *beam.* It is also scraped on the reverse with a *fleshing knife* for the removal of all fleshy particles which may have adhered to it during the skinning. It is then soaked for some forty-eight hours in a sulphuric acid solution, after which it is ready for the tanning pits.

The pits are dug in the earth of the tanyard, are oblong in shape, and anywhere from six to eight feet in depth. They are usually clay lined. The pit is filled with ground bark, or tannin powder, and water, forming a solution called *ooze.* Skins are soaked in this from three months to as much as a year and a half. The ooze is replenished with tannin powder monthly to maintain its strength. The hides are often pushed around, hauled up and down and drained with long hooks, during the soaking.

This is pretty rough treatment. Accordingly the more delicate pelts or skins are sometimes given a preparation less drastic than the tannin soaking, and never see the pit. This milder process is called *tawing*.

Subsequently the tanned hides are dried out, remaining, as a rule, as stiff as a board. This is where the currier's task begins. His job is actually a distinct phase in itself and is sometimes carried out by a specialist. More often, however, the currier and tanner are one and the same person, both processes being performed on the same premises.

The currier's work has many aspects and details depending upon the specific use for which he is preparing the leather. He takes the stiff hides from the tanner and soaks them, to soften the leather for working. His varied treatments are for permanent suppleness, graining, smoothing, and bringing out the color and lustre.

Parchment making is one of the finishing processes which is quite close to the currier's own province. Parchment is made from a fine grade of sheep or lambskin. It is stretched on racks of various shapes and angles and carefully shaved and thinned to uniform thickness, then variously treated for qualities of texture, color, and grain.

The first New England tannery was set up at Lynn, Massachusetts, in 1629. Such a basic process naturally spread, and by 1669 New York had so many thriving tanneries that a special part of the city was set apart for them. This is perhaps a euphemistic way of saying that the tanners were exiled and concentrated, for the potent effluvia of a tanyard are among the most noxious and sickening odors created by any manufacturing process.

Tanning was largely carried on, in early America, by the

processes described above. A good bit of small-scale tanning was done by farmers on their own establishments. The processes, at their best, were none too good and it was not until 1800 that the tanning of leather was accomplished in a really adequate manner. Since that time it has become a large-scale, wholly industrialized procedure.

The shoemaker, or cobbler, has always been one of the main consumers of leather since the abandonment of wood as a shoe material. Sole leather, heavy, sturdy and stiff enough to serve as the foundation of a shoe, comes directly from the tanner, requiring none of the currier's refinements. But leather is, of course, cellular animal tissue and is not naturally of sufficient density for such rough wear. Accordingly the thick slabs of stiff leather, removed from the tanning pit and dried, were pressed or rolled until they were brought to the required density. The leather was then sent to the shoemaker who cut it in rough soles to suit his need. The uppers were made of various types of softer, pliable leather.

A shoe is constructed around a *last,* or model, shaped in the contour of the foot for which the shoe is intended. In the modern ready-made shoe various sizes and models are manufactured on a variety of graded lasts. In the days of custom shoemaking by the hand craftsman, many a steady customer of the cobbler had his own last, carved from his special foot measurements by the shoemaker. When a new pair of shoes was needed the cobbler merely took down the last belonging to John Doe and made the shoes.

A shoe consists of the stiff, heavy sole and heel which are strongly stitched, nailed, or bound to the soft, pliant upper. Elaborate and powerful machinery now turns out shoes for a vast industry. The tools of the hand shoemaker are many and varied, involving the use of many punches and heavy needles required in the working of so tough and thick a material. Cobblers' benches, of which a good many are extant today among fanciers of antiques, are among the most interesting and charming relics of our earlier days. It is rare, however, to find such a bench with its full equipment.

The saddler and harness-maker is another consumer of leather. A saddle is constructed on a basic framework of light wood called a *tree*. Beechwood is one of the best woods for this purpose. It is shaped, and prepared to resist warping and splitting, by the use of canvas wrappings, glue, and metal fastenings. It is stuffed and padded, shaped to fit the horse's back, yet to avoid chafing or hurting the animal. The whole is then covered with pig- or sheep-skin, pig-skin being the more durable and desirable material. The leather is tooled in designs of varying richness to suit the taste of the owner. The harness, with its rather elaborate gear, is also of leather.

Saddle making was a high art practiced and judged by connoisseurs in the roistering days of the American west. A beautiful, though modern, specimen of the more ornate American saddle style is to be found in the Sante-Fe Saddle, wonderfully tooled and studded with handworked silver and gold.

Leather is tooled and shaped in a variety of methods of leather art work far too numerous to be examined here. The use of tooled leather as a bookbinding material is extremely ancient and received consideration in the chapter on Bookmaking.

CRAFT AIDS IN TRANSPORTATION

The field of transportation is perilous ground for the researcher in craft to tread. In the narrowest technical sense the story of American contributions to, or influences upon, modes of transportation belongs in a study of *invention,* or technological processes. But we have made the tenet that craft is a prerequisite to invention, in most cases. We further note that many American developments in transportation flourished almost spontaneously to meet specific needs. The ingenuity that rose to the occasion in answering such needs sprang often from the insight of the craftsman.

As early as the Revolutionary War ingenious Colonials were tinkering with the idea of submersible boats, as strategic means of attack upon the superior naval forces of the British. The idea of travel under water clung so tenaciously from one generation to another that the submarine inevitably evolved as an American invention.

To meet the needs of the Civil War, river and coastal vessels were sheathed with armor and sent forth to battle; the first ironclads in the world, ingeniously improvised to meet a need.

The development of the steam engine must largely be credited to the English, who had a necessity of their own, chiefly for stationary power to be used in industrial activity. It was in America, where great networks of vast rivers held the key to our inland exploitation, that steam was harnessed to boats, through the sum of the efforts of several individuals. The steamboat is truly American.

In the great overland push westward, the ingenuity of wheelwrights and waggoners contrived the many conveyances needed, not for the luxury of passenger carrying, but for freight hauling. These ranged from the hand-carts of the heroic Mormon advance to the Conestoga Wagon and the later familiar Covered Wagon or "Prairie Schooner."

The railroad had been used on a small scale in England. It was on the expanding continent of America, where the distances to be spanned and the directions to be taken could no longer be accommodated by rivers or artificial waterways, that the iron horse was set upon stretches of track worthy of his powers. The railroad, in its epic proportions, is American. The railroad for years was like a child whose developing strength exceeds his discretion. The need for speed and power outstripped the development of safety devices relating to switches, signal systems, and air brakes. American craft ingenuity hastened to keep up with the rolling cars, contriving devices to meet the continual appearance of new needs.

The fabulous Erie Canal, unfortunately destined to a swift doom by the railroads, is an astonishing record of the capacity of ingenious men to work by main strength and instinct. Reputedly the men who headed the construction were not "engineers" as we understand the term today. Nor were they trained in the secrets of vast-scale canal building. (Where could they have obtained such training? Where were comparable canals?) They sent out their work crews and did the job, devising means of solving each problem as they met it, never bothering to look for trouble they didn't find. Walter D. Edmonds has written a number of rich novels about the days of the "canawl," notably *Rome Haul* and *Chad Hanna*.

The French led the development of the automobile. Again the insatiable Americans with more country to cover, seized upon the idea, developed their own simpler and more efficient variants, and had begun to scatter cars over the face of the nation long before suitable roads could be made to accommodate them.

Roads, waterways, and tracks proved insufficient to the American need and the American energy. The Wright brothers tinkered around in a bicycle shop and came out with a flying contraption that revolutionized transportation and realized a dream which had haunted visionaries for centuries.

Deliberately removed from its more or less chronological sequence is the most sheerly romantic of all the American contributions to the rapid consumption of distance: the Yankee Clipper. It is an open question as to whether the clipper should be classified more accurately as a work of craft or a work of art. It was the most beautiful, the most noble type of ship ever built by man.

No one man was responsible for the clipper ship. It evolved, with a growing need, under the hands of far-seeing, daring, and loving craftsmen. The man who builds an iron boat is an engineer. But the man who builds a sailing vessel, of whatever proportions, is indisputably a craftsman, and a good bit of an artist. There is a lack of precision in the behavior of a sailing ship, an incalculable factor which can be called each ship's personality. There is an intimate, personal link between a sailing ship and its builder, and a sailing ship and its crew. The vast structure of legend, song, and poetry that has sprung from the sailing ship is testimony to this. The obscure and sometimes fanciful jargon of the old-time sailor reflects it.

The clipper ship grew out of the frigate and the packet. The frigate was a boat necessarily built for speed and strength. In the days of the Revolution, and the stormy years of sea-conflict with England that followed, the frigate was designed to carry guns and to outstrip the slower but formidable vessels of hostile British patrols. The frigate was the ship of the pirate and privateer.

The packet was a smaller and lighter vessel and became the traditional carrier of mail. When one of the major factors in the development of the clipper ship came along, the discovery of gold in California, the packets set up a speedy run between New York and Panama for the many who desired to rush westward via the Isthmus crossing.

Many authorities feel that the element of sheer sportsmanship was one of the greatest forces underlying the clipper ship. Races around Cape Horn, races to China, races around the world were the sport and trade of the fabulous Yankee skippers. The richest prizes in the Orient were often for the man who got there first. With the further impetus to carry freight and passengers around the Horn to gold-galvanized California the true clipper, or technically the *extreme clipper,* flourished.

For the lay understanding the principle of the clipper is fairly simple. It was a boat with an unusually slender hull and a considerable length. It was anything but a conservative vessel for it carried a disproportionate and sometimes dangerous amount of sail. The demoniacal skippers, (Melville's Captain Ahab, though not a clipper man, is the archetype), with the lust of speed and competition, often brutally driving their men, crammed sail onto the long, slender craft until they were nearly lifted out of the water. There are hair-raising accounts of legendary roundings of the Horn, passages through the Straits of Magellan with full sail in a hurricane, and the like. Never did the craftsmen-artists of America set their hands to a more beautiful and glamorous creation.

Several men made clipper ships. The greatest and most productive of them all, the man who led the development more than any other single person, was a Scotch-American, Donald McKay. Among his many beautiful clippers was the loveliest of all, the famous *Flying Cloud.*

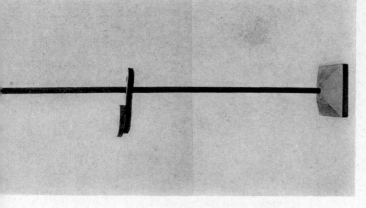

317. Candle Stand.

316. Adjustable Candlestand.

318. Candle Molds.

315. Betty Lamps and Tinder Box.

319. Whale Oil Lamps.

Metropolitan Museum

321. WOODEN BLOCK FOR PRINTING WALLPAPER.

320. WALLPAPER WITH PATRIOTIC DESIGN.

322, 3, & 4. EARLY WALLPAPERS WITH PATRIOTIC DESIGN.

325. TALL CLOCK BY
THOMAS HARLAND.

326. TALL CLOCK
BY SIMON
WILLARD.

327. WALL CLOCK BY AARON
WILLARD.

328. SHELF CLOCK BY AARON
WILLARD.

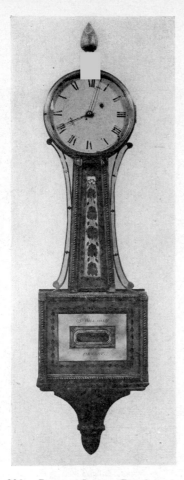

329. BANJO CLOCK BY SIMON
WILLARD. *Boston Museum*

330. LYRE CLOCK BY SAWIN &
DYER, BOSTON.
Metropolitan Museum

331. SHELF CLOCK BY AARON
WILLARD. *c.* 1790.

332. BANJO CLOCK BY
AARON WILLARD, JR.
c. 1815.

333. Yankee Peddler, Painting By John Whetton Ehninger. Note clock in wagon.

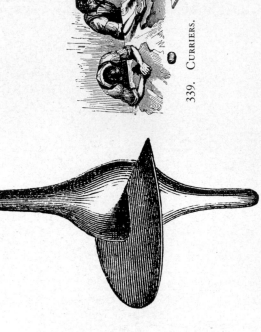

334. Tanner's Tools.

18"

4-6"

A

27" B

27" C

27" D

30"

Side View

Top View

20"

E

F

Windham County Court, June Term, A.D. 1748.

This Court grants License to Samuel
Lin .... to use the Art
of .... of Tanning Leather being ....
.... of his Skill & ability & that
....

Windham ..... A true Copy

....

Ebenezer Gray Clerk

335. Tanner's License.

336. Tanner "Scraping on the Beam."

337. Parchment Maker.

338. Parchment Maker's Half Moon Knife.

339. Curriers.

*From the Chronicle of
the Early Am. Ind. Assn.*

The Santa Fe Saddle, Elaborately Decorated in Hand Wrought Silver and Gold.

A. T. & S. F. R. R.

341. THE "FLYING CLOUD," EXTREME CLIPPER. Built at East Boston, in 1851, by Donald McKay.

Peabody Museum, Salem

. COBBLER'S BENCH, FULLY EQUIPPED.

N. Y. Historical Society

343. ADVERTISEMENT FOR THE "
KING."

Peabody Museu

CHAPTER 13

CRAFT TODAY

IN discussing the various separate crafts we have seen a scattered picture of the various trends toward increased or industrialized production, and a consequent lessening, in many cases, of the personal element of craftsmanship. The 19th century marked the beginning of the era of American industrialism. Hand production of most commodities was largely abandoned in favor of machine methods. Of course this didn't happen overnight. It is important, even though we have anticipated some of the findings, to take a backward look and survey this transition in very broad terms.

Originally the craftsman made things exclusively for local consumption; largely to individual order, often consulting with his customer on the details of the object. Naturally, under such a system, the integrity of craftsmanship was exceptionally high. *The workman identified himself intimately with his product.* Craft first manifests itself in the making of objects for *use,* rather than for *sale.*

The custom-made, or made-to-order stage, is second. Finally comes the object manufactured in quantity for extensive sale to unknown, wholly impersonal customers. In each stage of this cycle a diminishing of the craftsman's or maker's natural interest and pride in the work at hand occurs. When we add to this latter stage a new production method which usually allots to any one

177

workman only a single part or operation in the entire process he is almost wholly denied the enriching identification with his product. It is hard to feel a glow of workmanship over a machine-turned piston-ring which must be united with neighbor X's machine-stamped hub-cap and a thousand other milled parts to form one automobile to be purchased f. o. b. Detroit by an unknown customer.

Going back to our evolution; as towns and cities began to expand in the colonies, the early craftsman found it expedient to be prepared in advance for demands with which he might not be able to cope upon order. Accordingly the store, the retail establishment, came into existence, selling pottery, glassware, furniture, and even clothing and shoes, which clung somewhat more tenaciously to the tradition of personal transaction.

The line of craftsmanship had to be perpetuated and the busy craftsman needed a helper. Both problems were then solved by the apprentice system. The craftsman exchanged the knowledge of his craft for the labor of a boy, usually for seven years, but sometimes for a greater or lesser period. The boy started his tasks at an early age and received no cash compensation. On the other hand he was housed, clothed, fed, and trained so that, at the end of his indenture he found himself equipped with a trade in a good position to set up in business for himself in a steadily expanding world.

Here is a typical apprenticeship agreement: "This Indenture Witnesseth, that Nicolas Auger, Son of Nicolas Auger of ye Citty of New Yorke, Aged tenn years or thereabouts, with the Consent of his Parents and also of his own Full & Voluntary Will, in the Presence of Charles Lodwyck Esq., Mayor of ye said Citty, hath put himselfe Apprentice unto Wessell Evertson of ye same Citty, Cooper, and ye said Science or Trade which he, the said Wessell Evertson, now Useth, to be taught & with him after ye manner of an Apprentice to Dwell & Live from the day of the Date hereof until the full End and Terme of Seven Years, the said Apprenticeship the Sd. Nicolas Auger Well & Truely shall Serve the Commandments of his Master Lawfull & Honest. Everywhere he shall Gladly doe no hurte to his Said Master, he shall not Doe or Suffer to be done The Goods of his Said Master he Shall not Purloyn waste or Destroy nor them to any body lend at Dice or any other unlawful Game he Shall not play whereby his Master may incurr any hurte, Matrimony he Shall not Contract, Taverns he Shall not frequent, from ye Service of his Said Master day or Night he shall not absent himselfe but in all things as a good and faithfull Apprentice shall bear and behave himselfe, towards his Said Master and all dureing the Terme afore said. And ye said Wessell Evertson to Said Apprentice the Science or Trade of a Cooper which he now Useth Shall teach & Informe, Cause to be Taught & Informed the best way yt he may or Can & Also Shall finde to his Said Apprentice Apparell meate and drinke & bedding & all other Necessaries meet & Convenient for an Apprentice dureing the Terme Aforesaid & att ye Expiration of ye Said Terme to finde and Supply his said Apprentice with two good & Sufficient Suits of Wearing Apparell from head to foot.

"In Wittness whereof the Parties to these Present Indentures have Interchangeably Sett Their hands & Seals the Nineteenth day of February in the Sixth year of their Majesties Reign, Anno. Dom. 1694."

Occasionally there were added requirements in such agreements such as that the Master should teach his apprentice to "reade and write the English tongue . . ." and, more frequently, that he should present him with a complete set of tools upon the completion of his term.

The full importance of apprenticeship is further to be real-

ized by stressing the fact that in colonial America the burgher,
or freeman "right" or status, was not the inalienable and natural
birthright of the individual. Without this "right" no man could
practice a craft, trade, or business in the cities of early America.
It could be attained in only three ways: payment of a fee to
the city government, presentation as a Special Honor by the city
government, or the fulfillment of an apprenticeship with a local
craftsman. The freeman's right, we thus see, was automatically
bestowed upon the fulfillment of the terms and conditions of
indenture.

With the conditioning of modern competitive methods upon
us we might suppose that a craftsman would not be too anxious
to impart all the subtleties of his knowledge to an apprentice
who would probably grow up to be his competitor. Such was
not the case. This was that enviable period in which demand
exceeded supply. Moreover, should such a thing come to pass
as an overcrowding of the field the established man could
reasonably expect to hold his place. The apprentice could always
move on, not too far, to the ever present frontiers where the
demand for his services would be constantly and constantly
renewed.

Another aspect of the matter was pride of craftsmanship.
The boy would be known to all as the apprentice of a particular
craftsman and would probably advertise the fact when he first
established his own business, thus: "Nicolas Auger, formerly
apprenticed to Wessell Evertson." Lack of skill on the part of
the apprentice would be held to reflect shortcomings of his
master.

But in time the apprentice system became inadequate to the
demands of the relentlessly expanding market and the craftsman's increasing need for help. The first tendency to arise from

this was toward the forming of partnerships with somewhat less flourishing craftsmen. It was soon found to be more advantageous to pay wages. The craftsman became an employer.

At first he was the employer of *less established* craftsmen, possibly even taking his apprentices into service at a wage when they had freed themselves of indenture. But as the progress moved steadily forward it became necessary for him to divide up his work into its separate parts. With this he became the employer of *less skilful* craftsmen. In due time mechanical devices were invented to make parts of his work require practically no skill at all and with this he became an employer of *labor*. It is not much farther to the point where the original man becomes simply an employer and no longer a craftsman at all.

This was not yet wholly a "factory" system. Nearly all the work was still done by hand, even though divided into many stages of work requiring different degrees of skill. The artisan no longer owned what he produced, yet with the manual method there still remained a degree of individual pride in the work he was able to show. The whole thing was still operated on a relatively personal basis. Even though the owner did not work he usually had a knowledge of the craft. The workshop remained a closely-knit group of personalities. Often many of them were relatives of the employer or were related to one another. This stage was, in other words, essentially an extension of craft production.

Mechanization, we must understand, did not immediately supply the next factor. Power machinery, in the form of the steam engine, was first used only to prepare raw materials for manufacture rather than to produce finished goods. It was used to saw lumber, forge iron, grind grain and bark, to break hemp, etc., rather than to perform the final operations which fitted these commodities for direct consumption. Thus, between the mill, the furnace, the tannery, and the ultimate users of their products remained the stage of craft manufacture.

The much later mechanical application of power to milling machines of various orders basically altered the status of craft. We have seen that the glass-pressing machine greatly curtailed the honorable craft of glass-blowing. The horizontal lathe for clay objects reduced the mystical affinity between the potter and his handiwork. The power loom revolutionized weaving, and the stamping machine robbed metal work of its creativeness of execution, if not of design.

Industry flowered, if the term is apt for such a development. The resourceful and enterprising Americans were not handicapped by the feudal manufacturing tradition which hampered European factory methods. In England, for example, the major industries were broken up into their separate parts as though they were independent of one another. Thus, in the textile industry, there was carding and combing, spinning, weaving, dyeing, finishing. Each of these activities was housed in a separate building; possibly in a separate locality; was separately owned; had a separate organization; separate purchasing facilities, and separate marketing facilities. The American manufacturers regarded textiles as textiles and encompassed the whole within a single undertaking. This was the phenomenal American trend toward *industrial organization in manufacture*. So swift has it been that American workers are barely beginning to catch up with it in the present conflict between the somewhat outmoded form of craft union and the new mode of industrial union typified by the CIO.

AMERICAN THROWBACKS

We may not immediately realize that even the early crafts, in more or less their original forms, still exist widely in America today. They flourish in the general region of the Southern Highlands, including parts of Virginia, Georgia, Alabama, Maryland, West Virginia, Kentucky, North Carolina, South Carolina, and Tennessee. Many of the so-called "hill-billies" of this region exist under conditions which approximate those of the early American colonists. Their land is conducive neither to agriculture nor to manufacture. They seem to have been cut off from the entire stream of modern American achievement through lack of the resources or cash with which to participate. The Sears, Roebuck Catalogue, locally called the "wish book," is sometimes still their main contact with the general world; a contact which means little for they have little cash with which to buy.

Families have lived from year to year simply from their "patch of ground." Local crafts have been maintained to supply local needs. Here are to be found a good many of the old implements which we've had occasion to mention. Nearly all the crafts, even including pewtermaking, are found in their early phases.

Recently a number of government and private agencies have cooperated to develop this circumstance to the advantage of the people. They have organized craft guilds, instituted the teaching of crafts in local schools, and tried to create an outside market for the rare craft products of the region. The Russell Sage Foundation is one of the most powerful agents in this field.

Baskets, boxes, brooms, candlesticks, chairs and other types of simple furniture, lamps, pewter, and work in other metals, toys, and pottery are among the constant craft productions of these people. Their chairs are most often of the 17th century slat-back variety, and other products are similarly primitive, yet they are also of a conscientious craftsmanship associated almost entirely with the pre-machine era. Their potters work by the old methods, as do their pewterers, woodworkers, and so on. The generally extinct implements described in the section on early carpenter's tools are in use today throughout the Southern Highlands.

Folk-literature and folk-music still persist in their original forms. One of the genuinely indigenous articles of the region is the Dulcimer. Many musical instruments of the past have borne the same name but bear no other relation to the mountaineer instrument. It is an oblong box, usually strung with three strings. The box may be constructed with varying outlines, but it is always the length of the entire instrument. In other words, it has no appreciable neck. Its sad, nostalgic tone makes an appropriate simple accompaniment to the folk-songs of the region.

CRAFTSMANSHIP IN MODERN INDUSTRY

Striking a more truly contemporary note we find that craftsmanship must not be supposed to have wholly vanished from our industrial scene, as pessimists are prone to insist. Many highly mechanized industries still have necessary and vital aspects of their work in the form of manual processes, involving the skill and judgment of an individual worker, who can, to some degree, determine the result of the process in which he is engaged. Such a man is still a craftsman and is not to be classified with the mere machine operator, however skilled.

Such elements of craft in modern industry appear to be largely confined to two phases. One of these is the work of the "industrial designer." In the strictest sense of the word this is not necessarily craftsmanship. Industrial designers are men who carry on the creative tradition of craftsmanship without its manual phase. They are *architects of objects*. Everything, from automobiles to ash-trays, is designed by them before it is made in the factory.

More distinctly within our field is the model-maker. It must be remembered that for every factory-made object offered for sale there had first to be created a hand-made model. Most often this was made from the exact specifications of the industrial designer. Occasionally the man who makes the original model is himself the designer. In such a case he is a full-fledged craftsman.

Die-casting and tool-making both require craftsmen to perfect their original models. No branch of industry could be more vital than the manufacture of the very machines and machine tools upon which industry is based. It has been justly said that every new machine needs still another new machine to make it. The extension of this principle is limitless and here, indeed, the craftsman is indispensable. Whereas, in an earlier day, tools for various crafts were either manufactured to specification by the blacksmith or made by the craftsman himself, today the tool and machine industry paves the road for the march of all manufactures.

A significant example of the industrial use of craftsmanship is found in the shoe industry. A modern shoe is, so to speak, *cast* around a wooden last. The last is now made entirely by machinery, notwithstanding its irregular shape. But the original model of each last must be made by hand.

The need for the craftsman last-carver is characteristic of similar needs throughout many industries. It is a manual extension of the function of the industrial designer.

Some industries deliberately revert to early craft methods and charge an appropriately high price for their hand-made products. An outstanding example is the Steuben Glass Works, a subsidiary of the vast Corning Glass Works. Using the ancient, time-honored methods of hand-craftsmanship, Steuben produces magnificent and costly glass, the equal in every sense of the splendid Swedish and Danish glass. Modern chemical science here works hand in hand with the craftsman. At the Steuben Works the old craftsmanship is exalted by the availability of a chemically pure crystal glass used to realize the designs of famous American sculptors.

Beautiful hand-silversmithing is carried on today. In New York, Tommi Parzinger, an "American" craftsman, though of European origin, makes fine sterling silverware, in original modern designs, of such quality as to be regarded by many as a one-man renaissance of silversmithing. He maintains a silver-smithing shop in the heart of New York where fine hand work of his design is executed by a staff of silversmiths working in a manner that differs little from the old methods.

There are also large jewellers' firms, and custom furniture builders which execute to order the finest type of hand work. Even though only the wealthy can enjoy these products the old craftsmanship is thus kept alive in channels that do not often come to our attention.

Craftsmanship is still further nurtured in the field of amateur endeavor. Such work far transcends the ordinary "hobby" status in many instances. There are men in widely divergent walks of life who, for their own pleasure and relaxation, bind their own books, make furniture, or work in various metals. One aspect of the problem of revitalizing craft today on a still wider scale will be to make available to more persons, engaged in uninspiring routine work, the time to develop and practice such occupations.

Many efforts are now being directed toward the revival of craftsmanship. These efforts spring from a variety of sources and represent both sides of the major conflicting streams of social thought. There are those who dream of the "rugged individualism" of the era of craftsmanship; and there are those who anticipate the benefits to the worker of craftsmanship as contrasted to modern, proletarianizing industrialism.

We have spoken of the greater sense of identification of the workman with his product engendered by hand-craftsmanship. The advantage of the old method was in terms of conservation, creative impetus, and a certain inspiration calculated to make for good citizenship. We are only too familiar with the waste, destruction, and *ennui* of the modern world.

We must agree that any thought of destroying the machine is ridiculous. We are, or rather *could be,* much the better for the relative cheapness and unimportance of many material objects. The loss which we have suffered is not so much in the object itself as in the feeling of creative-workmanship which glorified craft-made objects, and which is largely denied to the modern workman.

Of course not every manufacturing process is inspiring to perform. It cannot be and never has been, even with manual methods. Machine methods definitely help take the onus from many phases of manufacturing dirty-work. It is to be doubted that the old-time tanner was ever exalted by his stench-plagued chores.

But at least he owned his work. True, a personal identification simply is not always possible in terms of the work itself. In such cases the modern loss has been more in terms of independence. The burden may lie just as heavily upon the workman who feels himself degraded by being a mere economic cog as upon the artisan who feels himself degraded by being a mere machine cog.

Restoring both values to the modern workman is partly a

matter of labor relations and social and economic enlightenment. Though rejected by revolutionaries as a capitalist ruse, and though no doubt abused and often faked, the worker-owner, or employee-shareholder system, successfully applied in some advanced industries, is an enormous step in the right direction. The direction is away from the mercilessly "efficient" industrial regimentation of totalitarianism in which the worker works for the state and the state is held greater than the worker.

Giving the workman a "stake" in his work, together with proper conditions of work, promises the ultimate answer to the psychological problem of the workman, in whose case literal crafts, arts, or special skills are not involved. The modern workman, like the old craftsman, must be allowed to "work for himself" in a more ennobling sense than mere subsistence bread-winning. He must feel some ownership of his tools, some security of employment, and some, even though remote, control over his production.

The problem of craft today is so complex that its answer will be found at the root of our whole social structure: our social structure now threatened by an appalling retrograde movement sweeping toward us from Europe and perhaps also from the Orient. If solved it must be solved as part of the problem of the whole and become an aspect of the joint task of workman, employer, artisan, artist, scientist, and statesman. Craftsmanship has a stake in Democracy, Democracy has a stake in craftsmanship.

CHECK-LISTS

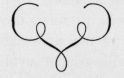

CHECK-LISTS

REPRESENTATIVE CHECK-LIST OF EARLY AMERICAN CABINETMAKERS.

ACKERMAN, JOHN   1798
New York City.

ACKLEY, JOHN   1792
New York City.

ADAMS, BENJAMIN   1800
Salem, Massachusetts.

ADAMS, JOHN   1740
Boston, Massachusetts.

ALDEN, JOHN   1600–1687
Plymouth, Massachusetts.

ALEXANDER, GILES   1800
Boston, Massachusetts.

ASH, GILBERT   1756
New York City.

ASH, THOMAS   1786–1815
New York City.

AYMER, JAMES   1789
New York City.

BACKHOUSE, EDWARD   1800
New York City.

BECK, MANASSES   1682
Boston, Massachusetts.

BELKNAP, SAMUEL   1665
Salem, Massachusetts.

BIDDLE, SILAS   1896
New York City.

BLAKE, JOHN   1680
Boston, Massachusetts.

BLAKE, SAMUEL   1789
Boston, Massachusetts.

BLAKE, WILLIAM   1800
Boston, Massachusetts.

BLISS, PELATIAH   1800
Springfield, Massachusetts.

BURLING, THOMAS   1787
New York City.

CARMER, HENRY   1774
New York City.

CARTER, ROBERT   1787
New York City.

CHAPIN, AARON   1783
Hartford, Connecticut.

CLARK, ELIPHALET   1791
New York City.

CONNELLY, HENRY   1770–1826
Philadelphia, Pennsylvania.

COWPERTHWAITE, JOHN K.   1818–1825
New York City.

DAVENPORT, THOMAS   1801
New York City.

DELAPLAINS, JOSHUA   1754
New York City.

DE WITT, JOHN   1794
New York City.

DISBROWE, NICHOLAS   c. 1612–1672
Hartford, Connecticut.

DIX, SAMUEL   1637
Boston, Massachusetts.

DOUGLAS, STEPHEN A.   1813–1861
Middlebury, Vermont. This was the "Little Giant", Lincoln's classic rival.

DURAND, WILLIAM   1816
New York City.

EGERTON, MATTHEW   1739–1802
New Brunswick, New Jersey. Succeeded by his son.

ELLISON, WILLIAM *New York City.*	1786	KIRKPATRICK, J. *New York City.*	1806
FELT, NATHANIEL *Salem, Massachusetts.*	1775	KIRKPATRICK, WILLIAM *New York City.*	1806
FERNSIDE, JACOB *Boston, Massachusetts.*	1700	LANNUIER, CHARLES HONORÉ *New York City.*	1805–1819
FROTHINGHAM, BENJAMIN *Boston, Massachusetts.*	1789	LAWTON, ROBERT *New York City.*	1794
FROTHINGHAM, SAMUEL *Salem, Massachusetts.*	1795	LIST, NATHANIEL *New York City.*	1811
GALER, ADAM *New York City.*	1774	LOW, MARINUS *New York City.*	1799
GAUTIER, ANDREW *New York City.*	1765	McINTIRE, SAMUEL *Salem, Massachusetts.*	1790
GODDARD, JOHN *Newport, Rhode Island.*	1723–1785	McINTIRE, SAMUEL F. *Salem, Massachusetts.*	1804
GODDARD, THOMAS *Newport, Rhode Island.*	1765–1858	MASON, ROGER *Boston, Massachusetts.*	1635
GOODALE, SAMUEL *Salem, Massachusetts.*	1707	MEEKS, EDWARD *New York City.*	1801
GOODHUE, JONATHAN *Gloucester, Massachusetts.*	1758	MILLS, WILLIAM *New York City.*	1801
GOSTELOWE, JONATHAN c. 1744–1795 *Philadelphia, Pennsylvania.*		MILLS & DEMING *New York City.*	1790
HAMPTON, JONATHAN *New York City.*	1768	NICKERSON, GEORGE *Boston, Massachusetts.*	1690
HAYS, SOLOMON *New York City.*	1754	PHYFE, DUNCAN *New York City.*	1793–1820
HICHBORNE, THOMAS *Boston, Massachusetts.*	1690	PRICE, WILLIAM *Boston, Massachusetts.*	1726
HITCHCOCK, LAMBERT 1818–1843 *Barkansted, Connecticut. Subse- quently Hitchcocksville; now Riverton.*		PRIMROSE, WILLIAM *New York City.*	1811
		PRINCE, SAMUEL *New York City.*	1773
HOES, JOHN *New York City.*	1801	PULCIFER, FRANCIS *Salem, Massachusetts.*	1795
HUBBEL, ISAAC *New York City.*	1774	PULCIFER, JAMES *Salem, Massachusetts.*	1795
HUBON, HENRY *Salem, Massachusetts.*	1820	PULSIFER, ISRAEL *Beverly, Massachusetts.*	1800
JONES, THOMAS *New York City.*	1771	RANDOLPH, BENJAMIN *Philadelphia, Pennsylvania.*	1762–1792
KELSO, JOHN *New York City.*	1774	RAWSON, JOSEPH & SON *Providence, Rhode Island.*	1790–1800

RIVINGTON, JAMES *New York City.*	1760	TOPPAM, ABNER *Newbury, Massachusetts.*	1764–1836
SAVERY, WILLIAM *Philadelphia, Pennsylvania.*	1721–1787	TOURNIER, DANIEL *New York City.*	1816
SEIGNOURET, FRANÇOIS *New Orleans, Louisiana.*	1810–1815	TOURNIER, HENRY *New York City.*	1816
SEYMOUR, JOHN & SON *Boston, Massachusetts.*	1800–1810	TOWNSEND, JOB *Newport, Rhode Island.*	1699–1765
SHADWELL, DANIEL *New York City.*	1793	TOWNSEND, JOHN *Newport, Rhode Island.*	c. 1730–1800
SHADWELL, DAVID *New York City.*	1792	TREMAIN, JOHN *New York City.*	1751
SHIPMAN, CHARLES *New York City.*	1767	VAN ALLEN, CORNELIUS *New York City.*	1794
SICKLES, THOMAS *New York City.*	1816	VANDERPOOL, JACOB *New York City.*	1789
SKILLIN, JOHN *Boston, Massachusetts.*	1789	WADSWORTH, JOHN *Hartford, Connecticut.*	1796
SKILLIN, SAMUEL *Boston, Massachusetts.*	1796	WARD, JOHN *Salem, Massachusetts.*	1780
SKILLIN, SIMEON *Boston, Massachusetts.*	1796	WARD, MILES *Salem, Massachusetts.*	1730
SPIES, HENRY *New York City.*	1811	WHITE, JOHN *Boston, Massachusetts.*	16—
SPOTSWOOD, WILLIAM *New York City.*	1811	WILLET & PEARSEY *New York City.*	1773
THAYER, ZIPHION *Boston, Massachusetts.*	1789	WILLET, COLONEL MARINUS *New York City.*	1773
TILYOU, WILLIAM & PETER *New York City.*	1791	WINSLOW, KENELM *Plymouth, Massachusetts.*	1634

REPRESENTATIVE CHECK-LIST OF EARLY AMERICAN GLASS MAKERS

For further or more detailed reference, see Bibliography.

ADAMS GLASS COMPANY *Adams, Massachusetts.*	1812	AMELUNG, JOHN FREDERICK (See New Bremen Glass Works).	
ADAMS, HOLMAN & DUTTON *Keene, New Hampshire.*	1831	BAMPER, LODEWYCK (See N. Y. Glass House Co.)	

BERKSHIRE GLASS COMPANY   1847–1857
Berkshire, Massachusetts.

BOSTON & SANDWICH GLASS COM-
PANY   1826–1888
*Sandwich, Massachusetts. Found-
ed by Deming Jarves and his
associates.*

BROWN, JOHN   c. 1790
India Point, Rhode Island.

CAPE COD GLASS COMPANY   1858–c. 1864
*Massachusetts. Founded by Dem-
ing Jarves upon withdrawal from
the Boston & Sandwich Company.*

CHAMPLAIN GLASS COMPANY   1827
Burlington, Vermont.

CHESHIRE CROWN GLASS WORKS   1813
Massachusetts.

CHESTER GLASS COMPANY   c. 1814–1815
Chester, Massachusetts.

CLEMENT'S GLASS WORKS   c. 1819–1825
Clementon, New Jersey.

COLONY, J. D. & COMPANY   1850
Keene, New Hampshire.

COLUMBIA GLASS WORKS   1812
*Near Paulinskill Creek, New
Jersey.*

CORNING GLASS WORKS   1875
*Corning, New York. The firm
had long been in operation in
Brooklyn, as the South Ferry
Glass Works. They are still in
operation and are owners of the
Steuben Glass Works.*

COVENTRY GLASS HOUSE   1813–1820
*Coventry, Connecticut. Succeeded
first by Stebbins & Chamberlin,
then by Gilbert, Turner & Company. Last firm discontinued
about 1848 upon exhaustion of
wood supply.*

DUNBARTON GLASS WORKS   1802
Near Durhamville, New York.

DUYCKING, EVERT   1638–1674
New Amsterdam and New York.

DYOTT, THOMAS W. (See Dyottville Glass Works).

DYOTTVILLE GLASS WORKS   1833–1838
*Kensington, Pennsylvania. For-
merly the Kensington Glass
Works.*

EXCELSIOR GLASSWORKS   1841–1857
Camden, New Jersey.

FARMER'S GLASS COMPANY   1814
Clarksburg, Massachusetts.

FOX, GREGORY AND COMPANY   1845
Durhamville, New York.

FRANKLIN, JOHN, AND ASSOCIATES   1754
*Lee, Massachusetts. Town named
long after disappearance of the
glassworks, about which nothing
is known.*

GALLATIN, ALBERT   1797
*Near Greensboro, Pennsylvania.
Subsequently moved his plant
two times.*

GORE, SAMUEL   1787
Boston, Massachusetts.

HAINES, JONATHAN   c. 1800
Clementon, New Jersey.

HARMONY GLASS WORKS   1813
Glassboro, New Jersey.

HEWES, ROBERT   1780–1830
*Temple, New Hampshire. His
blowers were said to be deserters
from the Hessian Army.*

HEWSON, CONNELL & COMPANY   1816
Kensington, Pennsylvania.

HOUGH, DAN.   c. 1825–1840
Keene, New Hampshire.

JAMESTOWN GLASS HOUSE (1st)   1606
Jamestown, Virginia.

JAMESTOWN GLASS HOUSE (2nd)   1620
Jamestown, Virginia.

JARVES, DEMING (See Boston &
Sandwich Glass Co.).

KENSINGTON GLASS WORKS   1771
Kensington, Pennsylvania.

LEE, JAMES AND ASSOCIATES   1806
Millville, New Jersey.

LIBBEY, W. L.   1878
Boston, Massachusetts. Libbey subsequently removed to Ohio. There he merged with the Owens Bottle Company. The firm is still in operation.

LUDLOW GLASS WORKS (date uncertain)
Ludlow, Massachusetts.

LYNDEBORO GLASS COMPANY   1866
South Lyndeboro, New Hampshire.

MOUNT WASHINGTON GLASS WORKS   1837
Massachusetts. Was founded by Deming Jarves.

NEW BREMEN GLASS WORKS (many variants to name)   1784–1789
New Bremen, Maryland. John Frederick Amelung, Proprietor.

NEW ENGLAND GLASS COMPANY   1817
Cambridge, Massachusetts.

NEW GRANITE GLASS FACTORY   1865–1871
Stoddard, New Hampshire.

NEW LONDON GLASS COMPANY   1856
New London, Connecticut.

NEW WINDSOR GLASS HOUSE (of the New York Glass House Company)   1753
New Windsor, New York.

NEW YORK GLASS HOUSE COMPANY   1754
New York City. Bamper's Enterprise.

PALMER, JOSEPH   1716–1760
Braintree, Massachusetts.

PERRY, JUSTUS   1817–1827
Keene, New Hampshire. Later, Perry & Wood, then Perry & Wheeler.

PITKIN, ELISHA & WILLIAM (Pitkin Glass Works)   1783–1830
Manchester, Connecticut. Samuel Bishop, partner. Taken over later

by Superintendent, J. P. Foster, 1810.

PORCELAIN AND GLASS MANUFACTURING COMPANY   1787
East Cambridge, Massachusetts. Subsequently moved to Ohio.

PROVIDENCE FLINT GLASS COMPANY   1830
Providence, Rhode Island.

RENSSELAER GLASS FACTORY   1806
Near Albany, New York.

SALEM GLASS HOUSE   1639–1642
Salem, Massachusetts. Concklin, Holmes and Southwick.

SCHOOLCRAFT, HENRY R.   1814
Keene, New Hampshire. Came with his father. In 1815 left New Hampshire Glass Factory to found his own. Later became Schoolcraft & Sprague.

SCHOOLCRAFT, LAWRENCE   1814
Keene, New Hampshire. Superintendent of New Hampshire Glass Factory. Father of Henry R. Schoolcraft.

SCHUYLKILL GLASS WORKS   1786
Near Philadelphia, Pennsylvania.

SCRIPTURE, WHITON & CURTIS   1844–1864
Stoddard, New Hampshire.

SOUTH BOSTON GLASS WORKS   1843
Boston, Massachusetts.

STEUBEN GLASS WORKS (See Corning Glass Works)

STIEGEL, HENRY WILLIAM   1762–1774
Manheim, Pennsylvania.

SMEDES, JAN   1654–1664
New Amsterdam and New York.

SMITH, PETER S.   1804
Peterboro, New York. Later, Smith & Solon.

STANGER BROTHERS (numerous spellings)   1781
Glassboro, New Jersey.

UNION GLASS WORKS 1859
New London, Connecticut. Apparently successors to the New London Glass Company.

VERMONT GLASS COMPANY 1812–1816
East Middlebury, Vermont.

WESTFORD GLASS COMPANY 1857
Westford, Connecticut.

WHALLEY, HUNNEWELL, PLUMBACH & KUPPER 1787
Essex Street, Boston, Massachusetts.

WHITNEY AND BROTHERS 1837
Glassboro, New Jersey. Later Whitney Glass Works. Now part of Libbey-Owens concern.

WILLINGTON GLASS COMPANY 1846
West Willington, Connecticut.

WINSLOW, ISAAC C. 1752
Providence, Rhode Island.

WISTAR GLASS HOUSE 1740–1775
Allowaystown (then Wistarberg), New Jersey. Caspar & Richard Wistar.

CHECK-LIST OF AMERICAN CLOCKMAKERS

For extensive literature on clocks, together with detailed data to augment this list (which does not pretend to be complete), see the numerous source books cited in the Bibliography.

ADAMS, NATHAN 1796–1825
Boston, Massachusetts.

ADAMS, THOMAS F. 1804
Baltimore, Maryland.

AGAR, EDWARD 1761
New York City.

AIKINSON, PEABODY 1790
Concord, Massachusetts.

AIRD, DAVID 1785
Middletown, Connecticut.

ALLAN, JAMES 1684
Boston, Massachusetts.

ALLEN, JOHN 1798
New York City.

ALRICHS, JACOB 1797
Wilmington, Delaware.

ALRICHS, JONAS 1780
Wilmington, Delaware.

AMANT, PETER 1793
Philadelphia, Pennsylvania.

ASHBY, JAMES 1769
Boston, Massachusetts.

ATHEATON, OTIS 1798
New York City.

ATKINSON, M. & A. 1804
Baltimore, Maryland.

AUSTIN, ISAAC 1785
Philadelphia, Pennsylvania.

AVERY, —— 1726
Boston, Massachusetts.

AVERY, JOHN, JR. 1750
Preston, Connecticut.

BACHELDER, EZRA 1820
Danvers, Massachusetts.

BADOLLET, PAUL 1798
New York City.

BAGNALL, BENJAMIN 1712–1740
Charlestown, Massachusetts.

BAGNALL, SAMUEL 1740–1760
Boston, Massachusetts.

BALCH, CHARLES HODGE 1817
Newburyport, Massachusetts.

BALCH, DANIEL 1760–1790
Newburyport, Massachusetts.
The Balch family was numerous
in clockmaking.

BALDWIN, ANTHONY 1810–1830
Lancaster, Pennsylvania.

BALDWIN, GEORGE 1808–1832
Sadsburyville, Pennsylvania.

BALDWIN, JABEZ 1812
Boston, Massachusetts.

BALDWIN, JEDEDIAH 1780
Hanover, New Hampshire.

BANSTEIN, JOHN 1791
Philadelphia, Pennsylvania.

BARKER, B. B. c. 1800
New York City.

BARNES, THOMAS c. 1800
Bristol, Connecticut.

BARNES, TIMOTHY 1790
Litchfield, Connecticut.

BATESON, JOHN 1720
Boston, Massachusetts.

BATTERSON, JAMES 1707–1730
Boston, Massachusetts.

BAYLEY (BAILEY), JOHN 1770–1815
Hanover, Massachusetts.

BEARD, DUNCAN 1755–1797
Appoquinnemink, Delaware.

BELL, JOHN 1734
New York City.

BIGGER & CLARKE 1784
Baltimore, Maryland.

BILLON & COMPANY 1797
Philadelphia, Pennsylvania.

BILLOW & COMPANY 1796
Boston, Massachusetts.

BINGHAM & BRICERLY 1778–1799
Philadelphia, Pennsylvania.

BISBEE, J. 1798–1825
Brunswick, Maine.

BIXLER, CHRISTIAN c. 1750
Easton, Pennsylvania.

BLASDELL, DAVID 1741
Amesburg, Massachusetts.

BODE, WILLIAM 1796
Philadelphia, Pennsylvania.

BOGARDUS, EVERARDUS 1698
New York City.

BOWMAN, JOSEPH 1821–1844
Lancaster, Pennsylvania.

BRASHER, ABRAHAM 1757
New York City.

BREARLEY, JAMES 1793–1811
Philadelphia, Pennsylvania.

BREWSTER, ELISHA C. 1833–1862
Bristol, Connecticut. Became
Brewster & Ingraham, later
Brewster again.

BRINCKERHOFF, DIRCK 1756
New York City.

BURNAP, DANIEL 1780–1838
East Windsor and Andover, Con-
necticut.

CAIRNS, JOHN 1784
Providence, Rhode Island.

CAMP, HIRAM 1829–1893
New Haven, Connecticut. (New
Haven Clock Company.)

CANBY, CHARLES 1820
Wilmington, Delaware.

CARVER, JACOB 1785–1799
Philadelphia, Pennsylvania.

CHANDLEE, JOHN 1795–1810
Wilmington, Delaware.

CHENEY, ASAHEL 1790
Northfield, Massachusetts.

CHENEY, BENJAMIN 1745–1780
East Hartford. The Cheneys
were a prolific brood of clock-
makers.

CLAGGET, WILLIAM 1726–1749
Newport, Rhode Island. There
were several clockmakers in the
family.

CLARK, BENJAMIN   1837–1850
*Wilmington, Delaware. Clark
and Clarke, are prolific names in
American clockmaking.*

CONANT, ELIAS   1776–1815
*Bridgewater, afterwards Lynn,
Massachusetts.*

CRANCH, RICHARD   1771–1789
*Boston, and Braintree, Massa-
chusetts.*

CROW, GEORGE   1740–1770
*Wilmington, Delaware. There
were several of this family working here.*

DAVIS, WILLIAM   1683
Boston, Massachusetts.

DOWNS, EPHRAIM   1811–1843
Bristol, Connecticut.

DROZ, HUMBERT   1797
Philadelphia, Pennsylvania.

DUFFIELD, EDWARD   1741–1801
*Philadelphia, and Lower Dublin,
Pennsylvania.*

DUPUY, ODRAN   1735
Philadelphia, Pennsylvania.

EBERMAN, JOHN   1780–1820
Lancaster, Pennsylvania.

EDWARDS, ABRAHAM   1794–1840
Ashby, Massachusetts.

ELIOT, WILLIAM   1799
Baltimore, Maryland.

ELSWORTH, DAVID   1780–1800
Windsor, Connecticut.

ENT, JOHN   1758
New York City.

ESSEX, JOSEPH   1712
Boston, Massachusetts.

EVANS, THOMAS   1766
New York City.

FARNUM, HENRY & RUFUS   1780
Boston, Massachusetts.

FESSLER, JOHN   1782–1820
*Fredericktown, Maryland. Suc-
ceeded by son.*

FLOWER, HENRY   1753
Philadelphia, Pennsylvania.

FRARY, OBADIAH   1745–1775
Southampton, Massachusetts.

FROST, OLIVER   1800
Providence, Rhode Island.

GALBRAITH, PATRICK   1795–1811
Philadelphia, Pennsylvania.

GALT, SAMUEL   1751
Williamsburg, Virginia.

GEDDES, CHARLES   1773
Boston, Massachusetts.

GILL, CALEB   1785
Hingham, Massachusetts.

GODFREY, WILLIAM   1750–1763
Philadelphia, Pennsylvania.

GORDON, THOMAS   1759
Boston, Massachusetts.

HAM, SUPPLY   1850
Portsmouth, New Hampshire.

HANKS, BENJAMIN   1778–1785
Litchfield, Connecticut.

HARLAND, THOMAS   1773–1807
Norwich, Connecticut.

HENDRICK, BARNES & COMPANY   1845
*Forestville, Connecticut. Origi-
nators of the marine clock.*

HENDRICKS, URIAH   1756
New York City.

HERON, ISAAC   1769–1780
New York City.

HILL, JOAKIM   1800
Flemington, New Jersey.

HILLER, JOSEPH   1770
Salem, Massachusetts.

HILLDROP (or HILLDRUP), THOMAS
        1774–1794
Hartford, Connecticut.

HOADLEY, SAMUEL & LUTHER
        1807–1813
Winchester, Connecticut.

HOADLEY, SILAS   1808–1849
Plymouth, Connecticut.

HOTCHKISS, HEZEKIAH 1748
New Haven, Connecticut.

HOWARD, THOMAS 1789–1791
Philadelphia, Pennsylvania.

HUTCHINS, ABEL 1788–1819
Concord, New Hampshire.

INGRAHAM, ELIAS 1835–1885
*Bristol, Connecticut. Founded the
company still manufacturing.*

JEROME, CHAUNCEY 1816–1860
New Haven, Connecticut.

KINCAIRD, THOMAS 1775
Christiana Bridge, Delaware.

KUMBELL, WILLIAM 1775–1789
New York City.

LEACH, CALEB 1776–1790
Plymouth, Massachusetts.

LEAVENWORTH, WILLIAM 1802–1815
Waterbury, Connecticut.

LEAVITT, DR. JOSIAH 1772
Hingham, Massachusetts.

LEE, WILLIAM 1717
Charleston, South Carolina.

LEFFERTS, CHARLES 1819
Philadelphia, Pennsylvania.

LUSCOMB, SAMUEL 1773
Salem, Massachusetts.

MARACHE, SOLOMON 1759
New York City.

MATLACK, WHITE C. 1769–1775
New York City.

MAYNARD, GEORGE 1702–1730
New York City.

MONTGOMERY, ROBERT 1786
New York City.

MORRIS, WILLIAM 1765–1775
Grafton, Massachusetts.

MULLIKEN, SAMUEL 1750–1756
*Newbury, Massachusetts. A pro-
lific family.*

NICHOLS, GEORGE 1728–1750
New York City.

NORTON, SAMUEL 1785
Hingham, Massachusetts.

PARKE, SOLOMON 1791–1819
Philadelphia, Pennsylvania.

PARKER, GARDNER (prior to Revolution)
Westborough, Massachusetts.

PARKER, ISAAC 1780
Deerfield, Massachusetts.

PARMELEE, EBENEZER 1726–1740
Guilford, Connecticut.

PAYNE, LAWRENCE 1732–1755
New York City.

PEARSON, WILLIAM, JR. 1775
New York City.

PECK, MOSES 1789
Boston, Massachusetts.

PERKINS, THOMAS 1785–1799
Philadelphia, Pennsylvania.

PERRY, MARVIN 1769–1780
New York City.

PERRY, THOMAS 1749–1775
New York City.

PHILLIPS, JOSEPH 1713–1735
New York City.

PITMAN, SAUNDERS 1780
Providence, Rhode Island.

PORTER, DANIEL 1799
Williamstown, Massachusetts.

POTTER, EPHRAIM 1775–1790
Concord, New Hampshire.

PRICE, ISAAC 1799
Philadelphia, Pennsylvania.

PROCTOR, CARDAN 1747–1775
New York City.

REED, SIMEON 1770
Cummington, Massachusetts.

RICHARDSON, FRANCIS 1736
Philadelphia, Pennsylvania.

RITTENHOUSE, DAVID
Norristown, Pennsylvania. 1751–1770
Philadelphia, Pennsylvania. 1770–1777

ROBERTS, GIDEON 1780–1804
Bristol, Connecticut.

ROCKWELL, SAMUEL 1750–1754
Providence, Rhode Island.

ROGERS, SAMUEL   1700–1804
  Plymouth, Massachusetts.

RUSSELL, MAJOR JOHN   1765
  Deerfield, Massachusetts.

SADD, THOMAS   1750
  East Windsor, Connecticut.

SANDS, STEPHEN   1772–1786
  New York City.

SANFORD, EATON   1760–1776
  Plymouth, Connecticut.

SAWIN & DYER   1800–1820
  Boston, Massachusetts.

SHEARMAN, ROBERT   1760–1770
  Wilmington, Delaware.

SHIPMAN, NATHANIEL   1789
  Norwich, Connecticut.

SIBLEY, GIBBS   1788
  Canandaigua, New York.

SINNETT, JOHN   1774
  New York City.

SOUERS, CHRISTOPHER   1724
  Philadelphia, Pennsylvania.

STAPLES, JOHN I.   1793
  New York City.

STILLMAN, WILLIAM   1789–1795
  Burlington, Connecticut.

STOWELL, ABEL   1790–1800
  *Worcester, Massachusetts. A pro-
  lific family.*

STRECH, PETER   1750–1780
  Philadelphia, Pennsylvania.

TABER, ELNATHAN   1784–1845
  *Roxbury, Massachusetts. Suc-
  ceeded by his sons.*

TAYLOR, SAMUEL   1799
  Philadelphia, Pennsylvania.

TERRY, ELI   1793–c. 1852
  *Plymouth, Connecticut. A pro-
  lific family, involving in addition
  many partnerships and firm
  names. See text, and other check-
  lists. (Bibl.)*

THOMAS, SETH   1809–1850
  *Plymouth Hollow, Connecticut.
  Founder of company still manu-
  facturing.*

TOWNSEND, CHRISTOPHER   1773
  Newport, Rhode Island.

VINTON, DAVID   1792
  Providence, Rhode Island.

VOGT, JOHN   1758
  New York City.

VOIGHT, HENRY   1775–1793
  Philadelphia, Pennsylvania.

VUILLE, ALEXANDER   1766
  Baltimore, Maryland.

WADY, JAMES   1750–1755
  Newport, Rhode Island.

WARD, ANTHONY   1724–1750
  New York City.

WARD, JOSEPH   1735–1760
  New York City.

WATERBURY CLOCK COMPANY   1855
  Waterbury, Connecticut.

WHITE, PEREGRINE   1774
  Woodstock, Connecticut.

WHITING, RILEY   1807–1835
  Winchester, Connecticut.

WHITTAKER, WILLIAM   1731–1755
  New York City.

WILDER, JOSHUA   1780–1800
  *Hingham, Massachusetts. Suc-
  ceeded by son.*

WILLARD, AARON   1780–1790
  *Roxbury, Massachusetts. Later
  Boston. Succeeded by his son,
  Aaron, Jr.*

WILLARD, BENJAMIN   1764–1803
  *Grafton, Massachusetts. Later,
  Lexington & Roxbury.*

WILLARD, EPHRAIM   1777–1805
  *Medford, Roxbury, and Boston,
  Massachusetts; and New York
  City.*

WILLARD, SIMON 1770–1839
*Grafton, Roxbury, and Boston,
Massachusetts. The Willard
family is made still more numerous by large numbers of children
and collateral branches.*

WILMURT, JOHN J. 1793–1798
New York City.

WOOD, DAVID 1790–1824
Newburyport, Massachusetts.

WOOD, JOHN 1770–1793
Philadelphia, Pennsylvania.

WRIGHT, JOHN 1712–1735
New York City.

YEOMANS, ELIJAH 1771–1783
Hadley, Massachusetts.

YOUNGS, EBENEZER 1778
Hebron, Connecticut.

CHECK-LIST OF COLONIAL IRON FURNACES

This representative but far from complete check-list is largely drawn from the unparalleled resources of Henry C. Mercer's catalogue, *The Bible in Iron* (see Bibliography for this and other references). It naturally cannot hope to include the later, more modern industrial beginnings. It neglects altogether a few scattered furnaces in southern states other than Virginia.

CONNECTICUT
LIME ROCK FURNACE 1740–1750
Litchfield County.

NEW HAVEN FURNACE 1658
New Haven.

DELAWARE
DEEP CREEK FURNACE 1763
Deep Creek, Sussex County.

PINE GROVE FURNACE 1764–c. 1785
Deep Creek, Sussex County.

MAINE
SHAPLEIGH FURNACE (no date)
York County.

MARYLAND
BUSH FURNACE 1760
Harford County.

CATOCTIN FURNACE 1774
Frederick County.

CURTIS CREEK FURNACE 1851
Patapsco County.

ELK RIDGE FURNACE, prior to Revolution
Patapsco River.

GREEN SPRING FURNACE 1770
Washington County.

GUNPOWDER RIVER FURNACE, prior to 1769

GWYNNS FALLS FURNACE 1723–1730

KINGSBURY FURNACE 1744
Herring Run, Baltimore County.

LANCASHIRE FURNACE 1751
Back River, Principio County.

LEGH FURNACE 1760–1765
Westminster.

MOUNT ETNA FURNACE 1770
*Antietam Creek, near Hagers-
town.*

MOUNT ROYAL FURNACE 1723–1730

NORTHAMPTON FURNACE 1760
Baltimore County.

OLD HAMPTON FURNACE 1760–1765
Near Emmetsburg.

PATUXENT FURNACE   1734
  Anne Arundel County.

PRINCIPIO FURNACE   1724–1780
  Principio Creek, Cecil County.

STEMMERS RUN FURNACE   (no date)
  Baltimore.

UNICORN FURNACE   1762
  Queen Anne County.

MASSACHUSETTS

BRAINTREE FURNACE   1646–1653
  Norfolk County, south of Boston.

CHARLOTTE FURNACE   1760–c. 1812
  South Carver.

DESPARDS FURNACE   1702
  *On Mattakeeset Pond Pembroke.
  Abandoned when wood supply
  was exhausted.*

FEDERAL FURNACE   1794
  Plymouth County.

FURNACE VILLAGE FURNACE, prior
  to 1773.
  Furnace Village.

KINGS FURNACE   c. 1724–1840
  *On Little North Brook, Taun-
  ton. Users of bog iron.*

LENOX FURNACE   1765–1881
  Berkshire County.

LYNN FURNACE   1645–1688
  *On Saugus River bank at Saugus
  Center.*

PLYMPTON (or CARVER) FURNACE 1730
  *Carver. Said to have made the
  first cast iron tea kettles in
  America.*

POPES POINT FURNACE   1733
  South Carver.

NEW HAMPSHIRE

FURNACE VILLAGE FURNACE   1795
  Exeter.

NEW JERSEY

ANDOVER FURNACE   c. 1760
  Andover.

ATSION FURNACE   1766
  Atsion Branch, Mullica River.

BATSTO FURNACE   1766–1846
  Batsto Branch, Mullica River.

BERGEN FURNACE   (no date)
  Monmouth County.

BLOOMINGDALE FURNACE   1765
  Passaic County.

CHARLOTTENBURG FURNACE   1767–1776
  West Branch, Pequannock Creek.

FRANKLIN FURNACE   1770
  Franklin.

HIBERNIA (or ADVENTURE) FUR-
  NACE   1765
  Pequannock Township.

LONG POND FURNACE   1768
  Greenwood Lake.

MOUNT HOLLY (or HANOVER)
  FURNACE   1730–1776
  Destroyed, possibly in Revolution.

MOUNT HOPE FURNACE   1772–1825
  Mount Hope.

OXFORD FURNACE   1742–1882
  Warren City.

POMPTON FURNACE   1768
  Pompton.

RINGWOOD (or OGDEN'S) FUR-
  NACE   1740–1776
  Greenwood Lake.

SHREWSBURY (or TINTON FALLS)
  FURNACE   1682
  Tinton Falls.

TAUNTON FURNACE   1766–1773
  Evesham Township.

UNION FURNACE   1750–1778
  *Hunterdon County. Abandoned
  during Revolution.*

NEW YORK

ANCRAM FURNACE   1750–1837
  *On Ancram Creek, east of the
  Hudson River.*

AMENIA FURNACE & FOUNDRY.
  Revolutionary period.
  Dutchess County.

COURTLAND MANOR FURNACES,
   prior to 1756.

CRAIGSVILLE FURNACE. Revolutionary period.

FOREST OF DEAN FURNACE 1756–1777
   Ramapo Creek, Orange County.

HAVERSTRAW FURNACE. Revolutionary period.
   Haverstraw.

PHILIPSBURG FURNACE   (no date)
   Westchester County.

QUEENSBOROUGH FURNACE c. 1770–1800
   Six miles south of West Point.

STERLING IRON WORKS (or WARD
   AND COULTON'S FURNACE)   1751
   Sterling Pond, Orange County.
   Makers of the great West Point
   Chain, under Ironmaster Peter
   Townsend.

PENNSYLVANIA

ABINGTON FURNACE   1727–1768
   On Christiana Creek, Delaware,
   formerly Pennsylvania.

CARLISLE FURNACE   1762
   Boiling Springs, Cumberland
   County.

CHRISTINE FURNACE (later RED-
   DING FURNACE)   c. 1720–1783
   French Creek, Chester County.

CODORUS (or HELLAM) FURNACE
                            1765–1850
   Codorus Creek, Hellam Town-
   ship, York County.

COLEBROOKDALE FURNACE 1720–c. 1793
   West of Pottstown, Berks County.

CORNWALL FURNACE, 1742, still
   existing up to 1914.
   Furnace Creek, Lebanon County.

DALE FURNACE   1791–1821
   West Branch, Perkiomen Creek,
   Berks County.

DISTRICT (or GERMAN) FURNACE
                         c. 1784–1797
   District Township, Berks County.

DURHAM FURNACE   1727–1897
   Durham Township, Bucks County.

ELIZABETH FURNACE   1750–1856
   Brickerville, Lancaster County.
   Jacob Huber and Baron Stiegel.

GREENWOOD FURNACE   1796
   Schuylkill Gap, Sharp Mountain,
   Schuylkill County.

HEREFORD FURNACE   1753
   Hereford Township, Berks County.

HOLLY FURNACE   1770
   Mount Holly Springs, Cumber-
   land County.

HOPEWELL FURNACE   c. 1759–1890
   Union Township, Berks County.

JOANNA FURNACE   1792
   Hay Creek, Robeson Township,
   Berks County.

KEITH'S FURNACE   1725–1728
   Christiana Creek, in what is now
   the State of Delaware, then part
   of Pennsylvania.

KURTZ'S FURNACE   c. 1726
   Lancaster County.

MARTIC FURNACE   1751–c. 1793
   Colemansville, Lancaster County.

MARY ANN FURNACE   c. 1761–1800
   Furnace Creek, West Manheim
   Township, York County.

MARY ANN NO. 2   c. 1789–1869
   Eight miles west of Trexlertown,
   Longswamp Township, Berks
   County.

MOUNT HOPE FURNACE   1786–1876
   Big Chickies Creek, Lancaster
   County.

MOUNT PLEASANT FURNACE   1738
   West Branch, Perkiomen Creek,
   Berks County.

MOUNT PLEASANT FURNACE
   No. 2.   1783
   Franklin County.

OLEY FURNACE   c. 1772–1884
Oley Township, Berks County.

PINE GROVE FURNACE   1770–1870
Mountain Creek Branch of Yellow Breeches Creek, Cumberland County.

POPADICKON (or POTTS GROVE)
FURNACE   c. 1745–1769
Pottstown.

ROXBOROUGH (or BERKSHIRE)
FURNACE   1755–1792
Heidelberg Township, Berks County. Later renamed Reading Furnace, still later Robesonia Furnace. Active until at least 1913.

SHEARWELL FURNACE   c. 1774–1783
Furnace Creek, Oley Township, Berks County.

WARWICK FURNACE   1738–1867
French Creek, Chester County.

WINDSOR FURNACE   (no date)
Conestoga Creek, Caernarvon Township, Lancaster County.

RHODE ISLAND

HOPE FURNACE   1735
North Branch, Pawtuxent River.

THREE FURNACES   1735
Cumberland Township.

VERMONT

THREE FURNACES   1794
Rutland County.

VIRGINIA

ACCOKEEK FURNACE (or ENGLAND'S IRON MINES FURNACE)
                    1750–1753
Twelve miles from Fredericksburg. Mercer calls this one of the most important Colonial furnaces and records that, in 1750, it shipped 410 tons of pig iron to England.

FREDERICKSVILLE FURNACE   1727
Spottsylvania County.

GERMANNA FURNACE   c. 1727
Spottsylvania County.

ISABELLA FURNACE   1760–1841
Page County.

MASSAPONAX FURNACE   1732
On Rappahannock, below Fredericksburg.

MOSSY CREEK FURNACE   1760–1841
Augusta County.

OLD DAVY ROSS FURNACE, prior to 1781.
Beaver Creek, near Lynchburg.

OLDS FURNACE   1777
Near Charlottesville.

POPLAR CAMP FURNACE   1778
Wythe County.

RAPPAHANNOCK FURNACE   c. 1732
Above Fredericksburg.

WESTHAM FURNACE   c. 1776–1781
James River, above Richmond.

ZANES FURNACE, prior to Revolution.
Frederick County.

CHECK-LIST OF AMERICAN POTTERS

This check-list does not pretend to be exhaustive. It constitutes a representative sampling of early American potters. It has been brought forward only as far as 1830, with a few exceptions, thus omitting the vast field of commercial pottery manufacture continuing from this date. Nor does the list include western Pennsylvania or the South, by far the bulk of whose potters are mid-, or late 19th century. For further reference see Bibliography. Note especially, for a far-reaching check-list, *American Potters and Pottery*, by John Ramsay. (Bibl.).

CONNECTICUT

BREWSTER AND SLEIGHT   c. 1810–1818
  Hartford. Successors to Peter Cross.

BROOKS, HERVEY C.   1753
  Litchfield.

CROSS, PETER   c. 1805–1808
  Hartford.

FISHER, J. C.   c. 1805–1812
  Hartford.

GOODALE, DANIEL   1818–1830
  Hartford.

GOODWIN, HORACE   1800–1810
  Hartford.

GOODWIN, SETH   c. 1795–1828
  Hartford. Brother of Horace. Succeeded by son.

HANFORD, ISAAC   c. 1796–1800
  Hartford.

HARRINGTON, T.   c. 1825
  Hartford.

LEFFINGWELL,   CHRISTOPHER
  (BEAN HILL POTTERY) c. 1779–1792
  Norwich. Succeeded by son-in-law, Charles Lothrop, 1792–1796; succeeded in turn by C. Potts & Son, 1796–1816.

MEADE, "DEACON" ABRAHAM 1760–1791
  Greenwich.

PIERCE, JOHN   c. 1753
  Litchfield.

SEYMOUR, NATHANIEL   1790–1825
  Hartford. Succeeded by son.

SMITH, ASA   c. 1780–1830
  Norwalk.

SOUTER, JOHN   1790–1805
  Hartford.

TRACY, ANDREW   c. 1790–1798
  Norwich. Three successors, Joseph Hosmer, William Cleveland, and Armstrong & Wentworth, to 1834.

WADHAM, JESSE   c. 1753
  Litchfield.

MAINE

PORTER, BENJAMIN   c. 1790–1805
  Wiscassett. Succeeded by son.

SMITH, HEZEKIAH   1782–1797
  Gorham.

MARYLAND

ADAMS, HENRY   c. 1812
  Hagerstown.

AUER (or AYER), NICOLAS   c. 1796
  Baltimore.

BAKER, THOMAS ("POT HOUSE") c. 1750
  St. Mary's.

BELL, PETER   1813–1825
  Hagerstown. Later, Winchester, Va.

BROWN, JAMES   1799–1807
  Baltimore.

BROWN, JOHN   c. 1796
  Baltimore.

FLOYD, CALEB   1799–1807
  Fells Point (Baltimore).

HUGHES,   DANIEL & WILLIAM
  RUSSEL   c. 1780
  Elk Ridge Landing.

JOHNSON & MASON   c. 1803
  Baltimore.

JONES, N. S.   1824–1832
  Baltimore.

KELLY, JOHN   1796–1807
  Old Town, Baltimore.

LEISINGER & BELL   1800–1813
Hagerstown.

MORGAN, THOMAS   1800–1837
Baltimore.

NEFF, CHRISTIAN   c. 1790–1810
Cumberland.

PARR, DAVID   1819–1829
Baltimore. Developed into a company active for years.

PERRINE, MAULDEN   c. 1796
Old Town, Baltimore. The beginning of a line, and firm of potters active at least until 1900.

REICHARD, DANIEL   c. 1813
Hagerstown.

SNAVELY, JOHN   c. 1813
Hagerstown.

WALLACE, RICHARD   1796–1803
Baltimore.

MASSACHUSETTS

BAILEY, JOSEPH   c. 1734–1760
Newbury. Succeeded by sons.

BOSTON PORCELAIN & GLASS MANU-
FACTURING COMPANY   1787–1788
Cambridge.

CLARK, PETER   c. 1745–1774
Braintree.

CRAFTS, THOMAS   c. 1802–1820
Whateley. Succeeded by son.

GOLDTHWAITE, WILLIAM   c. 1763–1808
Peabody.

HEWS, ABRAHAM   1765–1810
Weston. Succeeded by two generations.

KENDALL, MILES   c. 1740
Peabody.

KETTLE, JONATHAN   c. 1730
Peabody.

MORRISON, EBENEZER   c. 1750–1813
Newburyport.

ORCUTT, STEPHEN   c. 1777–1800
Whateley.

OSBORNE, JOSEPH   c. 1759–1800
Peabody. Succeeded by several generations.

PRIDE, JOHN   c. 1641
Salem.

SOUTHWICK, LAWRENCE   1639
Peabody. See also under "Glass."

SOUTHWICK, WILLIAM   c. 1735–1759
Peabody. Succeeded by two generations.

STONE, ROBERT   c. 1780–1811
Peabody.

SYMONDS, NATHANIEL   c. 1740–1790
Salem. Succeeded by two generations.

TARBELL, WILLIAM   c. 1790–1816
Beverley. Succeeded by son of same name, 1816–1819.

TRASK, JOSEPH   c. 1790–1813
Peabody.

VINSON, WILLIAM   c. 1641
Salem.

WHITTEMORE, JOSEPH   c. 1750
Peabody. Succeeded by son.

WILSON, JOB   c. 1780–1791
Peabody. Succeeded by son.

NEW HAMPSHIRE

BURPEE, JEREMIAH   c. 1804–1835
Boscawen.

CLARK, PETER   c. 1775–1826
Lyndeboro. Succeeded by two generations.

DODGE, JABESH   1800–1806
Exeter. Succeeded by three generations.

HUTCHINSON, EBENEZER   c. 1815
Lyndeboro.

NEW JERSEY

COXE, DANIEL   c. 1684–1691
Burlington.

JERSEY CITY PORCELAIN &
EARTHENWARE COMPANY   1825–1828
Jersey City.

PRICE, XERXES   c. 1802
Sayreville (or Roundabout).

VAN WINCKLE (or WINKLE), ———   1800
Old Bridge.

WARNE & LETTS   c. 1778–1820
South Amboy.

NEW YORK

BENSING, DIRICK   c. 1698
N. Y. C.

BENSON (possibly BENSING), HENRY   c. 1732
N. Y. C.

CAMPBELL, THOMAS   c. 1769
N. Y. C.

CLAESEN, DIRICK   c. 1675
N. Y. C.

COMMERAW, THOMAS   c. 1800
Corlear's Hook, N. Y. C.

CORSELIUS POTTERY   c. 1782
N. Y. C. See text on Remmey and Crolius.

CROLIUS, WILLIAM & PETER   1732–1762
N. Y. C. Succeeded by three generations. Clarkson Crolius, c. 1790–1830, most notable.

CROYLAS (possibly CROLIUS), WILLIAM   1698
N. Y. C.

CUSHMAN, PAUL   1805–1825
Albany.

DURRELL, JONATHAN   1753–1774
N. Y. C.

EUTATSE, JOHN   c. 1728
N. Y. C.

KEELER, BENJAMIN   1825–1827
Huntington. Successor to Moses Scudder. Followed in turn by three other successors.

MEAD, DR.   c. 1816–1819
N. Y. C.

MORGAN, D.   c. 1806
N. Y. C.

REMMEY, JOHN   1735–1762
N. Y. C. Succeeded by two generations.

SCUDDER, MOSES   c. 1810–1825
Huntington. Successor to Wetmore & Company.

SEYMOUR, ISRAEL   1806–1810
Albany. Later, Troy.

STATES, ADAM   c. 1751–1774
Huntington. Later, Connecticut.

TITUS, JONATHAN   c. 1784–1805
Huntington. Successor to Adam States.

WETMORE, SAMUEL J. & COMPANY   c. 1805–1810
Huntington. Successor to Jonathan Titus.

WILSON, ———   c. 1782
N. Y. C.

PENNSYLVANIA

ALBERT, HENRY   c. 1816–1825
Allentown, Lehigh County.

BELL, JOHN   1826–1830
Chambersburg, Franklin County.

BINNEY & RONALDSON   c. 1809
Philadelphia.

BONNIN, GOUSSIN & GEORGE A. MORRIS   1769–1771
Philadelphia.

BRICHDEL, CHRISTIAN   c. 1767
Tulpehocken Township, Berks County.

CURTIS, JOHN   1790–1811
Philadelphia.

DRACH, RUDOLPH   c. 1780–1800
Bedminster, Bucks County.

DUCHE, ANTHONY   1700–1762
Philadelphia.

FREYTAG, DANIEL   c. 1810–1830
Philadelphia.

FRY, JOHN   1768–1784
Reading, Berks County.

GILBERT, MORDECAI c. 1788
Philadelphia.

GREEN, BRANCH c. 1820
Philadelphia.

GROFF, JOSEPH c. 1815–1832
Franconia, Montgomery County.

HAIG, THOMAS 1812–1833
Philadelphia.

HEADMAN, ANDREW c. 1806–1840
Rock Hill, Bucks County. Succeeded by son.

HEADMAN, JOHN 1800–1830
Rock Hill, Bucks County. Brother of Andrew. Succeeded by two generations.

HERSTINE, CORNELIUS c. 1785–1810
Nockamixon, Bucks County. Succeeded by three more generations of Herstines, active until 1910.

HERRING (or HARRING), JOHN
c. 1818–1826
Nockamixon, Bucks County. Succeeded by son.

HORN, SAMUEL c. 1825–1835
Allentown, Lehigh County.

HUEBNER, GEORGE 1783–1798
Vincent, Chester County.

HUMSICKER, CHRISTIAN c. 1800
Hamlin, Lebanon County.

KINTNER, JACOB c. 1780–1840
Nockamixon, Bucks County.

KLINE, PHILLIP c. 1808
Carversville, Bucks County.

KLINKER, CHRISTIAN 1772
Bucksville, Bucks County.

KLOSTER OF THE UNITED BRETHREN c. 1750–1800
Ephrata, Lancaster County.

KRAUS, JOHN c. 1800
Krausdale, Lehigh County.

KRIMLER, HENRY c. 1767
Reading, Berks County.

KUCH, CONRAD 1767–1784
Reading, Berks County.

LEAMAN, GODFREY c. 1780
Reading, Berks County.

LEIDY, JOHN c. 1796–1815
Franconia, Montgomery County.

MELCHER, ———— c. 1790–1804
Dryville, Berks County. Succeeded by the family Dry, 1804.

MILLER, ANDREW 1785–1810
Philadelphia.

MULLOWNEY, "CAPTAIN" (WASHINGTON POTTERY) 1810–1817
Philadelphia.

MUMBAUER, CONRAD c. 1800
Haycock Township, Montgomery County.

NESSZ (or NEESZ), JOHANNES
1798–1829
Tylersport, Montgomery County. Succeeded by son, with name changed to "Nase."

PIERCEY, CHRISTIAN c. 1788–1794
Philadelphia.

RENNINGER, WENDELL c. 1800–1815
Gerysville, Bucks County.

RIEFF, CHRISTIAN c. 1767
Rockland Township, Berks County.

ROUDEBUTH, HENRY c. 1810–1820
Montgomery County.

SCHOLL (or SHOLL), MICHAEL
1818–1826
Tylersport, Montgomery County.

SCHULTZ, JOHANN THEOBALD c. 1790
Newmanstown, Lebanon County.

SEIXAS, DAVID G. 1816–1822
Philadelphia.

SMITH, JOSEPH 1763–1800
Wrightstown, Berks County.

SPINNER, DAVID 1800–1811
Willow Creek, Melford, Bucks County.

STOFFLET, HEINRICH c. 1814–1830
Rockland Township, Berks County. Succeeded by son.

STOUT, ABRAHAM   1760
  Gardenville, Bucks County.

STOUT, ISAAC   c. 1795–1810
  *Gardenville, Bucks County. Son
  of Abraham.*

STRADLEY, WILLIAM   c. 1785
  Philadelphia.

SWOPE, JACOB   c. 1820
  Bird-in-Hand, Lancaster County.

TAWNEY, JACOB   c. 1794
  Nockamixon, Bucks County.

TROTTER, ALEXANDER (COLUM-
  BIAN POTTERY)   1810–1812
  Philadelphia.

TROXELL, SAMUEL   1823–1835
  *Upper Hanover, Montgomery
  County.*

TUCKER, WILLIAM ELLIS (AMER-
  ICAN CHINA MANUFACTORY)
                         1826–1828
  Philadelphia.

VICKERS, JOHN & THOMAS   1740–1750
  Caln, Chester County.

VICKERS, THOMAS & SONS   c. 1809
  Downingtown, Chester County.

WARDER, JEREMIAH   c. 1780–1784
  Philadelphia.

RHODE ISLAND

WILSON, JAMES   c. 1767
  Providence.

VERMONT

BAILEY, CHARLES   c. 1800
  Hardwick.

FENTON, CHRISTOPHER WEBBER
                         1847–1849
  *Bennington. Worked as Lyman &
  Fenton, beginning 1849. Began
  as United States Pottery in 1852.*

FENTON, JACOB   c. 1801–1820
  Burlington.

FENTON, JONATHAN   1801–1834
  *Dorset. Other Fentons, including
  sons of Christopher Webber, were
  active in Vermont.*

JUDD, NORMAN L.   1806–1809
  Burlington. Later, Rome, N. Y.

NORTON, CAPTAIN JOHN   1793–1823
  *Bennington. Succeeded by a line
  of Nortons. Fenton and the
  United States Pottery may be
  regarded as an offshoot.*

UNITED STATES POTTERY (See
  Fenton, C. W.)

WOODMAN, SAMUEL   1800–1820
  Poultney.

REPRESENTATIVE CHECK-LIST OF EARLY AMERICAN
SILVERSMITHS

For a complete check-list and catalogue of marks, see *The Book of Old
Silver,* by Seymour B. Wyler, and other titles listed in Bibliography.

ADAMS, JONATHAN   1785
  Philadelphia, Pennsylvania.

ADAMS, PYGAN   1712–1776
  New London, Connecticut.

ALLEN, CHARLES   1760
  Boston, Massachusetts.

ALLEN, JAMES   1720
  Philadelphia, Pennsylvania.

ALLEN, JOHN   1691–1760
  Boston, Massachusetts.

ALLISON, PETER   1791
  New York City.

ALSTYNE, JERONIMUS   1787
  New York City.

ANDREW, JOHN   1747–1791
  Salem, Massachusetts.

ANDREWS, JEREMIAH   1776
  Philadelphia, Pennsylvania.

ANTHONY, ISAAC   1690–1773
  Newport, Rhode Island, and
  Swansea, Massachusetts.

ARMSTRONG, WILLIAM   1750
  Philadelphia, Pennsylvania.

ARNOLD, THOMAS   1739–1828
  Newport, Rhode Island.

AUSTIN, BENJAMIN   1775
  Portsmouth, New Hampshire.

AUSTIN, JOSEPH   1740
  Hartford, Connecticut.

AUSTIN, JOSIAH   1718–1780
  Charlestown, Massachusetts.

AVERY, JOHN   1732–1794
  Preston, Connecticut.

BAILEY, HENRY   1780
  Boston, Massachusetts.

BAILEY, JOHN   1762
  New York City.

BAILEY, LORING   1780
  Hingham, Massachusetts.

BALCH, EBENEZER   1744
  Hartford, Connecticut.

BALDWIN, EBENEZER   1723–1808
  Hartford, Connecticut.

BALDWIN, JEDEDIAH   1793
  Portsmouth, New Hampshire.

BALL, JOHN   1765
  Boston, Massachusetts.

BALL, WILLIAM   1752
  Philadelphia, Pennsylvania.

BANCKER, ADRIEN   1703–1772
  New York City.

BARNES, ABRAHAM   1716
  Boston, Massachusetts.

BARRET, JAMES   1717
  Norwich, Connecticut.

BARTLETT, NATHANIEL   1760
  Concord, Massachusetts.

BASSETT, FRANCIS   1774
  New York City.

BELKNAP, SAMUEL   1789
  Boston, Massachusetts.

BENTON, BENJAMIN   1659–1749
  Newport, Rhode Island.

BOELEN, HENRICUS   1684–1755
  New York City.

BOELEN, JACOB   1773
  New York City.

BOELEN, JAMES   1659–1729
  New York City.

BOGARDUS, EVERARDUS   1698
  New York City.

BOGERT, NICHOLAS J.   1801
  New York City.

BREVOORT, JOHN   1715–1775
  New York City.

BROADHURST, SAMUEL   1724
  New York City.

BUEL, ABEL   1742–1825
  New Haven, Connecticut.

BURNAP, DANIEL   1791
  East Windsor, Connecticut.

CARLISLE, ABRAHAM   1791
  Philadelphia, Pennsylvania.

CARMAN, JOHN   1771
  Philadelphia, Pennsylvania.

CARPENTER, CHARLES   1807
  Norwich, Connecticut.

CASEY, GIDEON   1753
  South Kingston, Rhode Island.

CASEY, GIDEON   1726–1786
  Providence, Rhode Island.

CASEY, SAMUEL   1724–1773
  South Kingston, Rhode Island.

CHALMERS, JAMES   1749
  Annapolis, Maryland.

CHALMERS, JOHN   1770
  Annapolis, Maryland.

CHITTENDEN, BERIAH   1787
  New Haven, Connecticut.

CHITTENDEN, EBENEZER *New Haven, Connecticut.*	1726–1812	FARRINGTON & HUNNEWELL *Boston, Massachusetts.*	1830
CODDINGTON, JOHN *Newport, Rhode Island.*	1690–1743	FELLOWS, ABRAHAM *Newport, Rhode Island.*	1826
COGSWELL, H. *Boston, Massachusetts.*	1760	FERRIER, JOHN *New Orleans, Louisiana.*	1802
CONEY, JOHN *Boston, Massachusetts.*	1655–1722	FIELDING, GEORGE *New York City.*	1731
COOPER, JOSEPH *New York City.*	1770	FORBES, ABRAHAM G. *New York City.*	1769
CORNELISON, CORNELIUS *New York City.*	1711	FOSTER, SAMUEL *Boston, Massachusetts.*	1676–1702
CROSBY, JONATHAN *Boston, Massachusetts.*	1743–1769	GARDINER, JOHN *New London, Connecticut.*	1734–1776
DAGGETT, HENRY *New Haven, Connecticut.*	1763	GARDINER, JOIIN J. *Boston, Massachusetts.*	1730–1776
DAVENPORT, SAMUEL *Milton, Massachusetts.*	1741	GAY, CHARLES *Baltimore, Maryland.*	1779
DAVIS, SAMUEL *Providence, Rhode Island.*	1801	GAY, NATHANIEL *Boston, Massachusetts.*	1664
DE SPIEGEL, JACOBUS VAN *New York City.*	1668–1703	GETTY, JAMES *Williamsburg, Virginia.*	1772
DUMMER, JEREMIAH *Boston, Massachusetts.*	1645–1718	GHISELIN, CESAR *Philadelphia, Pennsylvania.*	1695
DUPUY, DANIEL *Philadelphia, Pennsylvania.*	1719–1807	GHISELIN, WILLIAM *Philadelphia, Pennsylvania.*	1751
DUYCKINCK, DANIEL *New York City.*	1798	GILBERT, SAMUEL *Hebron, Connecticut.*	1798
DWIGHT, TIMOTHY *Boston, Massachusetts.*	1645–1691	GLIDDEN, JOSEPH *Boston, Massachusetts.*	1607–1780
EDWARDS, ABRAHAM *Ashby, Massachusetts.*	1763	GOELET, PHILIP *New York City.*	1731
EDWARDS, CALVIN *Ashby, Massachusetts.*	1710	GOODWIN, BENJAMIN *Boston, Massachusetts.*	1756
EDWARDS, JOHN *Boston, Massachusetts.*	1700	GORHAM, JABEZ *Providence, Rhode Island.*	1792
ELLIOT, JOSEPH *New Castle, Delaware.*	1768	GRAY, JOHN *New London, Connecticut.*	1692–1720
EMERY, STEPHEN *Boston, Massachusetts.*	1725–1801	HANCOCK, JOHN *Boston, Massachusetts.*	1732–1772
FAIRCHILD, CAPTAIN ROBERT *Durham, Connecticut.*	1703–1794	HARLAND, THOMAS *Norwich, Connecticut.*	1735–1807
FARIS, WILLIAM *Annapolis, Maryland.*	1728–1804	HAYS & MYERS *New York City.*	1770

HENDRICKS, AHASUERUS   1676
  New York City.

HEWS, ABRAHAM, JR.   1823
  Boston, Massachusetts.

HEWSON, JOHN D.   1815
  Albany, New York.

HOTCHKISS, HEZEKIAH   1754
  New Haven, Connecticut.

HOUGH, SAMUEL   1675–1717
  Boston, Massachusetts.

HULL, JOHN   1624–1683
  Boston, Massachusetts.

HULL & SANDERSON   1652
  Boston, Massachusetts.

HURD, BENJAMIN   1739–1781
  Boston, Massachusetts.

HURD, NATHANIEL   1730–1777
  Boston, Massachusetts.

JANVIER, LOUIS   1744
  Charleston, South Carolina.

JARVIS, MUNSON   1742–1824
  Stamford, Connecticut.

JESSE, DAVID   1670–1705
  Boston, Massachusetts.

JOHNSON, SAMUEL   1780
  New York City.

KIERSTEDE, CORNELIUS   1753
  New York City.

KIP, BENJAMIN   1702
  New York City.

KRIDER, PETER L.   1850
  Philadelphia, Pennsylvania.

LAMAR, BENJAMIN   1785
  Philadelphia, Pennsylvania.

LEACOCK, JOHN   1751
  Philadelphia, Pennsylvania.

LE ROUX, BARTHOLOMEW   1700
  New York City.

LE ROUX, CHARLES   1689–1745
  New York City.

LORING, HENRY   1773–1818
  Boston, Massachusetts.

LORING, JOSEPH   1743–1815
  Boston, Massachusetts.

MANSFIELD, JOHN   1634
  Boston, Massachusetts.

MARTIN, PETER   1756
  New York City.

MINOTT, SAMUEL   1732–1803
  Boston, Massachusetts.

MYERS, MYER   1723–1795
  New York City.

NEWKIRKE, JOHN VAN   1716
  New York City.

NORTON, ANDREW   1787
  Goshen, Connecticut.

NORTON, SAMUEL   1795
  Hingham, Massachusetts.

NOYES, JOHN   1695
  Boston, Massachusetts.

NOYES, JOSEPH   1719
  Philadelphia, Pennsylvania.

NUTTALL, JOSEPH   1778
  Maryland.

NYS, JOHANNIS   1695
  Philadelphia, Pennsylvania.

OTIS, JOHN   1703
  Barnstable, Massachusetts.

OTIS, JONATHAN   1723–1791
  Newport, Rhode Island.

PARKER, DANIEL   1726–1785
  Boston, Massachusetts.

PEARSE, SAMUEL   1783
  New York City.

PERKINS, ISAAC   1707
  Charlestown, Massachusetts.

PERKINS, JOSEPH   1770
  Little Rest, Rhode Island.

PHILLIPS, SAMUEL   1680
  Salem, Massachusetts.

PITMAN, BENJAMIN   1810
  Providence, Rhode Island.

PRICE, BENJAMIN   1767
  Boston, Massachusetts.

QUINCY, DANIEL   1651
  Braintree, Massachusetts.

QUINTARD, PETER   1731
New York City.
Norwalk, Connecticut, 1737.

REVERE, PAUL, SR.   1702–1754
Boston, Massachusetts.

REVERE, PAUL   1735–1818
Boston, Massachusetts.

REVERE, PAUL, 3RD   1795
Boston, Massachusetts.

RICHARDSON, JOSEPH   1711–1784
Philadelphia, Pennsylvania.

ROGERS, DANIEL   1753–1792
Newport, Rhode Island.

ROOSEVELT, NICHOLAS   1745–1769
New York City.

SANDERSON, BENJAMIN   1649–1678
Boston, Massachusetts.

SANDERSON, ROBERT   1693
Boston, Massachusetts.

SAYRE, JOEL   1778–1818
New York City.

SCHAATS, BARTHOLOMEW   1683–1758
New York City.

STEDMAN, ALEXANDER   1793
Philadelphia, Pennsylvania.

STEELE, JOHN   1710
Annapolis, Maryland.

STICKNEY, JONATHAN, JR.   1798
Newburyport, Massachusetts.

STILES, BENJAMIN   1831
Woodbury, Connecticut.

STOUT, SAMUEL   1779
Princeton, New Jersey.

STOW, JOHN   1772
Wilmington, Delaware.

SYNG, PHILIP   1676–1739
Philadelphia, Pennsylvania.

TANNER, JOHN   1740
Newport, Rhode Island.

TAYLOR, THOMAS   1727
Providence, Rhode Island.

TEN EYCK, JACOB   1704–1793
Albany, New York.

TEN EYCK, KOENRAT   1678–1753
New York City.

TROTT, THOMAS   1761–1777
Boston, Massachusetts.

VAN DYKE, PETER   1684–1750
New York City.

VERNON, SAMUEL   1683–1735
Newport, Rhode Island.

VOORHIS, DANIEL VAN   1769
New York City.

WAGSTAFF, THOMAS   1837
Philadelphia, Pennsylvania.

WAITE, JOHN   1770
Kingston, Rhode Island.

WAITE, WILLIAM   1760
Kingston, Rhode Island.

WALKER, WILLIAM   1793
Philadelphia, Pennsylvania.

WARD, TIMOTHY   1776
Middletown, Connecticut.

WARNER, JOSEPH   1768
Wilmington, Delaware.

WATERS, SAMUEL   1790
Philadelphia, Pennsylvania.

WEST, BENJAMIN   1770
Boston, Massachusetts.

WILMOT, SAMUEL   1777–1846
New Haven, Connecticut.

WINSLOW, EDWARD   1669–1753
Boston, Massachusetts.

WISHART, HUGH   1784
New York City.

WYNKOOP, BENJAMIN   1675–1751
New York City.

WYNKOOP, CORNELIUS   1724
New York City.

WYNKOOP, JACOBUS   1765
New York City.

CHECK-LIST OF AMERICAN PEWTERERS

This is a broadly representative list. For minutely detailed lists and further specialized data, see J. B. Kerfoot's authoritative and comprehensive *American Pewter*, and other titles in the Bibliography.

AUSTIN, NATHANIEL   1800
Boston, Massachusetts.

BABBITT, CROSSMAN & COMPANY   c. 1824
Taunton, Massachusetts.

BADGER, THOMAS   1789
Boston, Massachusetts.

BASSETT, FRANCIS   1786
New York City.

BASSETT, FREDERICK   1787
New York City.

BOARDMAN, HENRY S.   1845
Philadelphia, Pennsylvania.

BOARDMAN & HALL   1844
Philadelphia, Pennsylvania.
Boardman is a prolific name in
American pewter.

BOYLE, ROBERT   c. 1750
New York City.

BRADFORD, WILLIAM   c. 1770
New York City.

BUMPSTEED, THOMAS   1654
Boston, Massachusetts.

COMER, JOHN   1678
Boston, Massachusetts.

CROSSMAN, WEST & LEONARD   c. 1824
Taunton, Massachusetts.

CURTIS & COMPANY   1868
New York City.

DANFORTH, J.   c. 1825
Middletown, Connecticut.

DANFORTH, SAMUEL   c. 1810
Hartford, Connecticut.

DANFORTH, THOMAS   c. 1770
Norwich, Connecticut, and Taun-
ton, Massachusetts.

EDGELL, SIMON   1718
Philadelphia, Pennsylvania.

ENDICOTT & SUMNER   1846–1851
New York City.

EVERETT, JAMES   1717
Philadelphia, Pennsylvania.

GANTY (or GEANTY), LEWIS   c. 1830
Baltimore, Maryland.

GLEASON, ROSWELL   c. 1830
Dorchester, Massachusetts.

GRAME, SAMUEL   16—
Boston, Massachusetts.

GRAVES, RICHARD   1635–1669
Salem, Massachusetts.

GREEN, SAMUEL   1798–1810
Boston, Massachusetts.

GREEN, THOMAS   1789
Boston, Massachusetts.

HAMLIN, SAMUEL   c. 1825
Providence, Rhode Island.

HERA, CHRISTIAN & JOHN   1801
Philadelphia, Pennsylvania.

HOLDEN, JOHN   1743
New York City.

HORSEWELL, WILLIAM   1708
New York City.

JAGGER, DANIEL H.   1844
Hartford, Connecticut.

JAGGER, JAMES H.   1843
Hartford, Connecticut.

JAGGER, WALTER W.   1839
Hartford, Connecticut.

JONES, GERSHOM   (uncertain)
Providence, Rhode Island.

KILBOURNE & PORTER   1816
Baltimore, Maryland.

KIRBY, WILLIAM   1786–1793
New York City.

LEDDEL, JAMES   c. 1780
  New York City.

LEE, RICHARD   c. 1780
  Taunton, Massachusetts.

LOCKE & CARTER   1837–1845
  New York City.

LONGSTREET, BARTHOLOMEW   c. 1810
  Bucks County, Pennsylvania.

McEWEN, MALCOLM & DUNCAN   1793
  New York City.

MANNING, THADDEUS   1849
  Middletown, Connecticut.

METZGER, JOSHUA   c. 1810
  Germantown, Philadelphia.

MICHEL, ANDRÉ   1795–1797
  New York City.

MOREY & OBER   1834–1852
  Boston, Massachusetts.

PALETHORP, ROBERT, JR.   1817–1822
  Philadelphia, Pennsylvania.

PEARSE, ROBERT   1792
  New York City.

PORTER, EDMUND   c. 1800
  Taunton, Massachusetts.

PORTER, JAMES   1803
  Baltimore, Maryland.

REVERE, PAUL   1735–1818
  Boston, Massachusetts.

SHRIMPTON, HENRY   1665
  Boston, Massachusetts.

SIMPSON & BENHAM   c. 1850
  New York City.

SKINNER, JOHN   1789
  Boston, Massachusetts.

TRASK, ISRAEL   1825–1842
  Beverley, Massachusetts.

WILL, HENRY   1793
  New York City.

WILL, WILLIAM   c. 1778
  Philadelphia, Pennsylvania.

WOODBURY, J. B.   1837–1838
  Philadelphia, Pennsylvania.

YALE, CHARLES   1832
  New York City.

YALE & CURTIS   1838–1867
  New York City.

YOULE, GEORGE & COMPANY   1829
  New York City.

YOULE, THOMAS   1813–1820
  *New York City. Succeeded by
  his widow, 1821.*

CHECK-LIST OF EARLY AMERICAN GUNSMITHS

This selected list of early American gunsmiths owes a particular debt to the research of Captain John Grace Wolfe Dillin, and his splendid book *The Kentucky Rifle* (or "Pennsylvania Rifle"). For further reference, see Bibliography, with particular reference to two items cited from the Papers of the Lancaster County (Pennsylvania) Historical Society: *The Lancaster Rifles*, by F. R. Diffenderfer, and *The American Rifle*, by W. U. Hensel.

AGY, ———   c. 1780
  Pennsylvania.

ALDENDERFER, ———   1763
  Pennsylvania.

ALDENDERFER, M.   1817
  Lancaster, Pennsylvania.

ALLBRIGHT, HENRY   1744
  Durham, Pennsylvania.

ALLBRIGHT, J.   (no date)
Manheim, Pennsylvania. (Stiegel's town).

ALLEN, SILAS   (no date)
Shrewsbury, Massachusetts. Dillin cites him as a fine gunsmith.

ALLISON, T.   (no date)
Pennsylvania.

ANGSTADT, PETER   (early)
Pennsylvania. Highly rated by Dillin.

ARMSTRONG, JOHN   (no date)
Maryland.

BACKHOUSE, RICHARD   (early)
Easton, Pennsylvania.

BAER, J.   (no date)
Lancaster, Pennsylvania.

BAKER, JOHN   (early)
Lancaster, Pennsylvania.

BARLOW, J.   1840
Moscow, Indiana.

BARNHARDT, W.   c. 1780
Pennsylvania. Highly rated by Dillin.

BARTLETT, ———   (early)
Lancaster, Pennsylvania.

BAUER, GEORGE   (early)
Lancaster, Pennsylvania.

BEAN, BAXTER & JAMES   (no date)
East Tennessee.

BECK, C.   (early)
Well rated by Dillin.

BECK, ISAAC   c. 1835
Mifflinburg, Pennsylvania.

BENFER, ARNIG   (no date)
Beaverstown, Pennsylvania.

BERLIN, ABRAHAM   (no date)
Eastern Pennsylvania.

BERLIN, ISAAC   (no date)
Pennsylvania. Highly rated by Dillin.

BERRY, A. P.
Place and date unknown. Highly rated by Dillin.

BERSTROW, H. T.   1835
Buffalo, New York.

BILLIS, ———   (very early)
Lancaster, Pennsylvania.

BLOODGOOD, ———   (no date)
North Carolina.

BOONE, E.   1818
Oley Valley, Pennsylvania. Dillin identifies him as second cousin to Daniel Boone.

BOONE, SAMUEL   1768
Berks County, Pennsylvania. Daniel's nephew. (Dillin)

BOONE, SQUIRE   1800 and earlier
Rowan County, North Carolina. Daniel's brother. (Dillin)

BOSSWORTH, ———   (early)
Lancaster, Pennsylvania.

BOYER, D.   (no date)
Orwigsburg, Pennsylvania. One of a family of riflesmiths.

BREY, ELIDS
Place and date unknown. Highly rated by Dillin.

BRONG, PETER   1800
Lancaster, Pennsylvania.

BULOW, CHARLES   1797
Lancaster, Pennsylvania.

BURD, C.   (no date)
Philadelphia, Pennsylvania.

BYERS, N.   c. 1780–1800
Pennsylvania.

CHARLOTTESVILLE RIFLE WORKS   1740
Charlottesville, North Carolina.

CHARRINGTON, THOMAS   (no date)
Cattawissa, Pennsylvania. Highly rated by Dillin.

CHRIST, D.   (no date)
Lancaster, Pennsylvania.

CLAUSE, NATHAN   (early)
Pennsylvania. Highly rated by Dillin.

COLT, COLONEL SAMUEL 1814–1862
*Inventor of the revolver and
founder of Colt's Patent Firearms Manufacturing Company.
New Haven, Connecticut.*

DAUB, J. (early)
Berks County, Pennsylvania.

DECHARD, JACOB (variants in spelling) 1753
Lancaster, Pennsylvania.

DE HUFF, HENRY 1802
Lancaster, Pennsylvania.

DERINGER, HENRY (no date)
*Easton, Pennsylvania. Father of
the maker of the famous Deringer
pistol. (Dillin)*

DOYLE, JOHN c. 1784
Lancaster, Pennsylvania.

DREPPERD, HENRY (early)
Lancaster, Pennsylvania.

FARNOT, FRANK 1780
Pennsylvania.

FERREE, JACOB 1785
Lancaster, Pennsylvania.

FERREE, JOEL 1750
*Leacock Township, Lancaster
County, Pennsylvania.*

FONDERSMITH & SON, JOHN 1802
*Lancaster, Pennsylvania. Located
at Strassburg, 1749.*

FORD, J. (no date)
Virginia.

FORDNEY, MELCHIOR (no date)
Lancaster, Pennsylvania.

GOLCHER, JOHN (no date)
Easton, Pennsylvania.

GRAEFF, JOHN 1798
Lancaster, Pennsylvania.

GRAEFF, WILLIAM 1751
Lancaster, Pennsylvania.

HAINES, ISAAC c. 1730
Pennsylvania.

HALL, JOHN 1811
*Yarmouth, Maine. Maker of a
famous type of Breech-loading
flint-lock.*

HARPER'S FERRY RIFLE WORKS (no date)
Harper's Ferry, Virginia.

HAWKEN, JACOB c. 1822
*Louisville, Kentucky. His guns
famous in the west.*

HENRY, WILLIAM (1729–1786)
*Lancaster, Pennsylvania. First of
a long line of riflesmiths, involving a number of partnerships,
firm names, and uncertain collateral branches.*

KILE, NATHAN 1817
*Raccoon Creek, Jackson County,
Ohio.*

KRIDER, JOHN 1826
Philadelphia, Pennsylvania.

LEFEVRE, PHILIP 1731–1756
*Beaver Valley, Lancaster County,
Pennsylvania.*

MESSERSMITH, JOHN 1777
Lancaster, Pennsylvania.

MEYLAN, MARTIN 1719
Lancaster, Pennsylvania.

MILLER, SIMON (no date)
*Hamburg, Pennsylvania. Highly
rated by Dillin.*

PALM, JACOB 1768
Pennsylvania and New York.

RATHFONG, GEORGE 1774
Lancaster, Pennsylvania.

REED, TEMPLETON 1824
Milledgeville, Georgia.

ROESSER, MATTHEW 1744
Lancaster, Pennsylvania.

ROOP, JOHN 1775
Allentown, Pennsylvania.

SCHRIDT, JOHN 1758
Reading, Pennsylvania.

SHELL, JOHN
Leslie County, Kentucky.

SPITZER & SON   (no date)
  Newmarket, Virginia.

WHITNEY, ELI   1763–1825
  *Inventor of the interchangeable
  mechanism type of rifle. Whitney
  Arms Company, Whitneyville
  and New Haven, Connecticut.*

WITHERS, MICHAEL   1778
  Lancaster, Pennsylvania.

YOUNG, JOHN
  *Lehigh County, Pennsylvania.
  "The Youngs were skilled workmen. Received a contract for
  1000 rifles, from the Government
  in 1776 in association with Johnson Smith; and in April, 1776,
  with A. Foilke, contracted for
  130 rifles for the Virginia
  Colony." (Dillin)*

BIBLIOGRAPHIES

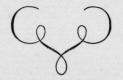

BIBLIOGRAPHIES

GENERAL

ADAMS, JAMES TRUSLOW, *Epic of America*. Boston: Little, Brown. 1931.

ADAMS, JAMES TRUSLOW, *The Founding of New England*. Boston: Atlantic Monthly Press. 1921.

ADAMS, JAMES TRUSLOW, *The March of Democracy*. N. Y.: Scribner's. 1932.

Arts and Crafts of New York. N. Y.: New York Historical Society. 1938.
> A detailed tabulation of New York's early crafts and craftsmen with all available statistics.

BEARD, CHARLES and MARY, *The Rise of American Civilization*. N. Y.: Macmillan. 1929.
> Unquestionably one of the finest histories of our country, representing new departures in the art of writing history.

BECKER, C. L., *Beginnings of the American People*. Boston: Houghton Mifflin. 1915.
> American history.

BISHOP, J. L., *A History of American Manufactures 1608-1860*. Philadelphia: Edward Young & Co. 1868.
> One of the important source books on our industrial background.

BRADFORD, *History of Plymouth Plantation*. In, *Original Narratives of Early American History*. N. Y.: Scribner's. 1908.
> One of Scribner's series of interesting contemporary accounts of early America. Splendid research source.

BRUCE, P. A., *Economic History of Virginia*. N. Y.: Macmillan. 1896.

Burghers of New Amsterdam and Freemen of New York. N. Y.: New York Historical Society. 1938.
> Splendid compilation of data on the early periods of the city.

BURLINGAME, ROGER, *March of the Iron Men*. N. Y.: Scribner's. 1938.
> An interesting study of American history in terms of the inventions which have contributed to its development.

CARMAN, H. J.: *Social and Economic History of the United States*. N. Y.: D. C. Heath. 1930.

CHASE, STUART, *Men and Machines*. N. Y.: Macmillan. 1930.
> A brilliant study of the influence of machines upon society and economy.

Chronicle. (A periodical) Early American Industries Association. N. Y. For information communicate with Editor, B. A. Kollmer, Historical Museum, Richmond, Staten Island, N. Y.
> A unique record of the early stages of nearly every form of American manufacture.

CLARK, VICTOR S., *History of Manufactures in the United States 1607-1860*. N. Y.: McGraw-Hill. 1929.
> Covers Bishop's ground with the advantage of added historical perspective.

DANKERS, JASPER, *Journal of Jasper Dankers and Peter Sluyter*. In, *Original Narratives of Early American History*. N. Y.: Scribner's. 1913.
> One of the best of all the early accounts.

DOW, G. F., *Arts and Crafts in New England*. Topsfield, Mass. 1927.
> A collection of excerpts from 18th Century newspapers.

DREPPERD, CARL W., *Early American Prints*. N. Y.: Century Co. 1930.

DUNLAP, WILLIAM, *Diary*. N. Y.: New York Historical Society. 1930.
> The personal record of one of early America's most extraordinary artists and public figures. Splendid contemporary account.

DYER, WALTER A., *Early American Craftsmen*. N. Y.: Century Co. 1915.

EARLE, ALICE MORSE, *Colonial Dames and Good Wives*. Boston: Houghton Mifflin. 1895.

EATON, A. H., *Handicrafts of the Southern Highlands*. N. Y.: Russell Sage Foundation. 1937.
> The record of the early crafts as they exist today in their original forms.

EDMONDS, WALTER D., *Erie Water*. Boston: Little, Brown. 1933.
> See below.

EDMONDS, WALTER D., *Chad Hanna*. Boston: Little, Brown. 1940.
> See below.

EDMONDS, WALTER D., *Rome Haul*. N. Y.: Modern Library.
> Three fine novels focussing upon the history or general background of the Erie Canal.

FARIS, J., *When America Was Young*. N. Y.: Harper. 1925.

FAY, BERNARD, *Franklin, the Apostle of Modern Times*. Boston: Little, Brown. 1929.
> A biography.

FELT, JOSEPH B., *The Customs of New England*. Boston: T. R. Marvin. 1853.
> An early record. Interesting research data.

FISHER, SYDNEY GEORGE, *Men, Women, and Manners in Colonial Times*. Philadelphia: Lippincott. 1898.
> A fairly early account.

FRANKLIN, BENJAMIN, *Autobiography*. N. Y.: Modern Library. 1932.

FRANKLIN, BENJAMIN, *The Ingenious Dr. Franklin*. Selected Scientific Letters of Benjamin Franklin. Edited by Nathan G. Goodman. Philadelphia: The University of Pennsylvania Press. 1931.

FRANKLIN, BENJAMIN, *The Writings of Benjamin Franklin*. Edited by Albert Henry Smyth. 10 Vols. N. Y.: Macmillan. 1905-1907.

GEISER, K. F., *Redemptioners in Pennsylvania*. New Haven, Conn.: 1901.
> A study of the religious cult and its way of life.

GILDER, RODMAN, *The Battery*. The story of the adventurers, artists, statesmen, grafters, songsters, mariners, pirates, guzzlers, Indians, thieves, stuffed shirts, turn-coats, millionaires, inventors, poets, heroes, soldiers, harlots, bootlicks, nobles, nonentities, burghers, martyrs, and murderers who played their parts during full four centuries on Manhattan Island's tip. Boston: Houghton Mifflin. 1936.

HAMILTON, ALEXANDER, *Report on Manufactures*. Philadelphia. 1791.
Part of Alexander Hamilton's general economic report on the financial state of the new American nation.

HAZEN, EDWARD, *Panorama of Professions and Trades*. Philadelphia. 1836.
A very interesting early account of American manufactures and similar occupations.

Indentures of Apprentices. N. Y.: New York Historical Society.
Records and examples of the documents characteristic of the apprentice system.

JOHNSON, CAPTAIN EDWARD, *Wonder-Working Providence of Sions Savior in New England*. N. Y.: Scribner's. 1910.
Early accounts of Colonial America by a contemporary traveller.

KALM, PEHR, *Travels in North America*. (1750.) N. Y.: Wilson-Erickson. 1937.
A Swedish traveller's account of early America.

KANE, JOSEPH NATHAN, *Famous First Facts*. N. Y.: H. W. Wilson. 1933.
A record of first happenings, discoveries, and inventions in the United States.

KELLY, JOHN FREDERICK, *Early Domestic Architecture of Connecticut*. New Haven: Yale University Press. 1933.
A small volume published for the Connecticut Tercentenary Commission.

KIMBALL, SIDNEY FISKE, *Domestic Architecture of the American Colonies and of the Early Republic*. N. Y.: Scribner's. 1922.

LARCOM, LUCY, *A New England Girlhood*. Boston: Houghton Mifflin. 1889.
A justly celebrated record, by a contemporary, of the unique and almost naïve blending of New England respectability and education with industry in the Lowell knitting mills.

McMASTER, J. B., *Acquisition of Political, Social and Industrial Rights of Man in America*. Cleveland. 1903.
Printing of lectures delivered at Western Reserve University under auspices of the D. A. R.

MILLER, WILLIAM DAVIS, *The Narragansett Planters*. Worcester, Mass.: American Antiquarian Society. 1934.
An account of an isolated and unusual economic and social phenomenon in the Northern Colonies.

MORTON, THOMAS, *The New English Canaan*. Force's Tracts, II. Washington. 1836.
Early narratives of America.

MUMFORD, LEWIS, *Technics and Civilization*. N. Y.: Harcourt, Brace. 1934.
A fascinating and distinguished study of the development of our civilization in terms of technics and machines.

MUNSELL, J., *Annals of Albany, New York*.
Scattered records of early New York State.

MYERS, ALBERT COOK (editor), *Narratives of Early Pennsylvania, West New Jersey, and Delaware. 1630-1707*. N. Y.: Scribner's. 1912.
Part of the Scribner series of Early American Narratives.

Original Narratives of Early American History. N. Y.: Scribner's.
A series of records and accounts, the bulk of which are separately cited in this bibliography.

Paintings of Life in America. N. Y.: Metropolitan Museum. 1939.
> Remarkably interesting pictorial record, with splendid notes, of a wide span in our history. Profusely illustrated, annotated catalogue of a distinguished exhibition.

PRIME, ALFRED COXE, *Arts and Crafts in Philadelphia, Maryland, and South Carolina. 1721-1800.* Topsfield, Mass.: 1929-32.
> Gleanings of craft activities from early newspapers.

PRIME, ALFRED COXE, *Colonial Craftsmen of Pennsylvania.* Reproductions of early newspaper advertisements from the author's private collection. Philadelphia: 1925.

RAWSON, MARION N., *Handwrought Ancestors.* The Story of Early American Shops and Those Who Worked Therein. N. Y.: Dutton. 1936.

RAYMOND, ELEANOR, *Early Domestic Architecture in Pennsylvania.* N. Y.: W. Helburn. 1931.
> With photographs and measured drawings.

RICKARD, T. A., *Men and Metals.* N. Y.: Whittelsey House. 1932.

SAVAGE, JAMES (Editor), *Governor Winthrop's Journal.* A history of New England from 1630-1642. Boston. 1825.

SHERMAN, FREDERIC FAIRCHILD, *Early Connecticut Artists and Craftsmen.* N. Y.: 1925.
> Small, privately printed volume.

SIMONS, A. M., *Social Forces in American History.* N. Y.: Macmillan. 1911.
> A splendid work, might be called, to some degree, a "leftist" interpretation.

SINGLETON, ESTHER, *The Collecting of Antiques.* New York: Macmillan.
> A general book for the layman, covering furniture, textiles, silver, and china. Not exclusively American.

SINGLETON, ESTHER, *Dutch New York.* N. Y.: Dodd, Mead. 1909.
> A history of New Amsterdam.

SINGLETON, ESTHER, *Social New York Under the Georges.* 1714-1776. Includes houses, streets, and country homes, together with chapters on Fashions. N. Y.: Appleton. 1902.

SLUYTER, PETER, *see* Dankers, Jasper. *Journal.*

SMITH, CAPTAIN JOHN, *Works.* E. Arber, Editor. London, 1886.
> The narratives of the leader of the Virginia colonists.

SMITH, HELEN EVERSON, *Colonial Days and Ways.* N. Y.: Century Co. 1900.
> Gleanings from old family papers.

STANARD, MARY NEWTON, *Colonial Virginia, Its Peoples and Customs.* Philadelphia: Lippincott. 1917.

STOKES, I. N. PHELPS, *Iconography of the Island of Manhattan.* N. Y.: R. H. Dodd. 1915-1928.
> An extensive work in six volumes, detailed study of Manhattan's history, manners and customs, in terms of data and illustrations compiled from obscure and original sources. Includes maps, plans, views and documents from public and private collections.

STURT, GEORGE, *The Wheelwright's Shop.* Cambridge University Press. 1923.
> An English work. Descriptions of the processes and implements of the wheelwright.

TAYLOR, REVEREND ISAAC, *Scenes of Wealth, or Views and Illustrations of Trades, Manufactures, Produce and Commerce.* 1826.
> An interesting old volume, extensively illustrated with contemporary prints.

TYLER, L. G. (Editor), *Narratives of Early Virginia.* N. Y.: Scribner's. 1907.
> Part of the Scribner series.

ULRICH, B. P., and COMMONS, J. R. (Editors), *Documentary History of American Industrial Society.*

USHER, A. P., *A History of Mechanical Inventions.* N. Y.: McGraw-Hill. 1929.
> An account, in detail, of the ingenuity which has built up our machine age. Illustrated.

VALENTINE, D. T., *History of the City of New York.* N. Y.: Putnam's. 1853.
> An early compilation of New York's history, bringing it down to about 1750.

VAN DOREN, CARL, *Benjamin Franklin.* N. Y.: Viking Press. 1938.
> A brilliant and distinguished biography. Probably the best work on Franklin.

VAN RENSSELAER, MRS. SCHUYLER, *History of the City of New York in the Seventeenth Century.* N. Y.: Macmillan. 1909.
> Two volumes, thoroughly studying New Amsterdam and the subsequent New York under the Stuarts.

VARNUM, WILLIAM HARRISON, *Industrial Arts Design.* N. Y.: Scott, Foresman. 1916.
> A practical handbook.

VARNUM, WILLIAM HARRISON, *Creative Design in Furniture: wood, metal, glass and plastics.* Peoria: Manual Arts Press. 1937.
> A comprehensive handbook.

WALLACE, P. B., *Colonial Churches and Meeting Houses. The Early Architecture of Pennsylvania, New Jersey, and Delaware.* N. Y. 1931.
> Illustrated.

WALLACE, P. B., *Colonial Houses, Philadelphia.* The pre-revolutionary period. N. Y. 1931.
> Illustrated. Introduction by Joseph Hergesheimer.

WANSEY, H., *Journal of an Excursion to the United States of North America in 1794.* London: 1796.
> Another early narrative, containing numerous genealogical records of the Colonies.

WEEDEN, W. B., *Economic and Social History of New England. 1620-1789.* Boston: Houghton Mifflin. 1890.
> One of the earlier studies of its kind.

BOOKMAKING

ANDREWS, WILLIAM LORING, *Bibliopegy in the United States, and Kindred Subjects.* N. Y.: Dodd, Mead. 1902. A limited edition. Essentially a study of early American book manufacture and binding.

ANDREWS, WILLIAM LORING, *The Old Booksellers of New York.* N. Y.: 1895.

ANDREWS, WILLIAM LORING, *A Short Historical Sketch of the Art of Bookbinding.* N. Y. 1895.

BOWDOIN, W. G., *American Book-Binders and Their Work*. The *Independent*. (A periodical). December 18, 1902.
> A magazine article, interesting for an account of the hand binders working at the time.

HOE, ROBERT, *A Short History of the Printing Press*. N. Y.: 1902.
> An account of the development of printing by one of the foremost contributors to the advance of modern printing in America.

THOMPSON, J. S., *History of Composing Machines*. Chicago: Inland Printer Co. 1904.
> The story of the amazing and complex machines behind modern, high speed printing.

WINTERICH, JOHN T., *Early American Books and Printing*. Boston: Houghton Mifflin. 1935.
> A noted book collector writes interestingly of our American background.

WROTH, LAWRENCE C., *The Colonial Printer*. N. Y.: Grolier Club. 1931.
> A highly interesting and very complete account of early American printing. Illustrated.

CABINETMAKING

ARONSON, JOSEPH, *The Book of Furniture and Decoration, Period and Modern*. N. Y.: Crown Publishers, Inc. 1936.
> A well known architect and designer writes of furniture and its use. Profusely illustrated.

ARONSON, JOSEPH, *The Encyclopedia of Furniture*. N. Y.: Crown Publishers, Inc. 1938.
> A comprehensive study of furniture of all types and periods. Profusely illustrated.

BENJAMIN, A., *The Practical House Carpenter*. Boston: L. Coffin. 1844.
> An old handbook of woodworking, interesting in its revelation of early method.

BURROUGHS, PAUL H., *Two Centuries of Massachusetts Furniture*. American Collector, vol. 6, Sept. 1937, pp. 4-5, 10-13.
> Including a valuable check-list of Massachusetts cabinetmakers.

CORNELIUS, C. O., *Early American Furniture*. N. Y.: Century Co. 1926.

CORNELIUS, C. O., *Furniture Masterpieces of Duncan Phyfe*. N. Y.: Doubleday Page. 1922.
> An extensive and authoritative study of Phyfe's work. Well illustrated.

DE ROZARIO, PEDRO, *Cabinetmakers and Chairmakers of New York City*. An exhaustive check-list. Typed sheets, bound as a book. New York Public Library.

HOPKINS, T. S. & COX, W. S., *Colonial Furniture of West New Jersey*. Haddonfield, N. J.: Historical Society of Haddonfield. 1936.

JOHNSTON, FRED J., *Ulster County Cabinet and Glassmakers*. New York History, v. 17, pp. 70-74. 1936.

LOCKWOOD, LUKE VINCENT, *Colonial Furniture in America*. 2 Vols. N. Y.: Scribner's. 1926.
> Accepted as the definitive work on the subject. Profusely illustrated.

LYON, IRVING WHITALL, *Colonial Furniture in New England*. Boston. 1891.
Seventeenth and Eighteenth century pieces. A relatively early work.

MERCER, HENRY C., *Ancient Carpenter's Tools*. Illustrated and explained together with the implements of the lumberman, joiner, and cabinet-maker, in use in the 18th Century. Doylestown, Pa.: Bucks County Historical Society.

MORSE, FRANCES CLARY, *Furniture of the Olden Time*. New York: Macmillan. 1937.
Deals with early American furniture.

ORMSBEE, THOMAS H., *Early American Furniture Makers*. N. Y.: T. Y. Crowell. 1930.
An excellent volume, with splendid biographical data in addition to a study of old pieces. Well illustrated.

ORMSBEE, THOMAS HAMILTON, *The Story of American Furniture*. New York: Macmillan. 1937.
A book for the layman.

CLOCKMAKING AND OTHER CRAFTS

BREARLEY, HARRY C., *Time Telling Through the Ages*. N. Y.: Doubleday Page. 1919.
A short history of clock-making, written for the Ingersoll Company.

CHAPPELLE, HOWARD I., *The History of American Sailing Ships*. N. Y.: W. W. Norton. 1935.
Contains data on the development of the Yankee Clipper.

CLARK, ARTHUR H., *The Clipper Ship Era*. N. Y.: Putnam's. 1910.
Splendid account of a thrilling period.

CONRAD, HENRY CLAY, *Old Delaware Clockmakers*. Papers of the Historical Society of Delaware. Wilmington. 1898.

CROSSMAN, CHARLES S., *A Complete History of Watch and Clock Making in America*. New York. 1886.

CUTLER, CARL C., *Greyhounds of the Sea,* N. Y.: Halcyon House. 1930.
The story of the Yankee Clippers.

DUNBAR, SEYMOUR, *A History of Travel in America*. Being an outline of the Development in Modes of Travel from Archaic Vehicles of Colonial Times to the Completion of the First Transcontinental Railroad. 4 Vols. Indianapolis: Bobbs Merrill. 1915.

GILFILLAN, S. C., *Inventing the Ship*. Chicago: Follett Publishing Co. 1935.
Traces the development, among others, of the Yankee Clipper ship.

HAYWARD, A. H., *Colonial Lighting*. Boston. 1923.
A study of early lamps and methods of household lighting.

HOOPES, PENROSE R., *Connecticut Clockmakers of the 18th Century*. New York: Dodd, Mead. 1930.

HOWARD AND COMPANY, *Watchmaking in America*. New York. 1870.

JEROME, CHAUNCEY, *History of the American Clock Business for the Past Sixty Years*. New Haven, Conn.: F. C. Rayton. 1860.

Written by a prominent clockmaker. Includes an account of Barnum's connection with the Yankee clock business.

MAGEE, D. F., *Grandfather's Clocks; Their Making and Their Makers, in Lancaster County*. Lancaster County (Pa.) Historical Society; Historical papers and addresses. v. 43, pp. 137-163. 1939.

MERCER, HENRY C., *Light and Fire Making*, with 45 illustrations explaining the rubbing of fire from wood, the striking of flint and steel, and some of the lamps, candles, torches and lanterns of the American pioneer. Philadelphia. 1898.

MILHAM, WILLIS ISBISTER, *Time and Timekeepers;* Including the history, construction, care, and accuracy of clocks and watches. New York: Macmillan. 1923.

MOORE, HANNAH, *The Old Clock Book*. New York: Stokes. 1911.

NUTTING, WALLACE, *The Clock Book;* being a description of foreign and American clocks, profusely illustrated. Framingham, Massachusetts: Old America Company. 1924.

PUBLIC CLOCKS COMMITTEE OF PHILADELPHIA, *Report of the Committee on Public Clocks*. Philadelphia. 1835.

RICHARDSON, ALBERT DEANE, *Ancient and Modern Time Keepers;* Containing an interesting notice of the works of the National Watch Co., at Elgin, Illinois. New York: R. T. Hutchinson. 1872.

SANDS, ANNA B., *Time Pieces of Old and New Connecticut*. Hartford: Manufacturers Association of Connecticut. 1926.

STRETCH, CAROLYN WOOD, *Early Colonial Clockmakers in Philadelphia*. Pennsylvania Magazine of History and Biography, v. 56, pp. 225-235. Philadelphia. 1932.

THRASHER, SAMUEL POWERS, *Connecticut Clocks*. A Sketch. Hartford. 1907.

WILLARD, JOHN WARE, *A History of Simon Willard, Inventor and Clockmaker;* Together with some account of his sons, his apprentices, and the workmen associated with him, with brief notices of other clockmakers of the family name. Boston: E. O. Cockayne. 1911.

GLASSMAKING

BARBER, E. A., *American Glassware*. Philadelphia: David McKay. 1900. One of the earlier standard works. Authoritative.

BASTOW, H., *American Glass Practice*. Pittsburgh, Pa.: 1920.

A practical book devoted to actual glass factory conditions, with problems discussed in a manner that will be readily understood by the layman.

BROWN, FRANK AND BRENDLE, A. S., *The Life of Baron Henry W. Stiegel;* iron and glass manufacturer, pioneer, philanthropist, preacher, teacher, etc. etc. Schaefferstown, Pa. c. 1900.

COGGESHALL, W. T., *Five Black Arts*. Columbus, Ohio. 1861.
> A study of glassmaking.

DYOTT, THOMAS W., *An Exposition of the System of Moral and Mental Labor Established at the Glass Factory at Dyottsville*. Philadelphia. 1833.
> The great quack doctor's personal formula for sanctimonious labor exploitation.

HUNTER, FREDERICK WILLIAM, *Stiegel Glass*. Boston: Houghton Mifflin. 1914. Illustrated by color plates by J. B. Kerfoot.

JARVES, DEMING, *Reminiscences of Glass Making*. Boston: Eastburn's Press. 1854.
> An account of the background and history of American pressed glass, Sandwich Glass in particular, by its pioneer manufacturer.

KNITTLE, RHEA M., *Early American Glass*. N. Y.: Century Co. 1927.
> Interesting work for the layman.

LEE, RUTH WEBB, *Early American Pressed Glass*. Pittsford, N. Y. 1931.
> A comprehensive and definitive work. Standard for collectors.

LEE, RUTH WEBB, *Sandwich Glass*. Pittsford, N. Y. 1939.
> An abridged, specialized study by the author of the comprehensive *Early American Pressed Glass*.

McMANNS, T. F., *A Century of Glass Manufacture. 1818-1918.*

VAN RENSSELAER, S., *Early American Bottles and Flasks,* Peterborough, N. H.: Transcript Printing Co. 1926.

IRONWORKING AND GUNSMITHING

CLARKSON, D. A., *Ancient Iron Work*. London: 1860.
> Early work. The background and general history of ironworking.

COPE, GILBERT AND FUTHEY, J. S., *History of Chester County, Pennsylvania*. Philadelphia: Evarts & Peck. 1881.

CURTIS, E. G., *Gateways and Doorways of Charleston, South Carolina*. N. Y. 1926.
> A specialized study of the beautiful wrought ironwork of the early South.

DIFFENDERFER, F. R., *The Lancaster Rifles*. Papers, vol. 9, pp. 67-73. Lancaster County (Pa.) Historical Society. 1904.

DILLIN, CAPTAIN JOHN G. W., *The Kentucky Rifle*. Washington: National Rifle Association of America.
> A well illustrated and highly interesting account of this famous American weapon and its makers.

DURFEE, W. F., *The History and Modern Development of the Art of Interchangeable Construction in Mechanism*. In, *Transactions,* American Society of Mechanical Engineering. Vol. XIV. N. Y. 1893. pp. 1225-1257.

ELLIS, F. AND EVANS, S., *History of Lancaster County, Pennsylvania*. Philadelphia: Evarts & Peck. 1883.

The File in History. Philadelphia. The Disston Company.
>A specially published study of rasp tools by one of America's big tool manufacturing firms.

GREENER, W. W., *The Gun and Its Development*. N. Y.: Scribner's. 1897.
>History of firearms by one of the foremost authorities in the field up to the 20th Century.

HENSEL, W. U., *The American Rifle*. Papers, vol. 9, pp. 59-66. Lancaster County (Pa.) Historical Society. 1904.

HORNOR, W. M. JR., *Obstructions of the Hudson River During the Revolution*. In, *American Collector*, II, 1926. pp. 436-445.
>An account of a particularly interesting phase of American improvised tactics during the struggle for Independence.

JOHNSON, G. W., *Ironwork in Charleston, South Carolina*.

LEONARD, JONATHAN N., *Tools of Tomorrow*. N. Y.: Viking Press. 1935.

MERCER, HENRY C., *The Bible in Iron;* or, the pictured stoves and stove plates of the Pennsylvania-Germans, with notes on Colonial fire-backs in the U. S., the ten-plate stove, Franklin's fire-place and the tile stoves of the Moravians in Pennsylvania, together with a list of Colonial furnaces in the U. S. & Canada. Profusely illustrated. Doylestown: Bucks County Historical Society. 1914.

MERCER, HENRY C., *Tools of the Nation Builder*. Doylestown, Pa.: Bucks County Historical Society. 1897.
>Descriptive catalogue of objects in the Museum of the Society at Doylestown. Valuable and interesting.

NORTON, C. B.: *American Inventions in Breech-loading Small Arms*. Springfield, Mass. 1880.
>Valuable source for data on our earlier firearms.

PEARSE, JOHN B., *Iron Manufacture in America*. Philadelphia: Allen & Scott. 1876.

ROE, JOSEPH WICKHAM, *English and American Tool Builders*. N. Y.: McGraw-Hill. 1926.

ROHAN, JACK, *Yankee Arms-maker,* The Incredible Career of Samuel Colt. N. Y.: Harper. 1935.
>A highly interesting biography constituting a worthwhile study of some aspects of developing high-pressure industrialism in America.

SAWYER, CHARLES WINTHROP, *Firearms in American History. 1600-1800*. Boston. 1910.
>An interesting and well illustrated book by a well known collector and authority.

SHARPE, PHILIP BURDETTE, *The Rifle in America*. New York: Morrow. 1938.
>A comprehensive, well illustrated history of American firearms.

SONN, ALBERT H., *Early American Wrought Iron*. 3 Vols. N. Y.: Scribner's. 1928.
>The definitive work on the subject. A splendid collection of drawings by the author of specimens of every type of early American iron work from all sections of the country.

SWANK, JAMES M., *Iron and Coal in Pennsylvania.* 1878.

SWANK, JAMES M., *Iron in All Ages.* Philadelphia. 1892.

WALLACE, PHILIP B., *Colonial Ironwork in Philadelphia.* N. Y.: 1930.
> The craftsmanship of the early days of the republic. Illustrated. Preface by Fiske Kimball.

WERLEIN, MRS. PHILIP, *The Wrought Iron Railings of le Vieux Carré, New Orleans.* New Orleans. 1925.
> An illustrated record of this famous southern ironwork. Pamphlet size. Illustrations not particularly outstanding.

WHELAN, TOWNSEND, *The American Rifle.* N. Y.: Century Co. 1918.
> Written by a military authority.

PEWTER

BELL, MALCOLM, *Old Pewter.* N. Y.: Scribner's. 1905.

CALDER, C. A., *Rhode Island Pewterers and Their Work.* Providence. 1924.
> The craftsmen of Rhode Island in some ways form a special group case. This is a valuable study of one section of them.

COTTERELL, H. H., *National Types of Old Pewter.* Boston. 1925.
> A study of the distinctively American aspects of this craft.

COTTERELL, H. H., *Pewter Down the Ages.* London: 1932.
> A general history.

KERFOOT, J. B., *American Pewter.* Boston: Houghton Mifflin. 1924. Illustrated by photographs of specimens in the author's noted collection. The standard definitive work on American pewter.

MYERS, LOUIS G., *Some Notes on American Pewterers.* N. Y.: 1926.
> A limited edition, privately printed.

VARNUM, WILLIAM HARRISON, *Pewter Design and Construction.* Milwaukee, Wisconsin: 1926.
> A handbook for practice.

POTTERY MAKING

BARBER, E. A., *Pottery and Porcelain in the United States.* N. Y.: Putnam's. 1893.
> An early standard work. Authoritative.

BARBER, E. A., *Tulip Ware of the Pennsylvania-German Potters.* Philadelphia: 1903.
> Standard work, as are the others by the same author.

JERVIS, W. P., *The Encyclopedia of Ceramics.* N. Y.: Blanchard. 1902.

PITKIN, ALBERT H., *Early American Folk Pottery.* Hartford, Conn.: Case, Lockwood, and Brainard. 1918.

RAMSAY, JOHN, *American Potters and Pottery.* Boston: Hale, Cushman & Flint. 1939.
> An excellent recent work. Well illustrated. Contains a comprehensive checklist.

SPARGO, J., *Early American Pottery and China.* N. Y.: Century Co. 1926.
   One of the excellent Century series.
YOUNG, JENNIE J., *The Ceramic Art.* N. Y.: Harper. 1878.
   A compendium of the history and manufacture of pottery and porcelain.

SILVERSMITHING

ANDREWS, WILLIAM LORING, *Paul Revere and His Engraving.* N. Y.: Scribner's. 1901.
AVERY, C. LOUISE, *Early American Silver.* N. Y.: Century Co. 1930.
   An interesting treatise for the layman.
BIGELOW, F. H., *Historic Silver of the Colonies.* N. Y.: Macmillan, 1917.
   A study and listing of important pieces, styles, and their makers.
BRIX, M., *List of Philadelphia Silversmiths.* Philadelphia: 1920.
   A specialized study, privately printed.
BURGESS, F. W., *Silver: Pewter: Sheffield Plate.* London. 1860.
   A very early work, primarily English.
CLARKE, H. F., *John Coney, Silversmith.* Boston: Houghton Mifflin. 1932.
   A biography of Paul Revere Senior's master and one of America's finest early craftsmen. Beautifully illustrated.
ENSKO, R., *Makers of Early American Silver.* N. Y. 1915.
ENSKO, STEPHEN G., *American Silversmiths and Their Marks.* N. Y. 1937.
GILLINGHAM, H. E., *The Cost of Old Silver.* Philadelphia. 1930.
GOSS, ELBRIDGE HENRY, *The Life of Colonel Paul Revere.* 2 Vols. Boston: Joseph George Cupples. 1891.
   A definitive biography.
MILLER, WILLIAM DAVIS, *Silversmiths of Little Rest.* Boston: Merrymount Press. 1928.
   Interesting account of the personalities and output of Samuel Casey and the other Rhode Island silversmiths.
TAYLOR, EMERSON, *Paul Revere.* N. Y.: Dodd, Mead. 1930.
   A biography.
WYLER, SEYMOUR, *The Book of Old Silver.* N. Y.: Crown Publishers, Inc. 1937.
   Profusely illustrated with specimens and a complete list of the identifying marks of silversmiths.

WEAVING AND TEXTILES

FINLEY, RUTH F., *Old Patchwork Quilts and the Men and Women Who Made Them.* Philadelphia: Lippincott. 1929.
   Illustrated.
HOES, R., *Catalogue of American Historical Costumes.* Washington. 1915.
   Exhibits in the National Museum. Includes costumes of the Presidents' wives.
LITTLE, FRANCES, *Early American Textiles.* N. Y.: Century Co. 1931.
   An interesting work for the layman.

PETO, FLORENCE, *Historic Quilts*. N. Y.: American Historical Co. 1939.
  A book about American handmade quilts and coverlets. Comprehensive and beautifully illustrated with cover plates.

STEARNS, MARTHA GENUNG, *Homespun Blue, a Study of American Crewel Embroidery*. N. Y.: Scribner's. 1940.
  Extensively illustrated.

TRYON, ROLLA M., *Household Manufactures in the United States*. Chicago: University of Chicago Press. 1917.
  A thorough study of the domestic aspects of early American industrial history.

WARE, CAROLINE, *Early New England Cotton Manufacture*. Boston: Houghton Mifflin. 1931.

WARWICK, EDWARD AND PITZ, HENRY, *Early American Costume*. N. Y.: Century Co., 1929.
  One of the Century series on early American objects.

WEBSTER, MARIE D., *Quilts, Their Story and How to Make Them*. N. Y.: Doubleday. 1928.
  Combination of a history and practical handbook.

WHEELER, MRS. CANDACE, *The Development of Embroidery in America*. N. Y.: Harpers. 1921.
  History of American needlework, including special accounts of the various European national groups in America.

INDEX